OUR FEDERAL GOVERNMENT

How It Works

D1403489

OUR FEDERAL GOVERNMENT
How It Works

An Introduction to the United States Government

PATRICIA C. ACHESON

Fourth edition, thoroughly revised

DODD, MEAD & COMPANY · NEW YORK

First published as a Dodd, Mead Quality Paperback in 1984
Copyright © 1958, 1969, 1978, 1984 by Patricia C. Acheson
Published by Dodd, Mead & Company, Inc.
79 Madison Avenue, New York, N.Y. 10016
Distributed in Canada by
McClelland and Stewart Limited, Toronto
Manufactured in the United States of America

Library of Congress Cataloging in Publication Data

Acheson, Patricia C.
Our federal government.

(A Dodd, Mead quality paperback)
Includes index.
Summary: Describes the complexities of the United States government, from the
basic elements of the Constitution, the three branches, and the Federal Judiciary
to the growth of the independent agencies.
1. United States—Politics and government. [1. United
States—Politics and government] I. Title.
JK274.A529   1984   320.973   84-1534
ISBN 0-396-08312-9 (pbk.)

CONTENTS

FOREWORD

The federal government of the United States today is vast and complicated. Because its responsibilities have expanded enormously over the years, many departments, agencies, administrations and bureaus, none of them described in the Constitution, have had to come into being in order to meet the needs of the American people. The very size of the government makes it difficult for the average citizen to understand, and it is not surprising that many feel overwhelmed by the federal structure. It is, however, of the greatest importance that Americans understand how their national government works and why it performs the functions it does. This book is an attempt to explain what some of the major divisions of our Washington government are, how they came into being and what services they provide. Because it would be impossible in a book of this sort to include every federal agency, selections, perforce, have had to be made, but with the intent of indicating the immense variety of government functions. In addition, it must be noted that because the government is constantly undergoing reorganization in order to better serve the American people, it is also virtually impossible to guarantee that by the time the book is published the contents will be 100 percent accurate. It is sincerely hoped, however, that those who read this book not only will have a clearer understanding and knowledge of the organization and the purpose of the federal government, but in addition a new appreciation of the genius of the Founding Fathers who through the Constitution created a system under which Americans have lived in freedom for almost two hundred years.

Patricia C. Acheson.

OUR FEDERAL GOVERNMENT

How It Works

WHY HAVE A GOVERNMENT?

EVERYONE KNOWS that there is a federal government of the United States and that this government is located in Washington, D.C. Everyone also grows up with the knowledge that the president of the United States lives in the White House at 1600 Pennsylvania Avenue and that at the end of that avenue, housed in a large and stately building, the Congress of the United States meets and makes laws for the people concerning all sorts of subjects. Some know, too, of the Supreme Court of the United States which is the guardian of all the rights of the American people and the highest court of justice in the land. Everyone certainly knows about taxes. But what does all this knowledge really mean? What does the government really do? Why does it exist? How does it affect the lives of all the American people? Why are taxes necessary?

Before the importance of what our federal government does, why it does it, and how its actions affect the lives of the over two hundred and twenty million people who are Americans can be made clear and have any real meaning, it is important to know and to understand what government is in the first place and what we must do to deserve government. The easiest way to realize what government in general is and to see why it is necessary to have it, is to imagine what life would be like without any government at all.

Without any sort of government there would be no nation. There would be no American citizenship with all the rights and privileges that come with it. There would be no patriotism, no flag, no "Star-Spangled Banner." Without a government there would be no order in our lives. Each person would

1

be alone and apart from his neighbors. No one would have any loyalty to anything other than his immediate circle of family and friends. All the things in our lives that we take for granted such as the post office, weather reports, passports and the armed forces would not exist. There would be no protection against crime or unlawful actions either at home or abroad. We would be at the mercy of everyone and everybody. Strong people could take advantage of the weaker ones. In other words, without government life would be full of uncertainty and danger. No one could go about in peace and safety, and we would be neither prosperous nor free. And, above all, we would not be Americans because there would be no United States.

A nation, therefore, to be a nation, must have some form of government in which all the people living in that nation can believe and which they want to support. This belief in government and the willingness to support it makes each person, whether native or naturalized, a citizen of the nation, giving him certain rights and privileges and a sense of belonging to a group. Citizenship means loyalty and pride and respect for our flag as a symbol of our nation. The existence of our government makes the United States an independent country and gives us as citizens individualism and a place in the world.

That, therefore, is what government means in the life of an individual living in our country. But there is something more to it than what it does for us. To have the advantages of government, each citizen must give in return something to that government. A country can be compared to a very large family. Each member of a family must abide by certain general rules in order to make the family successful. Each must share with the other members. Each has certain jobs and duties to perform to make the home a good one. So it is in a nation. Each citizen must fit into a general pattern, abide by certain rules or laws so that everyone can be sure of his rights and have freedom to live happily and in safety. As in a family, each citizen of our country must give up a bit of his personal freedom to do as he likes when he likes in order to make the country progress for the good of everyone. A topsy-turvy country would be to the advantage of no one. Government keeps our nation from being topsy-turvy, but not simply because it exists. It keeps our lives from being chaotic because we as citizens are willing to respect our government, to work for it, and to give up some of our individual, selfish freedom in order to make the government a success. A basic reason for any government at all, then, is to provide an organized system by which we can live as a nation in peace and prosperity. Equally important are two other reasons: to give us a voice through which all Americans may speak, and to give us a sense of importance and individuality. For these ends government does exist and must exist.

THE WRITING OF THE CONSTITUTION

WHAT IS the government of the United States exactly? How and when did it come to be? Who were the people who agreed to accept our government and why did they want to accept it?

The answers to these questions lie in the sequence of events that took place between 1775 and 1787. In 1775 the war against British domination began first in Massachusetts and then spread rapidly throughout the colonies. At that point there was no central American government established by law. There was only the Continental Congress made up of men who believed in independence and who were willing to fight for their cause. It was that Congress that took the daring step in July 1776, of declaring the colonies independent of Great Britain, and it was only after that momentous decision that the evolution of our present form of government began. The initial step was to establish legal governments in the states to replace the defunct colonial regimes. Each of the former colonies, therefore, called conventions whose task it was to write state constitutions which were then ratified by the citizens of each of the states. Because Americans were rebelling against the British Crown, there was little dispute over what kind of government the people wanted. They established republics, each of the thirteen new states having elected governors and representative assemblies.

The next step in the evolution of our American government came about more from the necessity of coordinating the war effort and preparing for the eventuality of peace than from any abstract political convictions. As mentioned above, the Continental Congress was without legal foundation, and it was clearly necessary to establish some form of overall government agreed to by the people capable of directing the war and speaking for all the states at the peace table. It would not be untrue, however, to say that the Americans of this period only reluctantly accepted this necessity as the majority believed wholeheartedly that they could guarantee their freedom from oppressive rule only if each state remained almost entirely independent of the others.

The first government, therefore, of the United States under the Articles of Confederation adopted in 1781 was very restricted in its authority. It consisted of a Congress made up of representatives from the states. Each state, regardless of its population, could only elect two to seven representatives, but no state had more than one vote when it came to passing laws. There was no president with certain specific powers, only a rotating chairman whose job it was to preside and to keep order. As far as power to do anything went, the Congress had very little. It was authorized to conduct the war, to make peace, to attend to relations with nations abroad, and it could run the affairs of the territories belonging to the United States, but not of those belonging to the states. It could offer its good services in resolving disputes between states, but there was no well-defined system of justice to which all states had to bow. In fact, the list of what powers the central government did not have is a great deal longer than those it did have. Congress could not pass tax laws; it did not have the sole authority to coin money for use by the states, nor could it regulate trade between the states. To carry out its activities, the members of the central government could only politely ask for money contributions from the states. If the states refused to help, then no money could be raised. Because it had no money of its own, the Congress could not pay any of its debts, and, indeed, it could not even borrow money successfully because who would lend money when it was quite clear that it would not be paid back? In addition, although Congress was charged with the responsibility of defending the nation, because it lacked a means of raising revenue, it could not pay an army or a navy.

In fact, one of the major debts that Congress faced was the money owed to the Continental forces who had fought the Revolutionary War.

One might well ask if this original government did actually achieve anything, and the list of their accomplishments is short. It did negotiate the peace treaty in Paris, France in 1783 which concluded the war; it did settle a dispute between Connecticut and Pennsylvania; and it did adopt a brilliant system of government for the territories by which they would evolve into states on an equal footing with the original thirteen, which was of great importance for the future of the nation. In addition, it established permanently the republican form of government for the United States. Unfortunately, however, its failures far outnumbered its successes, and within four years after the end of the war it became obvious that the system of government under the Articles of Confederation was not working out.

Perhaps the worst problem that was causing so much trouble and confusion was that of money. Each state was issuing its own kind, and trade, therefore, between the thirteen states was very difficult. A man, for instance, in New Jersey crossing over into New York to sell his goods might discover that his goods were worth something different in New York than in New Jersey. If he sold them anyway, he found that the money he received for them was not worth as much when he went home. Also, he might discover that the state of New York was taxing him for selling his produce in New York. If the only market for his goods happened to be in New York, he was obviously in a bind. He would never make much money as long as this system existed. This was typical of the situation all over the nation, and the farmers and businessmen were all suffering. In the colonial days trade had been brisk between the colonies, and many people were now dissatisfied.

The discontent and the fact that the new nation was extraordinarily weak without an adequate army or navy made thoughtful people realize that a better government must be worked out if the United States of America was to be a strong and rich nation. In Philadelphia in 1787 a meeting, or a convention as it was called, met in order to remold the government. It was there that our present system of government was born, and the Constitution of the United States was written. The people of the United States, the District of Columbia, Puerto Rico and the territories now in the Union are still governed today by the framework drawn up in that document almost two hundred years ago despite the changes in America over the years.

THE PREAMBLE

BEFORE SPELLING out the details of the new government, the men who designed the Constitution felt strongly the need to explain what an ideal government should be. The first paragraph of the Constitution, the Preamble, therefore, sets out the ideals for a government dedicated to serve its citizens. The people of the thirteen original states knew exactly what kind of government they were going to have and why they needed such a government before they were asked to adopt it as their own.

The Preamble begins with the words, "We the People of the United States." "We the People" meant exactly that. No one person or group was to accept the Constitution. The people of the nation who were going to be governed were the ones who had to agree to their government.

"In order to form a more perfect union" follows. "A more perfect union" was a direct reference to the less than satisfactory union established under the Articles of Confederation. The new government was to set up a union of closely allied states under a federal government instead of a loose confederation of semi-independent states. The states under this new union were to have their rights, but the union under the Constitution was to be strong and efficient.

In order to make this possible the Founding Fathers stated firmly the reasons for a good government in the Preamble. To be a strong and fine government, it must "establish justice, insure domestic tranquility, provide for the common defense, promote the general welfare, and secure the blessings of Liberty to ourselves and our posterity." No nation can be strong

8

without justice under law for all, without an army and a navy to protect its land and its people from foreign foes, without good, forward-looking laws to help the individual citizen lead a happier and better life, without the protection of the basic rights of a free, intelligent people. With these principles stated in the opening paragraph of the Constitution, the Founding Fathers, by incorporating the philosophy of Thomas Jefferson so magnificently spelled out in the Declaration of Independence, had guaranteed to the people of the United States a government based on the right of man to govern himself.

The Constitution established a democratic republic. The word "democracy" comes from the ancient Greek language. *Demos* means people, *Kratos* means strength or power, and the two words together mean the strength in or of the people. A republic is a government in which the chief of state is elected by the citizenry rather than inheriting his position as in a monarchy. A government based on democratic and republican principles is a government, therefore, in which the power rests in the people. They who are to be governed will form that government. They will be the ones who carry out the duties of that government. They will be the ones who will live under that government. Therefore, because the people of the United States are the government, that government must inevitably serve them. Should it fail to serve them, it is the people's right, in fact, their duty, as Jefferson said in the Declaration of Independence, to find out why it has failed and to correct what is wrong. In a democracy the government is only as good as its citizens, and, therefore, every citizen in a democracy must take responsibility and care about his government. The people of the United States have accepted this responsibility. Although the Constitution has been severely threatened repeatedly since its adoption—by secession and the ensuing Civil War in the nineteenth century, by external aggression twice in the twentieth century, World Wars I and II, and by the near subversion of the constitutional system itself in the Watergate affair a few years ago—it has survived because the people have cared and rallied around to reaffirm the faith of those who authored it two hundred years ago.

THE CONSTITUTION

THE PREAMBLE stated the fundamental principles to be followed by the United States government. It now remained to translate these ideals into a practical system. How was the government actually to be as Abraham Lincoln stated in his immortal Gettysburg Address, "of the people, by the people and for the people"? How was it to "Establish Justice, insure domestic Tranquility, provide for the common defense, promote the general Welfare, and secure the Blessings of Liberty . . ." for all? The actual government must put the principles of democracy into working day-to-day democracy in the lives of the people. The machinery of government must insure freedom, not only for the citizens of the United States in the eighteenth century, but for all times.

To create such a government was not an easy thing to do. Remember that in 1787 the men at the convention in Philadelphia were virtually pioneers in the setting up of a democratic republican government. They really only knew what they did not want. They did not want a king, and they did not want too strong a central government because they were afraid of losing their own freedoms. They certainly wanted to keep the states as they were. To erase them would have been impossible. Each colony has been founded for a different reason in the beginning, and each had individuality and pride that had gradually evolved over many years. There could be no question of making just one government and forgetting the individual states. On the other hand, the men in Philadelphia knew all too well that the first government set up after the Revolution under the Articles of Confederation had been a

10

miserable failure. It had had too little power to carry out its business. The states had bickered among themselves, and no one had been satisfied.

Here was a dilemma. On the one hand, it seemed that a strong central government was very undesirable. It might endanger the people's liberties. But, on the other hand, a weak central government had proven inadequate. It could not keep order, and the people were not able to make as much of their liberties as they should have. Americans since 1787 owe an everlasting debt of gratitude to those men who found the solution to this thorny problem. The system they worked out and wrote into the Constitution was the answer to the problem of how to have a democratic republican form of government to serve the people and to preserve their freedom, yet at the same time to avoid the danger of concentrating too much power in the federal government. The solution they found is called the "checks and balance" system, and it is the heart and soul of the Constitution.

The Checks and Balance System

The framers of the Constitution wanted to make sure that the people's rights would always be safe and that the central or federal government would never become too powerful. A government to work most efficiently and democratically ought to have three major powers: to make laws, to carry out those laws, and to provide justice under law for the best interests of the people. Should these three functions be in the hands of one person or one group, there would be great danger that that person or group could use the power for personal profit rather than for the people. To guard against this possibility, the Constitution provided for three major branches of government: the legislature, or Congress, to make laws; the executive to carry out the laws; and the judiciary to watch over the rights of the people as described in the Constitution.

The powers of these three branches of the government are described carefully in the Constitution. The men of 1787 were so afraid of too much power in the hands of a few that they worked hard and long to spell out each job for the three parts of the federal government. Nothing was to be left to chance. To make sure that the government should never take more power than what it was granted in the Constitution, it was carefully stated that any power not given to the government should forever belong to the states. This remarkably foresighted decision meant that, although the country could grow from a little one into a great nation over the years, the rights of the people could never be absorbed by the federal government. If changing times cause new problems to arise, the states or the people have the right to decide what to do. No one branch of the federal government can simply assume the power and not answer to the people.

Another reason for describing carefully the powers of the three branches was to prevent any one branch from becoming stronger than the others. Each job in the running of the country was balanced between the legislative, the executive and the judicial branches. The jobs were also intertwined. Each part of the government can only function in relation to the others. This system not only balances power between the three branches, but also provides a check on each branch by the others. For instance, a good example of the check system can be found in the manner in which laws become laws. The legislature, or Congress, has the job of drafting laws for the country. Once a bill, as a law is called before it is signed by the president, has been passed by the two houses, the Senate and the House of Representatives, the Congress must send a copy to the chief executive, the president of the United States, for his approval. He then has four options as to what he may do. He may agree with the bill and sign the copy, in which case the law goes into effect. Or, if he should feel that it is not a good law, he may veto it. Vetoing means that he refuses to sign. Should he do that, the copy is returned to the house of Congress in which it originated. If the Congress, sure that the proposed law is a necessary one, passes it again by a two-thirds majority, the bill becomes law regardless of the president's veto. The people are represented in Congress, and if they still favor the law, it is more democratic that they should have it. The foresighted writers of the Constitution saw that there would be times when the people could disagree with the president, and should this occur, the people in a democracy should have the last word. This is the meaning of democracy. There are also two other possibilities open to the president in the making of a law. He may ignore the bill and allow it to lie on his desk for ten days, excluding Sundays. Should he do this, he indicates his disapproval, but he does not veto it. After ten days that act becomes law, provided that Congress is in session. This course of action gives the president a chance to register an opinion between yes and no, and at times it is very important that he should have the opportunity of saying nothing instead of being forced to agree or disagree. His fourth option is to exercise what is called the "pocket veto." This means that if a bill comes to him and there are fewer than ten days remaining in the congressional session, the president may decide to leave it unsigned, and it automatically dies. Should the people through Congress still wish to enact the law, it must be reintroduced in the next legislative session, and the whole process begins anew.

The checks system goes further. The judicial branch has its say about the laws of the land. Once the Congress and the president have agreed upon a law, it must be enforced all over the United States. Should someone disagree with a federal law and challenge it by disobeying it, the case is brought into the court system of the United States. If the Supreme Court should decide to hear the case, it has the duty of examining the law and determining if it is constitutional, or, in other words, whether the law is in keeping with the rights of the people as outlined in the Constitution. It should be noted, however, that the right of judicial review, as this practice is called, is not stated as such in the Constitution. It became an enduring part of the checks and balance system as early as 1803 through an interpretation of the Constitution by Chief Justice John Marshall in the famous case of *Marbury* v. *Madison*.

This system of balanced power and of checks between the branches of the government reflects the political genius of the Founding Fathers. It has meant that at all times the people's rights and interests are being carefully guarded. There is virtually no chance that a strong man or a group of men can take over the government and force the rest of the people to do their will. It must be stressed, however, that as Jefferson said, "Eternal vigilance is the price of liberty," and if the people of the United States, their elected representatives, and their judges are not constantly vigilant, no mere words on paper are going to protect their freedom. The Watergate scandal more than proves the truth of Jefferson's observation.

THE THREE BRANCHES
OF GOVERNMENT

The Legislative Branch

THE FOUNDING Fathers had a deep belief in the people of the United States. They believed that government can only exist to serve the people. These beliefs are reflected in the Constitution. After the Preamble, the first Article of the Constitution is devoted to a description of the legislative branch of the federal government, the United States Congress. Legislative means the making of laws. The laws of a country are of the greatest importance. If the laws are good ones, the people of a nation will live in peace and prosperity, but if they are poor laws, everyone suffers. Therefore, the making of laws for the nation is a serious business. Because the federal laws affect every person in the land, the people in a democracy must have the right to make their own laws. It is in the legislature, or Congress, that the voice of the people is heard. It is not surprising, then, that Article I of the Constitution sets up the legislative branch.

The first sentence of Article I says that all lawmaking power in the United States will belong to a Congress made up of a Senate and a House of Representatives. In other words, there shall be two sections of the Congress of the United States. In that simple sentence lies one of the most important and wise decisions of the Founding Fathers. The decision to have two houses of Congress was not easily arrived at, and a great struggle took place in 1787 before the writers of the Constitution came to this agreement. The reasons for this struggle are threefold. For one thing, life in 1787 was very different than it

15

is now in the late twentieth century. There were few schools, and, hence, many people in the early days of our nation did not have much formal education. Some of the men in Philadelphia who cared deeply about good government worried that the privileges of democracy would be lost by giving too much responsibility to people who could not understand the difficult principles of lawmaking. Others felt quite the opposite. They said that unless all the people, regardless of their education, had a voice in the United States legislature, true democracy would not exist. They felt that, although the responsibility of making laws was a great one, the people would always be able to accept it.

The second problem which caused difference of opinion concerned how often the Congress should be elected. Some felt that frequent elections would mean a too rapid turnover and that the government would constantly be in a state of disorder. Others favored frequent elections of Congressmen to keep the lawmaking power close to the people.

The third point that caused argument was the problem of the unequal size of the states and whether they should have an equal number of votes in Congress. New York State, for instance, is and always has been a large state. Rhode Island and Delaware are very much smaller. If the federal Congress were made up of representatives elected according to the number of people living in a state, New York would obviously have many more votes than either Rhode Island or Delaware. This disparity was not just, and the small states felt very strongly about this issue.

These three differences of opinion created, indeed, a hard problem because when the argument started, the men were thinking in terms of just one elected assembly to make all the laws. After long and often angry debates, a solution was finally arrived at. Why not have two houses or assemblies in the Congress, one to be made up of two men chosen from every state regardless of its size to remain in office for a longer term (see Seventeenth Amendment), the other, to have members elected from the various states, the number depending on the number of people living in the state, and to have shorter terms in office? This compromise resulted in each point of view being satisfied, and out of this solution came the Congress of the United States made up of two bodies, the House of Representatives and the Senate.

The House of Representatives is the section of the federal government closest to the people of the United States. The men or women (see Nineteenth Amendment) who go to the House, as it is called for short, are elected by the people in their districts in their state every two years. A representative must be a resident of the state and district which he represents. This last requirement was an American innovation. In Britain members of Parliament, the equivalent of our representatives, did not then nor do they even today have to be residents of the constituency they represent. The Founding Fathers, however, wisely saw that the interests of the people would be better served if the person they sent to Congress was extremely familiar with their problems and wishes. In keeping with the nature of the House of Representatives, the powers allotted to this body are those nearest and dearest to the interests of the people of the nation. A very important job given only to the House is the right to start all tax bills. The power to tax, or to tell the citizenry how much money they must pay to make their government work, is almost the most important power in a government. Because as Chief Justice John Marshall stated in the famous case of *McCulloch* v. *Maryland* in 1819 "The power to tax is the power to destroy," the tax power must be jealously guarded and controlled. Should a government have the power to tax unwisely or too freely, the people would suffer, and the writers of the Constitution were all too well aware of this fact because one of the major causes of the War of Independence had been that the British Parliament had imposed taxes on the colonies without their consent. It must be the people who decide how much the taxes should be. They are the guardians against tyranny or dictatorship in this case, and as it is the voice of the people, the House of Representatives must have the power to initiate or begin all revenue laws.

Another important task belonging to the House alone is the authority to impeach the president of the United States. Impeach means to charge an individual with a crime. If the president should break his oath of office or fail to carry out the duties of the office, the House of Representatives charges him, much as a policeman arrests a person who breaks the law. Once again, this power was given to the House in order to give the people a way to protect their rights should a president dare to overstep the limits of his office. When such a situation arises, and it has only occurred twice in the history of the nation, the Judiciary Committee of the House of Representatives is responsible for conducting a careful investigation as to the truth of the charges against the president. All accusations of malfeasance, or misconduct in office, must be examined in detail, and if in the judgment of a majority of the committee the allegations have sufficient substance, a bill of particulars is then drawn up and presented to the full House. If the bill is adopted by a majority vote, the president must then face a trial which the Constitution dictates must be held by the Senate. In 1974 a bill of particulars was voted against Mr. Nixon, but his resignation from office precluded a full House vote, and because there was no vote, a trial before the Senate never occurred.

In addition, the House has several other special privileges. It has the right to elect its own officers. The Speaker of the House is the chairman of the assembly, and he is elected by the members of the House each time a new Congress convenes. Traditionally, he is the leader of the political party which has the most members in Congress. The House also is permitted to make its own rules and to run its affairs as it sees fit. Lastly, the House is constitutionally responsible for determining the outcome of a presidential election, should there be no electoral majority. When that situation arises, which it has twice in our history, in 1800 and 1824, the system of voting in the House changes. Each state gets one vote, and that vote is determined by the delegates of each state meeting and voting between the candidates. The one with the majority of votes receives the state's vote. In 1800, Thomas Jefferson won the presidency this way, and in 1824, John Quincy Adams.

Across the Capitol Building from the House of Representatives sits the other section of Congress, the Senate of the United States. It is made up of two senators from every state regardless of its population. The term of a senator is six years as against the two for a representative. He must be at least thirty years of age; he must have been a citizen of the United States for nine years; and he, too, must be a resident of the state from which he is elected.

The Senate is organized differently from the House. Although senators may choose some of their officers, the president of the Senate, the chief presiding officer, is not elected by that body. The Constitution dictates that he is always the vice-president of the United States. The reason for this rule is to knit together the legislative and executive branches of the government. This keeps the two from operating completely independently of each other. The vice-president, or the president of the Senate, does not vote except in the case of a tie, when he is mandated to cast a vote in order to break it. To provide for a president of the Senate should the vice-president be absent or should he become president due to the death, incapacity or resignation of the president, the Senate has the right to elect from its members a president pro tempore, thereby enabling the Senate to continue its work without pause.

The Senate, like the House, has its own special jobs shared by no other body in the federal government. It has the sole power to try the president of the United States should the House decide to impeach him. When the Senate is forced to sit as a court of law and decide whether the president is guilty or not, the Senate organization changes. The vice-president steps down from his job as president of the Senate, and in his place sits the chief justice of the United States. This substitution is another example of the intertwining of the three branches of the government. The trial of a president is of such a serious nature that the people should sit in judgment. The senators, with their added years and longer terms serving their country, are the best suited for this heavy responsibility. The vice-president cannot judge as he is second to the president, and it would not be right to force him to voice an opinion in a matter so close to himself and his future. The chief justice replaces him to avoid that situation and is in a position to give the president the fairest trial under law. Since the founding of the federal government of the United States, the Senate has exercised this power only once, in the case of Andrew Johnson immediately after the Civil War and he was acquitted by one vote. Although it is to be hoped that no president in the future will ever have an impeachment and a trial, the importance of the power to try a president is obvious. It is the only safeguard against the abuse of presidential authority and the guarantee of the protection of the people's right to be free.

Another of the Senate's special jobs is to serve as a check on and a balance to the power of the president of the United States as he carries out his constitutional duties. The Senate must confirm, or agree to, the appointment of the persons whom the president selects for certain jobs. All ambassadors, and ministers who represent the nation abroad, the justices of the Supreme Court as well as all the judges of the lower federal courts, the cabinet and sub-cabinet officers, members of independent agencies and senior officers of the armed forces must receive senatorial approval before they can assume their responsibilities. Again, the Founding Fathers took great care to make sure that those who would hold positions of great authority would serve the interests of the nation rather than their own. It must be pointed out, however, that it is up to the Senate to carry out this responsibility with the care that the Founding Fathers expected, and upon occasion senators have viewed the confirmation requirement lightly and have simply rubber-stamped the president's choices without a thoughtful and complete review of the candidate's qualifications.

In addition, in the area of foreign affairs, the Constitution authorizes the president to make treaties, but the Senate must ratify them by a two-thirds vote before they become legally binding. This senatorial power was designed by the Founding Fathers to serve as a brake on the executive's authority to commit the United States unless the Senate agreed that it was in the best interests of the nation. This is one case, however, where what the authors of the Constitution had in mind has not, in fact, been strictly followed, and today far more international commitments are made by executive agreement which does not require senatorial approval than by treaty which does. The practice of executive agreement arose partly because treaties have been legally defined as only those agreements which are to last forever, whereas executive agreements are considered temporary, and partly because of the time involved in having the Senate ratify every single international compact entered into by the United States in today's complex and interdependent world. Over the years the formal power of the Senate has also been diluted by the practice of a resolution voted by both houses of Congress agreeing to presidential actions in the foreign field. In the nineteenth century the annexation of Texas and Hawaii was accomplished in this manner because the two presidents involved, James Polk and William McKinley, knew that they could not get a two-thirds vote in the Senate. In recent years, President Lyndon Johnson sought congressional approval for the escalation of the American commitment to the war in Vietnam by getting a joint resolution. At the present time, however, largely because of the tragedy of the Vietnam War, there is considerable feeling among senators that they should exercise their authority to ratify agreements with foreign nations to a far greater degree in order to restore their constitutional role as a check and a balance to executive power and in keeping with the intent of the Founding Fathers to safeguard the rights of the people.

Following the outline of the organization and the separate powers of the House of Representatives and the Senate, the Constitution then lists the powers of Congress as a whole. Congress shall and must meet by law annually. To us in the latter part of the twentieth century, this provision seems to be an obvious necessity. How could laws be made and kept up to date if Congress, the only lawmaking body, failed to meet? In the eighteenth century, however, the inclusion of this specific requirement was of great importance. The framers of the Constitution, most of whom had a broad knowledge of history, were influenced by European experience. Although many of the nations in the Old World did have representative assemblies to help the kings make laws, they did not have constitutions which required that those bodies be convened. If the king wanted advice, he would call them into session, but if he chose to govern alone, he could whether the people liked it or not. In Britain, when the people did rebel, it took a civil war and the execution of one king and the subsequent deposition of another before they could establish the right of their Parliament to meet annually. In France, at the time of the writing of our Constitution, the monarchy had such absolute power that the Estates General, the French representative assembly, had not been convened since 1614! The Founding Fathers, therefore, were going to make certain from the start that the Congress of the United States would meet annually by law, thus preventing the president from ever governing single-handedly. Indeed, it would be impossible for the chief executive to govern alone because the Constitution places all legislative power in the Congress and the president cannot pass laws at all.

Originally, the Constitution said that Congress was to meet each year on the first Monday in December, but in 1933 that date was changed to the third day of January (see Twentieth Amendment). So, on that day each year the many congressmen and senators return to Washington, D.C., from their various homes to begin another session of Congress and to resume the responsibilities of lawmaking. As each term of a Congress lasts two years, it is only every other year that a new Congress assembles. In the in-between years the reconvening of Congress in January only signifies the opening of the second session of a given Congress. That is why, although the nation is almost two hundred years old as far as the Constitution is concerned, we have had under one hundred Congresses to date.

The work of Congress is controlled closely by the Constitution. The fundamental powers are carefully enumerated. Each house has the right to organize itself, to determine the way in which it shall do its business, to see that its members are properly elected, to punish them for bad behavior and to expel, if necessary, by a two-thirds vote. The Senate, for instance, has always allowed unlimited debate which can only be cut off by a cloture vote of the body. The House, on the other hand, has traditionally limited the time that a member has to speak to five minutes unless he can arrange for a sympathetic friend or friends to grant him their time. At the beginning of each new

Congress, all members of the House of Representatives must produce their election certification to the clerk of the House, and if there should be a dispute, it is referred to the appropriate committee for resolution. Should that committee find reason to suspect that the individual's credentials are, in fact, questionable, it can refuse to seat the member and can call for a new election in his or her congressional district. In the Senate, however, only one-third of the body is new at the beginning of each new session. This is because in the original Senate, in order to create the overlapping of the six-year terms, as required by the Constitution, the twenty-six senators drew straws to determine whether they would have two-year, four-year or six-year terms. The reason behind this staggering of the terms was that the Founding Fathers thought that because their work involved many ongoing problems, there should never be a time when the entire Senate was made up of new people. The House, however, as it was designed to be the closest to the electorate, must always be reelected in its entirety. When a new senator arrives, he or she, too, must present credentials to prove that she or he is the legal victor in the election. If there is any reason for doubt, another election must be held before the seat in question can be filled. A state, however, does not have to comply if it does not choose to, and many years ago the state of Mississippi actually chose not to hold another election when one of their senators was refused his seat in Washington, and until his death, the state was represented by only one senator. Again, in 1977 the House of Representatives refused to accept the credentials of a member from Louisiana, and his district held another election in which another man was chosen. Although the present Congress has 535 members, which is an enormous number compared to the first Congress, every effort is made to conform to the careful planning of the Founding Fathers whose intent it was to design a government of integrity.

Both the Senate and the House must keep a record or journal of its debates which is printed by the Government Printing Office and is available to the public. The *Congressional Record* is a day-to-day record of the affairs of Congress as well as a repository for anything of interest that a representative or a senator may wish to insert. Only discussions which touch on matters of national security which should remain secret are not printed. Otherwise anyone who is interested may follow the course of the making of laws and may find out exactly what his senator or representative is doing at all times. The keeping of an open record is another means of insuring democracy. Each voter has the right to check on his representatives in Congress at will.

The Constitution not only describes the duties and responsibilities of the congressmen, but also grants them certain protections and immunities while in government service. They are to be paid for their services by the United States Treasury, but the amount of their salaries is determined by their own action, a situation which is often extremely sensitive politically. The decision to give a salary to congressmen, however, was a very wise one. Obviously people coming to serve their constituents in Washington must live while they are away from their homes. Many who would wish to be lawmakers would not be men of private means and could not afford to give up their jobs at home if they were not paid for their work in Washington. A federal salary guaranteed to the people who enter government service has meant that men and women of all backgrounds could enter politics, and that has been one of the great strengths of the United States.

Congressmen are also guaranteed freedom from arrest while pursuing their duties in Congress. Naturally, major crimes such as treason or murder would not go unpunished, but one important result of this privilege granted to members of Congress is to guarantee their right to express their opinions freely while either in the Capitol or on their way to and from it. Laws which grow out of free discussion are always better than those resulting from inhibited debate. No man should be penalized for giving his opinion in the course of doing his duty. Therefore, it is another safeguard to democracy to have the lawmakers at liberty to speak their minds.

The Constitution then goes on to list the responsibilities that Congress must bear. The list is exact because the fear of losing the people's freedom is ever present. To give too much power to the federal government of the United States would perhaps endanger the rights of the states and the citizenry. The original states were jealous of their autonomy and wished only certain lawmaking powers to be granted to the federal Congress. The powers or rights not listed specifically in the Constitution belonged automatically to the states. This check on the power of Congress keeps that body from interfering with matters that are strictly the states' affairs. The powers listed as belonging to the federal legislature are those which affect all the people of the country equally and are important to the peace, the safety and the prosperity of the nation.

The powers relating to money and to financial affairs that are granted to the federal Congress are of the greatest importance. No government is a good one if it is not sound financially. It is not surprising, therefore, that the list of the powers of Congress relating to money is an impressive one. Congress, and Congress alone, has the right to coin money and to fix its value. Also, the punishments for counterfeiting or copying the currency of the United States are to be fixed by Congress. This central control over the currency of the nation was of great importance in 1787 because, as was mentioned above, before the Constitution each state had its own currency, and confusion prevailed. Now every state and its citizens could do business easily with one legal form of money everywhere.

The right to decide the amount of federal taxes and to collect them belongs solely to Congress. Since 1862 the Internal Revenue Service, established by an act of Congress, collects all federal taxes excepting those relating to alcohol, firearms, tobacco, and explosives. If money is to be borrowed by the United States government for any reason, only Congress can give permission for the loan to be arranged, and Congress is authorized to pay the debts of the United States. Commerce both between the states and with foreign nations is regulated by the Senate and the House of Representatives. These powers enable the federal government to regulate trade for the benefit of all the people in the nation and to keep commerce on an orderly basis. In today's world, which the Founding Fathers could not possibly have anticipated, this control over commerce has become one of Congress's most difficult and thorny problems in that what certain states want and need for their own prosperity often comes into direct conflict with the goals of American foreign policy, which are to maintain a stable and peaceful world. There are many examples of this sort of dilemma, but one good one is the case of the imports of Japanese television sets and other electronic equipment. The Japanese can produce at a lower cost than American firms because of a much lower wage scale, and, therefore, can sell at a better price in the United States. Although popular with the consumer, this situation places an economic hardship on American producers. They, quite naturally, turn to Congress for protection of their interests while the State Department is pressing for consideration for one of our staunchest allies whose economy depends heavily on exports. The same problem exists in the shoe and clothing industries. The importation of cheaper shoes from Taiwan and Korea in particular has hurt the shoe manufacturers in New England, and the garment industry, which used to be one of New York City's major industries, has suffered badly with the flood of imported clothes from Europe and the Far East.

Equal in importance to the financial responsibilities of the Congress is its duty to provide for the defense of the nation. Congress has the job of establishing an army, navy and, in the twentieth century, an air force for the protection of our land. Although the executive branch actually runs these services, Congress plays an important role in the formulation of defense policy because it funds the armed forces by appropriating money annually from the general revenue of the United States. Those responsible for the defense establishment must, therefore, justify their budgets to the satisfaction of the legislature, and the members of the congressional committees responsible for defense must become experts on weaponry and strategic needs in order to make the proper decisions in this extremely critical area.

Closely allied with its role in defense is Congress's constitutional responsibility of declaring war. In the eighteenth century wars were formally declared by a nation's government. In Britain the monarch had the sole power to take such a step, and it was not surprising that the Founding Fathers, always intent on curbing and checking the power of the executive, should split the serious responsibility of declaring war between the Congress and the president. The Constitution, therefore, dictates that the president, if he sees no alternative, must ask Congress for a declaration of war, and then Congress must vote for the declaration if its members agree with the chief executive's assessment of the situation. On Monday, December 8th, 1941, the day after Pearl Harbor was bombed, President Roosevelt went to the Capitol and asked a joint session of Congress to declare war against imperial Japan, which it did by an almost unanimous vote.*

Since that day, however, the world has changed radically, and although the Constitution has not been amended, the United States has actually engaged in two wars, neither of which was declared in the manner prescribed by the Constitution. Each came about due to the involvement of the United States in international organizations in the post–World War II era. In 1945 the United States became a founding member of the United Nations and by so doing pledged to protect member nations from aggression. In 1950, therefore, when the frontier between North and South Korea, which had been guaranteed by the United Nations, was violated by the North Koreans, the United States together with other member nations of the United Nations fought an undeclared war until 1953 when the fighting was terminated by negotiations. A permanent settlement has still to be determined, however, and to date American troops are still stationed in Korea. In 1954 the United States, concerned with the spread of communism in the Far East, became a member of the Southeast Asia Treaty Organization in an effort to protect the independent countries of that area. And, once again, in the 1960s the United States became entangled in a foreign war in Vietnam partly because of her membership in SEATO. Although Congress had not formally acquiesced in the decision to participate militarily in Vietnam, it did, however, support administration policy both by appropriating funds for the conflict and in 1964 by voting the Gulf of Tonkin Resolution which authorized President

---

*The sole nay vote was from a conscientious objector.

Johnson to escalate the war to protect the Americans already fighting there.

The Vietnam War proved to be a turning point in the nation's history in that it was the first time that a large proportion of the American public did not support their nation's participation in a land many thousands of miles away, and pressure mounted to the extent that Congress was forced to take steps to limit the authority of the executive to engage the country in military operations without its approval. Recognizing, however, the fact that in today's world of high speed airplanes and missiles the traditional system of declaring war was for all practical purposes outmoded, Congress passed the War Powers Act which, although it permits the president to respond to a crisis by deploying American forces, requires him to come to Congress after sixty days for authorization to continue the operation. Quite obviously, this solution, enacted in a highly emotional atmosphere, is not ideal in that if American troops were indeed engaged in combat, it would be most unlikely that a Congress would deny them the means by which to defend themselves. All that can be said at this time is that both the executive and legislative branches of the government have learned that there must be mutual trust and a sharing of responsibility in the whole area of defense and military engagement in order to carry out faithfully the intent of the Constitution to safeguard the American people from irresponsible military ventures.

Congress has many responsibilities other than defense and finance. It must establish post offices and post roads to enable the citizens to communicate with each other and to travel safely within the boundaries of the country. Congress is also given the power to encourage the development of the arts and sciences. By issuing patents and copyrights for inventions and artistic works, Congress protects the individual from having his discovery or creation used by others and grants him any financial benefits derived from his idea for a given period of time. This kind of protection encourages people to contribute to the progress of the whole nation and is one of the main reasons for the extraordinary scientific, technological, and cultural advances of the United States. Also in line with keeping the nation up to date, Congress has the responsibility of creating more federal courts under the Supreme Court when they are required. In the nineteenth century, as the country spread from the eastern seaboard to the Pacific Coast and beyond, because of this foresighted constitutional clause Congress was able to establish federal district and appellate courts across the nation so that Americans, wherever they were, were guaranteed access to the federal judiciary. Today, however, in spite of the fact that there are, in addition to the Supreme Court, twelve courts of appeal, ninety-one district courts, plus other specialized courts, with a total of 648 judges and justices, there is considerable pressure on Congress to create additional judgeships. Over two hundred and twenty million people now live in the United States, and the litigation they bring taxes the present judiciary to the hilt. It would seem an easy thing to add more judges to take some of the burden off the present judges, but because the Constitution requires that appointments to the federal judiciary be for life, politics play a considerable role in Congressional considerations, particularly if the executive is of one party and the majority of the legislature of the other. Under President Carter, however, both branches were held by the Democratic Party, and Congress created 110 new district and thirty-five new circuit judgeships. Because a basic tenet of American law is the right to speedy justice, which depends to a large extent on an adequate number of judges, it was important that Congress enact this law.

The fact that the Founding Fathers were well aware that the United States would grow led them to empower Congress to regulate naturalization laws for the whole country. Naturalization means the becoming of an American citizen of a person by birth the citizen of a foreign land. As people from other nations were pouring into the new nation in the Western Hemisphere, there had to be a system for making them Americans. Congress must set up these laws and see that they are carried out uniformly across the nation. A person desiring to become an American citizen must have resided here for five years in good standing. He or she must learn all about the American system of government and take a test proving an understanding of the obligations and rights of an American citizen. An oath is then administered by a federal judge, and much ceremony usually surrounds such occasions because they are very important events in the lives of the new Americans, especially in these days when many come to the United States in search of freedom which was denied them in the land of their birth.

Another Congressional responsibility is to decide whether to admit new states to the Union. This authority was extremely important in the nineteenth century as the nation was expanding so rapidly across the continent and was the source of much of the political friction which preceded the actual outbreak of the Civil War. The Founding Fathers did not foresee that the issue of slavery would become so divisive when they incorporated the procedures by which territories were to become states from the Articles of Confederation into the Constitution. Although many of the framers were strongly anti-slavery, they realized that the institution had to be accepted if the Constitution were to be ratified, and they also really believed that slavery was on the decline and would disappear in the near future. Unfortunately it did not, and the question over the admission of slave or free states had grown into the most burning political issue of the 1850s, one which in the end could not be resolved by compromise, only by war. After the war the admission of new states was mainly routine until the mid-twentieth century when Alaska and Hawaii applied. Not only were they noncontiguous, which posed a new situation for the forty-eight continental states, but their admission involved political and social problems as well, and it was not until 1959, long after they had actually qualified for statehood, that Congress finally voted them into the Union, Alaska in January, Hawaii in August.

Having decided the powers that Congress had to have to make the new nation strong, the writers of the Constitution still worried about the possibility of the federal government becoming too powerful. They then made a list of all the things that Congress might never do. This list is of equal importance as the list of Congress's responsibilities because it reinsures the freedom of the states and their citizens and prevents the federal government from ever becoming dictatorial. Congress can never suspend the writ of habeas corpus except in cases of extreme national emergency. Habeas corpus is the law prohibiting the imprisonment of any individual without a specific cause. The writ of habeas corpus is one of the greatest safeguards of liberty in that it protects the rights of the individual before the law.

Furthermore, Congress can never pass a law relating to criminal matters that would apply retroactively or to the past. All criminal laws, in other words, take effect at the time of their passage and cannot be applied to a situation which occurred before that date. The power to tax is also restricted. Congress is expressly forbidden to tax any articles exported from any state, and no preference can be shown for one state over another in any commercial way. A last restriction placed on the powers of Congress is that at no time can that body create or bestow on any individual any title of nobility. This particular restriction seems to be very eighteenth century in its concept, but had it not been included, the citizens of the twentieth century might well not be each other's peers. It should be pointed out also that the clause is not entirely outmoded because whenever a person from a foreign nation who wants to be naturalized comes before the judge, he must renounce his title if he has one before he can take the oath of allegiance to the United States of America.

Toward the end of the long list of powers and responsibilities of the legislative branch of the government, there is the instruction to the Congress to find a suitable site for the capital of the United States. The Constitution had been written in the old colonial city of Philadelphia, and the first capital was New York where George Washington took the first inaugural oath. There had to be a permanent home, preferably a new site established for the sole purpose of housing the federal government and which would be under the jurisdiction of Congress as the Constitution specified. Congress found that it was not easy to locate such a district in that there was argument over whether the capital should be in the North or the South, and, in addition, states were somewhat reluctant to give up taxable property. Finally, Virginia and Maryland were persuaded to turn over some of their land along the Potomac River, and out of this territory the District of Columbia was formed. From 1800 to today Washington, D.C., has been the nation's capital, and the clause in the Constitution (Article I, Section 8) which ordered Congress to find the permanent site also granted Congress the right to rule the home of the federal government. Over the years, however, the people who live in the District and who are not necessarily connected with the federal government have clamored for self-government. In the nineteenth century they elected officials who handled local affairs, but in 1874 Congress revoked this privilege, and the city was administered by three presidentially appointed commissioners, one of whom by law had to be an officer in the Army Corps of Engineers. After World War II pressure began again to grow for home rule, but it was not until 1974 that Congress relented and abolished the "last colony."

The present government of the District of Columbia consists of an elected mayor and city council, and it is represented by an elected delegate to Congress, but he cannot vote. He can only speak for Washingtonians and urge the passage of legislation which they support. Congress still retains final legislative authority over the District, and it is not surprising that the District's representative introduces a bill for complete self-government every session. If such a bill were enacted, it would have to be in the form of a constitutional amendment because it is the Constitution which gives Congress the ultimate control, and unfortunately to date, the representatives and senators from the fifty states have not been very concerned with the problems of the citizens of the District of Columbia. In 1960, however, Washingtonians did gain the privilege of voting in presidential elections through the Twenty-third Amendment to the Constitution, so it is possible that someday the District will enjoy the same status as the fifty states. Not only do the residents of our national capital deserve the privileges of all American citizens, but if the District had the status of a state, it would save Congress a lot of trouble. As it stands today, every time Congress passes a law applying to the states, it has to include a special provision so that it will apply to the District of Columbia as well, which is a nuisance and time consuming.

The same clause which ordered Congress to find a location for the capital city also granted Congress the right to take land for the use of the government for forts, arsenals, dockyards and the like, but it must compensate the owner, either the state or a private citizen. All federal land in the United States is governed by Congress unless a special arrangement is made with the state in which the land is located. One of the famous federal sites was Fort Sumter at the mouth of the harbor of Charleston, South Carolina. Because it was a federal fort, President Lincoln had no choice in 1861 but to reinforce it, thus bringing about the opening salvos of the Civil War.

The very last power given to Congress in Article I deserves special attention in that it probably was the most important of all the powers of Congress to the future of the country and has contributed to the lasting success of the Constitution. Whereas all the other charges to Congress are very specific, the last is not. It simply states that Congress is authorized "to make all laws which shall be necessary and proper for carrying into Execution the foregoing Powers, and all other Powers vested by this Constitution in the Government of the United States, or in any Department or Officer thereof." What this means is that Congress could exercise implied power or pass legislation not specifically authorized but necessary to carrying out an authorized power. An example is that Congress is ordered to pay the debt of the United States, but it is not told how precisely it is to do this. Early in our federal history, the first secretary of the treasury, Alexander Hamilton, whose task it was to pay the nation's debts, wished to establish a bank under federal auspices by which to raise the money with which to meet the new nation's obligations. Because it was not specifically within the enumerated powers of Congress to charter a bank, there was widespread opposition to the idea, but George Washington decided that under the Necessary and Proper Clause, or the Elastic Clause as it has been nicknamed, Congress did have the right to pass such legislation authorizing a bank. He was later vindicated in his judgment by Chief Justice John Marshall in *McCulloch* v. *Maryland* in 1819, and since then this clause has enabled Congress to meet the challenges of changing times within the Constitution. Had the framers not included this "Elastic Clause," it is quite possible that the Constitution would have been outmoded in short order.

Thus were the organization, duties and responsibilities of the legislative branch so carefully worked out. Not a detail was omitted by the Founding Fathers in their attempt to create a working Congress able to carry out its functions, but at the same time restricted from ever becoming too powerful. From 1789 to the present, in spite of the fact that the country has grown enormously and the problems facing the nation today were inconceivable to the framers of the Constitution, Congress still legislates under exactly the same rules they prescribed so many years ago.

The Executive Branch

Laws are a basic necessity to the democratic way of life. Therefore, the making of laws is a vital function in a democracy. If those laws, however, are not carried out, they would be of no value whatsoever. The job of carrying out the laws is, then, of great importance. Who should be responsible for enforcing the acts passed by the legislature?

This question was a serious one to the people of the late eighteenth century in the newly independent United States. The thirteen colonies had waged a long and expensive war against the arbitrary rule of one man, a king. Immediately following that war, the colonies had created a form of government without a central executive empowered to carry out laws and had found that system to be far from satisfactory. The answer to the problem of how to carry out laws had to lie between the two extremes. There should be neither an arbitrary ruler nor no ruler at all, but a chief executive with carefully specified powers and a limited term in office.

Article II of the Constitution describes the executive branch of the federal government in as careful detail as possible. The Constitution places the executive power in the hands of a president. To guard against the possible tyranny of one man, the president's term is limited to four years. No matter what the situation, every four years an election is held to fill the office of the president. War is no deterrent, and in the middle of the Civil War and World War II, Abraham Lincoln and Franklin Roosevelt had to stand for reelection. In the Constitution as written in 1787 there was no limitation placed on the number of terms one president might have. George Washington, however, set a precedent by stepping down after two terms, and no president until Franklin Roosevelt had more than two. Roosevelt had four, although he died shortly after his election to the fourth. The American people then decided that it was better for the country to limit the terms to two in a row, and in 1951 the Twenty-second Amendment to the Constitution was added restricting any future president from being elected to more than two consecutive terms. That amendment also restricts a vice-president who accedes to the presidency. If he fills more than two years of the presidential term, it counts as a full term, and he can only be reelected once more. If he fills less than two years, however, he is then eligible for two four-year terms of his own. President Ford is a case in point. He had filled less than two years of President Nixon's term and was, therefore, eligible to run in 1976, and, had he won, again in 1980. It should be pointed out, however, that the amendment is unclear as to whether a president could have two consecutive terms, then step down for four years, and run again later. This issue might have been decided had President Kennedy lived. He was the youngest man ever to be elected to the White House, and it would have been quite possible for him to have served two terms, gone out of office, and then sought another term at a later date. The situation, however, never arose due to his tragic death, and the issue is yet to be resolved.

Who may be elected to the presidency and the manner in which he shall be elected were carefully specified in the Constitution. Anyone aspiring to the highest office in the land must have been born in the United States, and he must be at least thirty-five years of age. To insure the fact that his interests really lie within the country, the Constitution also demands that the candidate have lived in the United States for fourteen years prior to his running for office. The framers realized very sensibly that only a person whose life was centered in the land of his birth could be best suited to be the chief executive. Again, however, it is possible that with travel as rapid as it is today and the world so intertwined that an individual whose business had carried him abroad either in government service or as a private citizen for protracted periods of time who chose to run for president might indeed not have resided in the United States for fourteen consecutive years. If that case should ever arise, it is likely that if his party considered him the best candidate, the constitutional restriction would be lifted.

The importance of the job of the president of the United States is so great that the manner in which he is elected had to be devised with great care. Before the system of how the president is elected can be understood, it is important to remember the vast difference between the United States in the eighteenth century and in the twentieth century. Communications were extremely poor in the eighteenth century. There were few newspapers, no telegraph, no radio, no television. It was difficult, if not wholly impossible, for residents in one part of the country to know people well from far off sections. This was a matter of great concern to the Founding Fathers because they knew a democratic republican government depended entirely on the care with which the citizenry chose their leaders. They felt that the representatives to the House could be directly elected because the districts for which they were to speak were small, and the voter would know the candidates. They showed their concern, however, in the manner by which the senators were elected in the original Constitution. They were chosen by the state legislatures, and that system was not changed until the twentieth century with the ratification of the Seventeenth Amendment in 1913. No wonder, then, that the framers worked out an extremely complicated system for the election of the president called the electoral college. Every four years on election day, which by constitutional dictate is always the first Tuesday after the first Monday in November of even years, the voters go to the polls and cast their ballot for a man who will choose the president. He is called an elector. The number of electors a state will have is determined by the number of representatives it is permitted in the House of Representatives plus the two senators. All the electors in a state meet in their state capital in December following the November election and cast their ballots for the president. These ballots are then sealed in a chest and are carried to Washington where they are counted by the president of the Senate, the vice-president of the United States, in front of the assembled Senate in January. When he has finished, the person who has the majority of electoral votes is then declared officially to be the next president of the United States.* The original idea behind this scheme was that the electors should be men known to the voters for their intelligence and their integrity, and that they would exercise extreme caution to make sure that the best qualified person would be president. Although this system is clearly outmoded today with television and radio in everyone's homes, many newspapers, magazines, and speedy air transportation so that every voter knows the candidates well, it is still the way that Americans elect their president. The only real changes today are that everybody knows who the two major candidates are as soon as the political parties have held their conventions; their names are on the ballot that the voter marks; the winner is known generally before election night is out; and the electors are virtually unknown to everyone. Every four years there is a great deal of comment on the need to abolish the electoral college, but somehow the furor dies down, and everybody forgets it until next time.

Although the Constitution lays down certain rules as to the age, nationality and manner of election of the president, it specifies nothing as to the individual's political beliefs. When the Constitution was written, there were no organized political parties in this country. George Washington, the first president under the Constitution, was elected unanimously by the electors purely on his personal record, not because of any political affiliation. But today the president of the United States is the head of his political party, and he is elected by electors who

---

*This task of the vice-president can be painful. Both Richard Nixon and Hubert Humphrey, while vice-president, had to count the ballots which elected their opponent to the presidency. Nixon lost to John Kennedy in 1960 and Humphrey lost to Nixon in 1968.

are chosen because of their political allegiance. In fact, a candidate for the presidency only becomes a serious contender because he has been selected by his political party. Independents, although men whom a great many admire, actually have little chance against the party candidates. Washington's election was, therefore, unique because as soon as he had taken office, political differences arose, and the party system of American politics began.

In a democracy in which freedom to think and to speak are the basic rights of each citizen, a political party is a natural development. People are very vocal as to how their government should be run and which policies should be adopted. That there should be differences of opinion in such a broad and important field is only natural, and out of these differences of opinion, political parties were born. Men who agreed tended to band together apart from those who held opposite views. These groups as early as the end of the eighteenth century became organized into what we call parties and began to play a significant role in American government. By the third presidential election, held in 1800, the advent of political parties forced an amendment to the Constitution. Originally, the runner-up in a presidential contest became the vice-president, but when politics became a factor, it was absurd to have a president of one party and a vice-president of the other. The Twelfth Amendment, therefore, caused the electors to cast two ballots, one for the president and the second for the vice-president, thus insuring that the victors would be of the same political persuasion. For many years presidential candidates for the parties were chosen by the party supporters in Congress, but in 1831 a new system was introduced, that of conventions held for the sole purpose of having members of the party vote for the man of their choice. That system has been followed ever since. It should be noted, however, that in spite of the major role that parties play in American government, there is absolutely no mention of them in the Constitution. They are simply an integral part of the American political tradition. It should also be emphasized that party membership is not a prerequisite for voting. A basic civil right of an American, provided he is eligible (age, residence,

THE THREE BRANCHES OF GOVERNMENT

etc.) is the right to vote, and, indeed, in recent years party membership has actually fallen off sharply and an increasing number of Americans list themselves as independents. These voters scrutinize candidates for political office from the Presidency on down to the local dogcatcher extremely carefully, and because their votes cannot be taken for granted, they have become a very important factor in American elections.

Whoever he may be or to whatever party he may belong, the president of the United States has certain powers and responsibilities, and he must abide by his oath to carry them out. Every president, following his election, must be inaugurated before he can legally take over his job. The chief justice of the United States administers the oath of office to the president-elect. He swears, often on a family Bible, in front of the American people to "faithfully execute the office of President of the United States, and . . . to preserve, protect and defend the Constitution of the United States." Once he has taken the oath, he is the president and for four years must carry out the responsibilities of his office and the law of the land.

His job as president is carefully outlined in the Constitution so that there would be little chance of his taking over any powers belonging to either Congress or to the states. He is the chief executive of the federal government. He is the commander in chief of the armed forces and of any state militia should it be called into federal service. This responsibility is of great importance. Over the course of history many a military man with the power of the armed forces behind him has taken over the government of a country and has ruled by might instead of by right. The president of the United States is and must be a civilian, and the fact that he is in supreme command over the generals and admirals of the armed forces serves as a guarantee against military dictatorship in the United States. Should a military man be elected president of the country, he must resign his commission and command before taking the oath of office. He is elected as a civilian and remains one while in the White House despite his past profession. Americans have had a penchant for electing military men beginning with George Washington. Andrew Jackson, William Henry Harrison, Zachary Taylor, Ulysses Grant, Theodore Roosevelt, and Dwight Eisenhower had all been military heroes before becoming president, but all served their country faithfully as civilians once in that exalted office.

The president is entrusted with the job of appointing all those who serve their country as ambassadors, ministers, consuls, judges of the federal bench and all other offices of the United States. Before they can take the oath of their office, however, they must be approved by a two-thirds vote in the Senate. As was pointed out above, this restriction checks the power of the president to appoint just anyone to an important job. He must be acceptable to the people through their elected senators. When a new president takes office, however, the Senate is apt to confirm his cabinet appointments rather perfunctorily as it is considered his right to have whom he chooses serve him in these advisory capacities. In recent years, however, in the wake of Watergate, the Lance resignation early in President Carter's administration, and the resignation of two top officials of the Environmental Protection Agency appointed by President Reagan, the Senate has begun to take a much closer look at the individuals chosen, and it is probably fair to say that standards of ethics and consideration of an individual's expertise are going to be more strictly adhered to. Should the Senate not be in session when a vacancy occurs, the president is permitted to make a recess appointment so that the work of government may go on without interruption, but the appointees must be confirmed as soon as the Senate reconvenes.

As chief executive of the land, the president also has the power to grant pardons and reprieves for crimes committed against the United States. To the Founding Fathers, mercy, a characteristic of civilized society, was a basic tenet of a democratic republic, and they considered it morally right that the president should have it within his power to forgive those who had committed in the eyes of the law crimes against the state if there were extenuating circumstances. The inclusion of clemency in the Constitution distinguished the new government from many of its counterparts in the Old World where punishments were often arbitrary, harsh and irrevocable. Important as this power is, however, it was probably the least known and understood by the general public. That is until the present. Few Americans can be unaware today of the right of the president to pardon after President Ford's pardon of Richard Nixon shortly after Ford took office in August of 1974. Although many people disagreed with the decision, Ford believed that by exercising his prerogative, he had saved the nation from a continuation of the Watergate trauma which was ripping the country apart. Until President Ford, the only other president to use the pardon power frequently was Abraham Lincoln during the exceptional days of the Civil War. In both cases the presidents were, in fact, carrying out the intent of the Founding Fathers to make the United States government a compassionate one for the good of the nation.

Because the president is the chief executive and responsible for the condition of the nation, he is also required by the Constitution to report to Congress, and through Congress to the people, on the state of the Union. At this time he not only reports on the state of affairs, but also suggests and recommends programs to Congress which he thinks advisable for the good of the country. In this way, the president becomes a policy maker. As the political party system in the United States has evolved, the president's State of the Union address has become the traditional way in which he asks for laws by which his party's platform or his own campaign promises can be enacted. Congress does not have to follow the president's suggestions or heed his requests, but the speech is a guide to what the nation's leader thinks should be done. The State of the Union address is traditionally given in person by the president in the Capitol at the beginning of each new congressional session in January. It is always attended by the justices of the Supreme Court in their judicial robes, the cabinet, foreign ambassadors and other dignitaries as well as by the Senate and the House of Representatives. And today, because of television, it is usually given in the evening during prime time so that the American people can see it and hear their president's message. This major address is followed by any number of special messages from the White House to Congress dealing with specific problems confronting the nation. In addition, if there is some particularly important reason, the president can address a special session of Congress at any time.

As was noted above, the Constitution also requires the president to ask Congress for a declaration of war. As also stated above, in recent years presidents, in fact, have deployed American forces abroad without the formality of a request for a declaration of war, and, as a result, Congress has attempted to control this presidential practice by the War Powers Act of 1975. In all likelihood presidents in the future will meet the spirit of the act and will consult with the congressional leaders if tense international situations threaten to involve the United States. The president also has the responsibility of drawing up peace treaties at the end of hostilities which cannot become binding until the Senate ratifies by at least a two-thirds majority.

The president's treaty-making power extends to all international agreements which will be permanently binding on the United States. The newly negotiated Panama Canal treaties are a recent example of this power. In 1903 the original treaty with Panama was drawn up by Theodore Roosevelt, then the president, and was ratified by the Senate. Under the terms of this treaty the United States built the Panama Canal, operated it, and governed a zone bordering the Canal. The United States paid an annual rent to Panama for these privileges. For some time the Panamanians have been very eager to regain control over the zone which bisects their country and to have more say in the operation of the Canal as well as more income. For many years now the United States has been negotiating a new treaty; in fact four presidents have worked toward a satisfactory agreement. Finally the two nations came to an agreement and President Carter and General Torrijos of Panama signed the texts. The Senate of the United States, after a prolonged debate, ratified the treaties in the winter of 1978. This is a classic example of the checks and balances system in operation.

All the executive authority and responsibility are vested in the president of the United States. Constitutionally, no one can share his power. But what if the president should die, become totally incapacitated, or be forced to resign within the four years in which he is the chief executive? To prevent a complete breakdown of the executive department, the Constitution provides for a vice-president who shall become president in case of the latter's death, illness, or resignation. The Constitution, as it was first written, did not provide for the situation in which there is no vice-president because the elected vice-president has become president. By the 1960s this situation had occurred seven times in the history of the United States, and in view of the dangers inherent in the world today, Congress felt it was necessary to amend the Constitution to provide for a new vice-president should the incumbent have to move to the presidency. The Twenty-fifth Amendment, ratified in 1967 by the necessary three-quarters of the states, decrees that in such circumstances the new president nominate a vice-president who then must be confirmed by a majority vote of both houses of Congress. Before this amendment was adopted, had both the president and the vice-president died or become incapacitated, the presidency would have passed to the Speaker of the House of Representatives. There were two major problems to that practice: one, the Speaker could be a member of the opposite political party from the man who had won the presidency in the last election, and, two, he could be unqualified for the job due to age or some other reason. Therefore, it seemed a better idea to allow the new president to pick a man of his own party and to let his competency and acceptability rest on the judgment of Congress. Little did anyone think in 1967 that the new system would be almost immediately put to the test and that for the first time in history the nation would have an unelected president. In 1973 the vice-president of the United States, Spiro Agnew, was forced to resign due to legal improprieties. President Nixon then nominated Gerald Ford, a representative from Grand Rapids, Michigan, to take his place, and he was duly accepted by the Congress. In 1974 he became the thirty-seventh president of the United States upon the resignation of Mr. Nixon. The wisdom of the authors of the amendment was proven in that President Ford, although not elected to office, arrived at the White House via the Constitution which enhanced his acceptability to the American people who were stunned by the series of untoward events. President Ford, then, in his turn nominated Nelson Rockefeller to the vice-presidency, and, once again, Congress confirmed his choice. The executive branch of the government was able to function within the Constitution without faltering in spite of the series of exceptional events which had shaken it.

What does the vice-president do as vice-president? Unless he should become president of the United States, he has only one constitutional role. He is the president of the Senate. Otherwise he has no defined job at all, and until very recently vice-presidents were known as the forgotten men of Washington. Since World War II, however, because of the unrest and tension in the world, presidents have seen fit to give their vice-presidents more assignments and have brought them into the highest councils of the government so that they would be prepared in case they had to take over. For some years now they have regularly attended cabinet meetings, something they never did in the past. Also they usually have important assignments in the area of national security and membership in other councils of state.* The vice-president is apt to travel a great deal as the president's personal emissary. Vice-presidential trips are very important for two reasons. One, as he is the vice-president, he outranks the secretary of state and ambassadors, and when abroad, he can hold high level discussions with heads of state and speak with almost as much authority as the president. Two, his getting to know foreign leaders personally can be extremely important should he be catapulted into the presidency at some point. It must be stressed, however, that his responsibilities are what the president desires, not prescribed by the Constitution, except for his role in the Senate. All the executive responsibility belongs to the president and to the president alone.

Today, the presidency of the United States is probably the most important and yet the most difficult job in the world. Not only does the president have to try to solve the many serious domestic problems which face the nation, but he is responsible for maintaining a strong and free America in a very turbulent world. All during his term in office he is not only burdened by

---

*He is also a Regent of the Smithsonian Institution

the great pressure of ceaseless work, but is also under the scrutiny of the citizens of the United States, and he is the target of all who disagree with him politically. He cannot even move about freely, but is surrounded at all times by a phalanx of secret service officers. No wonder that the president has been described as the loneliest man in the United States, but at no time has there been a dearth of candidates for the office in spite of its onerous nature.

The Judicial Branch

The third branch of the United States government is the judiciary, and it is the greatest testament to the political genius of the Founding Fathers. When they were designing the legislative and executive branches, to a certain extent they had models to guide them. After all, the British Parliament was a legislative body and the monarch an executive. From personal experience with both, the framers of the Constitution knew what they did not like in the British system, and, therefore, adjusted the legislative and executive branches in the Constitution to suit America's needs. They had, however, absolutely no experience with a separate judiciary because none existed at the time of the writing of the Constitution. The Founding Fathers were familiar, however, with the writings of the French philosopher Montesquieu who, in his treatise *The Spirit of the Laws,* had argued for the establishment of a separate judiciary in an ideal form of government. As the Founding Fathers were embarked on a completely new venture of writing out a constitution from scratch, they wanted very much, should it be ratified by the American people, to build into it the means by which it could be made permanent and not subject to the whims of the times. They believed that the way to best protect the Constitution was through the establishment of the separate judiciary that Montesquieu had urged. An independent federal judicial system could adjudicate or resolve the disputes over the Constitution that would surely arise between the other two branches as well as among the states, and it would insure liberty and justice for the American people for all time. Article III, therefore, establishing the judicial branch of the federal government is one of the key reasons that the Constitution has been able to withstand all the vicissitudes of history for nearly two hundred years. It is the reason that Chief Justice John Marshall could say that the United States government was a government "of laws, not of men."

Article III is surprisingly brief, considering its importance. It simply states that "the judicial Power of the United States, shall be vested in one Supreme Court, and in such inferior Courts, as the Congress may from time to time ordain and establish" and goes on to say that judges are to be appointed for life on the condition of good behavior and that they are to be paid, but that their salaries may not be lowered while they serve on the bench. Life tenure and the restriction of their salaries were included to insure the immunity of the federal judiciary from political pressure in order to guarantee really impartial justice.

As soon as the first administration under the Constitution took office in 1789, George Washington appointed the first justices of the Supreme Court, thereby breathing life into Article III. The first Congress established two inferior courts, the district and the circuit, to bring justice to the states and the people, and then the president appointed judges to the district bench. The circuit courts, of which there were three initially, had no special judges, but were manned by one Supreme Court justice and two district judges. Not until late in the nineteenth century did Congress establish separate judgeships for the circuit courts of appeal, of which there are now twelve in the United States, presided over by 132 judges. And today there are ninety-one district courts in the fifty states, in the District of Columbia, and in Puerto Rico. In addition, there are the territorial courts in Guam, the Virgin Islands, the former Canal Zone, and the northern Mariana Islands, which the United States hold under a United Nations Trusteeship. These courts handle all federal criminal and civil cases which come under their jurisdiction. The district courts hear cases initially, and if there is proper cause, decisions from these courts may be appealed to the circuit courts. (Appellate cases from the federal territories are assigned to either the first, third, fifth, or ninth circuits.)

Circuit court decisions in very specific circumstances may be reviewed by the Supreme Court. The decision of the Supreme Court is final.

As the nation has grown in size and governmental affairs have become infinitely more complicated, Congress has seen fit to add other courts to handle special kinds of cases. At present, in addition to the federal courts just described, there are the United States Tax Court, the Court of Claims, the Court of Customs and Patent Appeals, the Court of International Trade, the Court of Military Appeals, and the Temporary Emergency Court of Appeals. The president appoints the judges of these special courts subject to Senate approval, but in some cases the appointments are for a term of years rather than for life.

Today the Supreme Court, by congressional statute, is made up of nine persons, eight associate justices* and the chief justice of the United States. The chief justice is actually on a par with the other justices as they all have but one vote in deciding cases, but he is responsible for all the administrative details involved with the functioning of the Court and is chairman of the annual conference of the federal judiciary and, as such, receives a slightly larger salary than the other justices. He has, of course, tremendous prestige, and if he has a strong personality is apt to be very influential on the bench.

The jurisdiction of the Supreme Court as defined in the Constitution is both original and appellate. The cases which must be heard by the highest court are those involving ambassadors, ministers, or consuls and the states. The appellate jurisdiction covers a broader range. All cases having to do with the laws of the United States, treaties, admiralty and maritime jurisdiction, cases involving the United States, disputes between states, between the citizens of different states, between citizens of one state claiming lands under grants of other states, and between states or their citizens against foreign nations or their citizens may be appealed to the Supreme Court for final disposition. This list originally included disputes be-

---

*Seven are men and the eighth, appointed by President Reagan, is the first woman to serve on the Supreme Court.

tween a state and the citizens of another state, but as early as 1798, because the Court found it impossible to carry out, this jurisdiction was removed by the Eleventh Amendment. Finally, the Supreme Court may order that a case brought in a lower court be remanded to the highest Court immediately for adjudication. This occurs very rarely and only in exceptional circumstances.

The bulk of the cases heard by the Court are presented in a manner prescribed by Congress, petition for certiorari as part of the appellate jurisdiction. A writ is an order issued in the name of the Court and certiorari means to call up for a review. The review on a writ of certiorari is not a right, but a privilege granted by judicial discretion if there are sound reasons behind the petition. One reason for granting such a writ would be that a lower court had decided a federal question which had not hitherto been decided by the Supreme Court. Another would be that a federal appellate court had made a decision in conflict with another court of appeals on the same question. There are certain criteria for the granting of certiorari (published in the *Rules of the Court*) but it is, in the end, up to the justices's discretion. All petitions for certiorari are reviewed by the justices at their weekly conference, and if four or more vote to take the case, the writ is granted.

Once a case has been accepted by the Supreme Court, it is placed on the docket, and the lawyers involved are given a schedule of dates. Each side must prepare comprehensive briefs, their case in writing, and forty copies must be presented to the clerk of the Court. After the justices have studied the arguments, they may request that the case be presented orally, and, if they do, the opposing lawyers are given a very short time to make the salient points of their case. One hour is generally the limit, and it is an extremely tense time for the attorney as he not only must speak to the point, but must be prepared to answer any questions from the bench to the satisfaction of the justices. Once the time allotted for the case is up, no matter what has been left unsaid, the lawyer must step down, and the next case begins. After oral argument is heard, the justices then decide the outcome, and at some later date without advance notice announce their decisions from the bench. The decision becomes part of the law of the land and everyone must abide by it.

It would not be correct, however, to leave the impression that a Supreme Court decision can never be changed. In fact, there are two ways by which law as determined by the Court in a particular case can be adjusted: congressional action, and the reversal of a decision by the Court's own action at a later date. In the first instance, should the Supreme Court decide that an act of Congress is unconstitutional for a specific reason, Congress can reenact the law and make it constitutional by omitting the offending section. A case in point is the Agricultural Adjustment Act passed by Congress in 1934 in the days of the New Deal. As the act was first written, it decreed that payments made to the farmers of the nation, to whom the act applied, would be funded by a tax levied on food processors. The Court immediately declared that the tax was unconstitutional because it was a discriminatory use of the tax power of Congress. Taxes must be uniformly levied according to the Constitution. After the act was declared invalid, Congress proceeded to reenact the law, but without the discriminatory tax, and it stood uncontested.

In the second case, changes do occur in American life brought about by the passage of time, circumstances and different personalities on the Court which result in reevaluations of earlier doctrine. Perhaps the most famous example of the Court's reversing an earlier decision is the school desegregation case, *Brown* v. *The School Board of Topeka, Kansas,* 1954. In 1896, not long after the Civil War and the Reconstruction period which followed it, the Supreme Court decided in a case called *Plessy* v. *Ferguson* that it was constitutional for states to segregate public facilities, provided the facilities were equal. For over fifty years the doctrine of "separate but equal" stood, and segregation of the races was the accepted custom in public places, including schools, in certain areas of the nation. By the mid-twentieth century in the aftermath of the Second World War and in a world in which people were demanding equality, the United States of America, the bastion of liberty and justice, could no longer countenance racial segregation as a matter of law. In the *Brown* case, the argument for desegregation of schools rested on the logical point that segregation by definition produced second-class citizenship, which is inherently unequal and violated the equal protection of the laws guaranteed to all Americans under the Fourteenth Amendment. The Court agreed unanimously and overturned *Plessy,* and today deliberate segregation in public schools is against the law.

The importance of the federal judiciary and particularly of the Supreme Court to the stability of the United States cannot be underestimated, and we owe the Founding Fathers an incalculable debt for their prescience in recognizing the power of law and devising the system under which we live. Although every case that the Supreme Court adjudicates is of vital importance to the persons concerned, there is one recent case upon which the future of the Constitution and the American democracy depended. It was *The United States* v. *Richard Nixon.*

It was mentioned above that in extremely rare and exceptional circumstances the Supreme Court will intervene and ask that a case in a lower court come directly to the highest court. No situation could have been more exceptional than that which occurred in the summer of 1974 when the special prosecutor, appointed by Congress to see that justice was done in the Watergate affair, asked the president of the United States to turn over his private tape recordings to the federal district court in the District of Columbia which was hearing the case of those accused of complicity in the attempted break-in of the Democratic party's national headquarters. Because of the extreme seriousness of the constitutional issue involved, the Supreme Court accepted its full responsibility as the highest court of the land and exercised its option of taking over the case. The whole country held its breath as the special prosecutor argued that not even the president of the United States was above the law and the president's attorney countered with the argument that executive privilege protected Mr. Nixon's private documents. Had the president of the United States, in fact, gone beyond his constitutional bounds? It was up to the Court, to the eight men who heard the argument* to decide

---

*Mr. Justice Rehnquist, having served as an assistant attorney general in the Nixon Administration prior to his elevation to the Supreme Court, chose to absent himself in this case.

what was probably the single most important case ever to come before the Court. It was made more difficult because not only had the chief justice been appointed by the man whose case was before the Court, but two of the associate justices as well. Historically, the Supreme Court justices have had a remarkable record of objectivity and the highest level of integrity, and the justices hearing the case of *The United States* v. *Richard Nixon* adhered to the tradition. Unanimously they declared that the president was not above the law and that the doctrine of executive privilege did not enable him to withhold evidence from a federal court.

The importance of this case is historic. The decision led to a peaceful denouement of the Watergate affair. As the evidence in the tapes was conclusive as to the knowledge on the part of Mr. Nixon of the Watergate break-in in the first place and then to his role in the obstruction of justice, the president was forced to resign or to stand trial before the Senate as a result of the threat of impeachment by the House of Representatives. He chose to resign, and the presidency passed peaceably to the vice-president, Mr. Gerald Ford. Such a transfer of power is only possible in a nation governed by constitutional law.

Thus does the Constitution describe the organization and powers of the federal government. On close examination, however, it becomes clear that the Constitution draws up a broad framework for the government. Important and basic powers are incorporated in the document, but there is no attempt to spell out or to explain every last detail as to how each of the three branches is to carry out its job. Only general patterns are laid down. For instance, Congress must legislate on a variety of subjects, but the method by which this legislation is to be arrived at is omitted. The president also is, indeed, responsible for many specific tasks, but, again, the way in which he is to accomplish these or with whose help is not specified. The Supreme Court is given certain definite areas of jurisdiction, but it, too, has leeway in that it can decide which cases it will hear and which it will leave to the inferior courts.

The genius of those who designed the Constitution lies in their willingness to believe in change and their unwillingness to impede the free development and progress of the nation by imposing crippling restrictions and limitations prescribing the methods by which the three branches would carry out their duties. The flexibility and elasticity of the Constitution have meant that for almost two hundred years the nation could be governed by the pattern set forth in 1787.

One specific article in the Constitution is devoted to the principle that change is necessary and good. Article V describes the methods by which the Constitution may be amended, and the power to amend has kept the document as alive and as meaningful today as it was in the eighteenth century. There are two ways in which an amendment can be made to the Constitution. By a two-thirds vote both houses of Congress can propose an amendment, and, if the proposal is passed by three-quarters of the state legislatures or by conventions called in three-quarters of the states, it becomes law and part of the Constitution. The states may also propose changes if two-thirds of them so desire by requesting that Congress call a convention to draft an amendment. If the proposed amendment is passed in this way, it also becomes law. The systems of amending the Constitution are sufficiently complicated to prevent any irresponsible changes. In the many years in which the Constitution has existed, only twenty-six amendments have been made. The first ten, the Bill of Rights, were drafted and adopted in 1791, or almost immediately following the ratification of the Constitution by the necessary three-quarters, or nine, of the original states. These amendments specifically guarantee certain rights and privileges to the American people and are the bedrock of our freedoms.

We owe the Bill of Rights primarily to Thomas Jefferson. His first reaction to the Constitution when he read it was one of dismay. Where were the inalienable rights of the American people specifically mentioned? Nowhere in the body of the Constitution could he find guarantees against the infringement of certain basic liberties. His clear reasoning influenced many, and as soon as the Constitution was ratified, the first Congress drew up the Bill of Rights, safeguarding the rights which Jefferson had so clearly enunciated in the Declaration of Independence.

The other sixteen amendments have been added over the

years as changing times and conditions have demanded new fundamental laws. Prior to the Civil War, only twice was the original language of the Constitution altered. The Eleventh Amendment, adopted in 1798, removed one type of case from the jurisdiction of the Supreme Court because experience had proved that its inclusion had been a mistake. The Twelfth Amendment, 1804, came as a result of the evolution of political parties and has already been described.

Following the Civil War three amendments were adopted, each dealing with the great changes brought about by that conflict. The Thirteenth Amendment abolished involuntary servitude (slavery) except for punishment for crime. It was lucky that the authors in their haste to end slavery remembered to include the exception. Otherwise, it would be unconstitutional to put criminal offenders in prison. The Fourteenth Amendment is an extremely important one. Although its primary intent at the time it was written was to bestow citizenship on the newly freed slaves, by its definition of citizenship and its rights and privileges, it continues to be applicable in every situation where the right or privilege of a citizen of the United States is in question. The Fifth Amendment of the Bill of Rights guarantees every person protection against the arbitrary exercise of power by the federal government, and the Fourteenth extends this guarantee to protect Americans against arbitrary state authority. In addition, this amendment guarantees to everyone due process of law and equal protection of the laws. The Fifteenth Amendment, the last of the Civil War amendments, declares that no man may be deprived of the right to vote "on account of race, color or previous condition of servitude." This was another attempt to protect the new black citizens from loss of a constitutional right.

The remaining eleven amendments all reflect the great social, economic and technological changes of the twentieth century. The Sixteenth legalized the income tax which had been expressly forbidden in the Constitution as a direct tax on the people. By the twentieth century, however, the increased responsibilities of the federal government required greater sources of revenue, and the income tax became a necessity. The Seventeenth Amendment provided for the direct election of senators and reflected the tremendous advances that had been made in communications as well as the growth of the spirit of democracy which made men demand the right to choose their own senators. The Eighteenth Amendment is the exceptional one in that it is the only one that was repealed at a later date. It outlawed the manufacture, transportation and sale of intoxicating beverages, and came about due to the pressure of women's temperance societies and the pressing need to send as much grain, the source of alcoholic beverages, as possible to Europe during World War I. Very quickly it became apparent that it was virtually impossible to enforce, and the growth of criminal syndicates and what was known as bootlegging were so much worse for the country than the legal imbibing of alcohol that it was repealed by the Twenty-first Amendment in 1934. The Nineteenth Amendment, the product of the then women's liberation movement, grants women the right to vote in federal elections, and the Twentieth changes the dates of the opening of Congress and the inauguration of the president and vice-president. The Twenty-second restricts the number of terms a president may have consecutively, and the Twenty-third gives citizens of the District of Columbia the right to vote in presidential elections. The Twenty-fourth is a cousin, so to speak, of the Civil War amendments in that it came about as a result of the civil rights movement in the 1960s and outlaws the poll tax in federal elections. The poll tax had been widely used by some states to circumvent the Fifteenth Amendment by permitting only those who had paid it to vote—the tax, if cumulative, could amount to a sizable sum of money. Many poor citizens, particularly black citizens in the South, had been disenfranchised, and the amendment was a necessity to guarantee the right to vote. The Twenty-fifth, part of which has already been described, also sets up a system by which the vice-president can take over if the president should become physically handicapped. The last one to date, the Twenty-sixth, again reflects changing times and the youth movement of recent years by granting eighteen-year-olds the right to vote in federal elections. The argument in favor of lowering the voting age from twenty-one was that if a person were old enough to fight, he was old enough to cast a vote for people in the government that was sending him to war. The draft age was eighteen. Recently, intensive efforts were being made to get the requisite number of states to ratify a twenty-seventh amendment that would grant sexual equality under the law. This proposed amendment reflects the powerful women's liberation movement of today. Its supporters are determined to gain their equal rights in all fields by embedding the privilege in the Constitution, and although they failed to win ratification by 1983, the last year in which ratification was possible, they plan to reintroduce the amendment in the next session of Congress. If Congress passes it, which undoubtedly it will as 1984 is a presidential election year, it will again be presented to the states. Thirty-eight states must ratify it before it can become part of the Constitution. As should be clear, in recent years the number of constitutional amendments have increased dramatically, and the reason is obviously the speed with which change overtakes society in today's world. One would hope, however, that Americans would be careful to distinguish between really important changes which can only be accomplished through constitutional guarantee and the lighter and more transient problems which can be dealt with best by statutory law.

The flexibility and adaptability of the Constitution to respond to changing times is not limited to the amendment privilege. As the nation has grown in size and has entered more importantly into world affairs, many government changes have taken place. Any of the writers of the Constitution, even George Washington himself, would be overwhelmed by the workings of the United States government today and would hardly recognize it to be the one they designed so long ago. Many of the ways in which the business of government is carried out today were never conceived of by the men of 1787, nor is there any mention of them in the Constitution. Washington, D.C., and indeed the country, is full of departments, agencies, bureaus, commissions and offices whose existence we do not even question, but which were never mentioned in the Constitution. Their legality is made possible by the foresighted language of the framers. Congress has developed the committee system under the constitutional power "to determine rules of its proceedings." Congress also has passed laws about subjects not specifically listed in Article I under the Elastic Clause, but as they are always subject to possible review by the judiciary, the spirit of the Constitution has been kept intact. In addition, there are now, under the supervision of Congress, a myriad of offices whose existence was never decreed by the Founding Fathers who could never have conceived of the functions they fulfill.

The executive branch has also changed almost beyond recognition. The responsibilities of governing the country have grown so tremendously since 1789 that the president requires much more assistance in order to be able to do the job. Whereas in George Washington's day the cabinet numbered four, today it numbers thirteen. Washington and most of his successors in the nineteenth century made do with a small staff, a secretary or two and a few assistants, but today the president is served by literally hundreds of men and women in the White House and the adjacent Executive Office Building. In addition, there are a multiplicity of advisory groups, each with its own staff, which have proliferated over the years. While there is no question that many of these positions and groups are essential to the president's being able to keep up with all the problems which face him, there is no guarantee that uncontrolled expansion of the bureaucracy results in greater efficiency. In recent years both President Carter and President Reagan have vowed to cut back White House personnel and to reorganize the executive department to make it less costly to the taxpayer and more responsible to the demands of the times.

They are not the first presidents to try to streamline the executive department, and undoubtedly they will not be the last. Although the federal government is now the single largest business in the United States, employing well over two million people, efforts are continually being made to make the structure of government more responsive to the needs of the people. Repeatedly, commissions of wise and experienced Americans have been appointed to examine the government and to recommend ways of increasing its efficiency. This constant reappraisal is of the greatest importance to the continued success of the constitutional system, and, although the government may seem monolithic and unresponsive at times, the two hundred and twenty million plus Americans who live under it enjoy more freedom to live and work as they choose than the citizens of almost every other nation in the world.

THE DEVELOPMENT OF THE EXECUTIVE BRANCH

THE CONSTITUTION requires that the president of the United States bear the responsibility for the executive branch of the federal government, and he alone must answer to the American people and to Congress for the executive policies and actions. Nowhere, however, does the Constitution declare that the president must actually do all the work in carrying out his job single-handedly. From the very beginning of the federal government the presidents have been assisted by persons in an advisory capacity, some officially responsible for a particular department and others simply close friends who help him unofficially.

The president's "official" family dates back to George Washington's first administration. Aware that the day-to-day business of running the federal government was an impossible task for one man, he divided the work logically into departments and appointed men he trusted and believed capable of serving the American people to head them. In his day there were four departments: State, Treasury, War, and Justice, and the title of secretary was given to the department heads except for attorney general, the title for the head of Justice. These gentlemen formed the first cabinet. Cabinet rank, which is still in force today, was determined by the order in which the departments were created. The first was the Department of State. Today we associate the State Department entirely with foreign affairs, but, in fact, the secretary of state's other job was and still is to hold the Great Seal of the United States. He is, in fact, the secretary of state which is why when both the vice-president and the president of the United States resigned their offices recently, their letters of resignation were addressed to the secretary of state. This role of the secretary also accounts for the name of the department. In other nations the person in charge of foreign affairs is called a foreign minister and heads a ministry of foreign affairs. Originally our secretary of state was responsible for many internal state matters such as the census which have gradually been assigned to other departments, and he is now primarily concerned with foreign policy. The secretary of the treasury was the second appointment because the financial situation of the United States was desperate and required immediate attention if the new nation were to become economically viable. The War Department came next. Under Washington, both the army and the navy were the responsibility of the secretary of war, but in John Adams's presidency, because of the conflict with the Barbary pirates and the quasi-naval war with France, the navy's importance was such to warrant its own department. Consequently, in 1798 Congress established it with its own secretary, and the secretary of war directed only the affairs of the army. Washington also appointed the attorney general in his first administration. The new Constitution was a complex legal document, and Washington, who was not an attorney, wanted a lawyer at his side to guide him in the conduct of his office as well as to see that justice for the American people was carried out as designed by the Founding Fathers. Washington's other major appointment was the postmaster general, who directed the post office, but he was not of cabinet rank in the early years of our constitutional history.

The other executive departments were established over the course of time by Congress and each came into being to answer a new need. In 1849 the Department of the Interior was necessary as the frontier receded; in 1862 the importance of the nation's farmers was recognized by the creation of the Department of Agriculture, and in 1872 the post office was elevated to department status. In the early twentieth century the Industrial Revolution produced the necessity for the Departments of Commerce and of Labor, and after World War

II the revolutions in the science and technology of warfare resulted in the combining of all the armed forces into a Department of Defense, with the secretaries of the army, navy and air force being demoted from cabinet rank. More recently, an increasingly urbanized population and a new emphasis on social problems caused the establishment of the Departments of Health, Education and Welfare and of Housing and Urban Development. In answer to the need to coordinate all modes of transportation and their regulation in an age where rapid and safe communication is imperative, Congress created the Department of Transportation. Finally, under President Carter, in response to two critical problems which confronted the nation, Congress authorized the Department of Energy and a separate Department of Education. HEW, therefore, became the Department of Health and Human Services. Changing times have also caused the deletion of cabinet posts, and today the post office has been reorganized into a government corporation, and the postmaster general no longer sits in the cabinet.

From Washington's day the cabinet has functioned as an advisory board to the president, but the extent of its role and its influence has depended entirely on each individual president's desires. Some have used the cabinet heavily in policy determination, asking each member his opinion and following the majority vote. Other presidents have felt that the cabinet officers' primary duties were to run their departments and have seldom sought their advice as to general administration policy. In addition, at any time the president wishes, he can call other government officials to join the cabinet, and in recent years the vice-president has become a permanent member. The United States Representative to the United Nations and the Special Representative for Trade Negotiations also have been granted cabinet rank. Cabinet meetings are held entirely at the president's discretion, and no law, in fact, requires him to call the cabinet together. It is, however, a great honor to receive a cabinet appointment, and the cabinet room is one of the most impressive in the west wing of the White House with a magnificent antique table surrounded by chairs especially made for each officer with his or her name on it which is received as a gift from the government when the recipient leaves his post.

With the cabinet officers so engrossed in the management of their departments, all of which have grown into gigantic bureaucracies responsible for a myriad of different day-to-day problems, modern presidents have had to increase their own staffs enormously to carry out the work of the office of chief executive. Members of the White House staff are called the president's "unofficial" family because they do not require Senate confirmation. Their positions, however, have all been authorized by Congress in that it is Congress which appropriates the money for their salaries. Unlike cabinet officers, they are not required to make reports to Congress, and, in fact, if asked to appear before a congressional committee, they do so only if the president gives his permission. The men and women who hold these White House staff jobs are usually personal friends of the president and enjoy his close confidence and trust, and they, therefore, are extremely influential people in Washington. They assist the president in various ways to carry the burden of his office. They have no responsibility except to the president himself, and they serve at his pleasure. They act, in general, as go-betweens. They maintain close liaisons with the executive departments and agencies, the Congress and with individual senators and congressmen, and with the general public. As a rule each assistant is assigned a subject for which he is responsible. National security, educational, health, scientific, technological, ethnic, minority women, and consumer affairs are a few of the areas covered by the staff. Much of the assistants' time is devoted to drafting speeches for the president and collaborating on messages to Congress suggesting legislation. At any given moment the special assignments of the president's staff will reflect the subjects of particular importance facing the nation. There is no set number of assistants, each president having as many as he feels he needs and for whom Congress is willing to budget salaries. During Nixon's White House days, the staff reached the unheard of number of over six hundred. President Ford cut it back to 485, and Presidents Carter and Reagan both promised during their campaigns to pare it to the bone. The smaller the staff, the more control the president can exercise, and that control should be important to him because it is he who at all times is responsible for its actions. Being on the White House staff is one of the most exciting and challenging jobs in Washington, and, although the hours are unconscionably long and the work terribly exacting, there are few who turn down such an opportunity.

Probably one of the most sensitive areas for any modern president is that of his relations with the public, particularly with the news media. In the early days of the nation the presidents handled their own relations with the public because they were pretty much available to any American seeking an interview. One of the most trying problems that vexed Abraham Lincoln, for instance, was that of dealing with the numbers of people who constantly clogged the White House corridors, all waiting to catch his ear. In the twentieth century, however, easy, informal access to the president has had to stop for two main reasons. For one, his personal safety and that of his family are of paramount importance, and the secret service and the White House police force must know who everyone is who enters the White House grounds. In addition, the work load of the president has increased to such an extent that he cannot be as available as were his nineteenth-century predecessors. Every minute of his day is carefully scheduled so that he can attend to all his duties as chief executive. In our democracy, however, the American people have the right to know what the president is doing and the right to question him, and today the public exercises this right to a large extent through the press. Therefore, the job of the president's press secretary is probably the most difficult and demanding of all his personal staff.

As his office is responsible for all White House news, the press secretary has many tasks. It is he who accredits the members of the White House press corps. This is a ticklish task in that choices have to be made because not every newsperson in the United States can be accommodated. It is the secretary who briefs the press daily on the president's schedule, his actions, and his policies, and, again, it is not as easy as it sounds. Many of the president's visitors, for instance, may be involved in extremely sensitive matters which for reasons of national security should not be publicized. In addition, the press secretary's words must at all times be carefully chosen when describing presidential policies or reactions because a mistake can have serious repercussions. The press secretary is also responsible for setting up nationally broadcast press conferences for the president when he wants to talk to the American people. In the 1930s the radio was the new medium, and Franklin Roosevelt was the first president to make extensive use of it to explain his New Deal programs to the nation. Since then, the advent of television has meant that the president, whenever he wants, can hold a live press conference so that the public can not only hear him, but see his every facial expression as well. It is at these press conferences that the people through the White House press corps have the opportunity of asking the president direct questions on any subject. The president, therefore, must be carefully prepared, and again it is the press secretary who must know what sort of questions the press will be most likely to ask. The secretary generally prepares a long list for the president's briefing, and other presidential aides provide him with the facts and figures that he will need to know.

Of course, in any presidential press conference it is the president himself who makes the impact on the viewers, but the relations between the chief executive and the media and the atmosphere surrounding press conferences are influenced by the way the press secretary handles his job. If he tends to be brusque or uncommunicative, the press's attitude toward the president will reflect it, so it is imperative for the president's relations with the public that the press secretary be a person of tact and sensitivity as well as being astute and intelligent.

Other members of the president's staff include military aides, doctors, counselors, and a large secretarial group. At special functions, diplomatic receptions, presentations of medals, dinners, etc., other members of the armed forces assist in various ways, and it is considered a great honor to be chosen for the White House detail. It can also have romantic connotations: During President Johnson's administration, his Marine

Corps aide met his daughter and married her in a spectacular White House wedding. The president's doctors are on call twenty-four hours a day as they are responsible for the president's health which is of vital importance for the whole country, and whenever the president travels either at home or abroad, one of his doctors always accompanies him. Should the president require medical treatment, he goes to one of the military hospitals in Washington. President Eisenhower, as an army man, made use of Walter Reed, and Presidents Roosevelt, Kennedy, Johnson, Nixon, Ford, Carter, and Reagan* used the Bethesda Naval Hospital because of their association with the navy. The secretarial staff handles all the White House clerical work, which is voluminous: correspondence, documents, and the like. The counselors, each with many assistants, serve the president in many different capacities, and one of the most important is the legal counselor whose task it is to see that the president always acts within the bounds of his constitutional responsibilities. And another key staff person is the president's political counselor. Although the president is the president of all the people, he is the head of his political party, and his political adviser keeps him constantly in touch with the leaders of the party and with the various groups that make it up. The president cannot forget his supporters if he wishes to be reelected.

One of the more recent developments within the White House is the greater role in national affairs played by the First Ladies. They, too, have had need for a staff, and, apart from secretaries, a housekeeper and household help, they have been assigned an assistant who deals with the press and a social secretary who arranges the First Lady's calendar. These aides are generally close personal friends of the First Family and are responsible for any task the president's wife sets. Gone are the days when the First Lady was expected simply to

---

*When President Reagan was shot, however, he was taken to George Washington University Hospital because it was the nearest to the Washington Hilton Hotel where the shooting occurred. The President's life, as well as that of his press secretary, was saved because of the proximity of the hospital.

be a gracious hostess. Her changed role reflects the general acceptance and, indeed, expectation that women have responsible jobs beyond those of wife and mother. In recent years each of the First Ladies has chosen a particular area of interest and has worked hard to accomplish her goal. Mrs. Johnson, for instance, was particularly concerned with the environment and the beautification of America, and any visitor to Washington cannot help being impressed with the legacy she left to the nation's capital—the exquisite flower beds all over the city. Mrs. Carter was not only concerned with mental health, but assisted her husband politically, and upon one occasion undertook a diplomatic mission for him in Latin America. Mrs. Reagan's particular programs for which she has worked extremely diligently are Foster Grandparents, a part of ACTION*, and anti-drug counseling for young people.

The expansion of the White House staff over the years illustrates the growth in the size and number of presidential responsibilities, and it would be absurd to suppose that one mortal man could attend to every detail alone. The staff performs the vital function of studying problems, reading voluminous amounts of material, preparing memoranda for the president and keeping him up to date on all the many problems with which he is confronted. It must never be forgotten, however, that the staff is purely a work-saving organization, and no member can ever take over any of the executive authority. White House staff members, in fact, must guard against overstepping their role by coming between the president and the country he serves. They do him no favor if they shield him and allow him to know only the things that he would like to hear.

---

*See page 274.

OTHER WHITE HOUSE GROUPS

THE PROBLEMS affecting the government of the United States which have arisen in the twentieth century are of such a vast nature and of such complexity that it has been found necessary to create many more advisory groups to help the president with his job of running the nation. In 1939 Congress first recognized this need and by the Executive Reorganization Act of that year established the Executive Office of the President, and in response to the demands of changing times has authorized the inclusion of new offices by subsequent legislation. Because Congress was concerned during the Watergate affair that President Nixon had abused his presidential authority, his power to reorganize the executive branch was rescinded. Later the power was restored, but any reorganization plan a president might choose to adopt must be submitted to Congress, and if neither the House nor the Senate rejects it within sixty days, it automatically goes into effect.*

Each president usually makes some changes in the organization of the Executive Office to suit his style of leadership and to reflect his priorities, but in recent years the following groups have been included: The Bureau of Management and Budget, the Council of Economic Advisers, the Special Representative for Trade Negotiations, the National Security Council, the Office of Policy Development, which at present includes the Office of Drug Abuse Policy and the Office of Policy Information, the Office of Science and Technology,

---

*A presidential proposal for a new executive department, however, must be voted on by both houses of Congress.

the Council on Environmental Quality, the Office of Administration, and the Office of the Vice-President. Each of these offices in the Executive Office is directly responsible to the president, and, with the exception of the Bureau of Management and Budget, serves only to advise him in detail on the specific problems within its jurisdiction. When he has all the facts and suggested courses of action before him, the president is then in a position to make policy decisions in the best interests of the people.

The Bureau of Management and Budget performs a different function from the others. This bureau was originally established in 1921 as the Bureau of the Budget and was then placed in the Department of the Treasury. In 1939 it was relocated and made part of the Executive Office of the President, and under the Reorganization Plan of 1970 its title was changed to the Bureau of Management and Budget to reflect more accurately its present responsibilities. These are basically twofold: to prepare the annual budget for the executive branch of the government, which involves acting as a clearinghouse for any proposals for legislation coming from any of the departments or agencies, and to work on the improvement of management and organization of the executive branch.

An annual budget is a necessity for any well-run business or home, and the same is true for the United States government. Each year the executive branch must decide what expenses it will incur, and then, if Congress agrees, it must raise the necessary revenue through taxes and borrowing to pay the bills. If the income matches the expenses, the budget is balanced. If less revenue, however, is raised than the expenses incurred, the budget is in deficit, and should the revenue exceed the outlay, there is a surplus. The preparation is really the single most important job of the executive branch each year as it is, in fact, a detailed plan of the president's goals. Presidential candidates may present the electorate with a broad and glowing picture of the programs they would enact as president, but when the victor becomes the president, he must then add up to the last penny the cost of his desired programs and then see whether the nation can afford them. Whether or not it can depends entirely on the state of the economy, and federal expenditures have a tremendously important influence on the nation's economy. Higher government spending will stimulate a sluggish economy, and yet it may cause inflation to soar which means higher prices for the American people. Lower government spending will reverse the process and will have a more depressing effect on the nation's economic life. The national budget, then, is a very complex thing, and because it will affect everyone of the two hundred and sixteen million Americans, it must be prepared with the greatest care.

The government's fiscal, or financial, year is October 1 to September 30th. The reason for this particular twelve-month period is that Congress, as has already been noted above, comes into session early in January, and it must have time in which to analyze the president's budget, to decide which programs it will fund, to vote the necessary tax bills and to appropriate funds for the executive branch. Because of the necessary time involved in the passage of the budget, each new budget applies to the year ahead. In other words, when President Reagan took office in January 1981, the budget for 1981-82 had already been presented by President Carter, and Reagan's first budget was for 1982-83.

How is the budget arrived at? The first step is for the president to determine the outside figure for the budget under consideration. He sets that figure on the basis of forecasts made by his economic advisers and the Federal Reserve Board as to the probable state of the economy eighteen months in the future and on his policy priorities. Once he has determined the figure within which he hopes to work, the Bureau of Management and Budget notifies all the departments, agencies, commissions, offices, etc., of the executive branch that they must determine their needs within that figure. The second step, then, is for all the component parts of the executive branch to make up their budgets, including all their fixed expenses and the programs that they want to see legislated. These budgets are then subjected to an intensive review by the Bureau of Management and Budget and are adjusted to meet the president's priorities. When the final budget is ready, the president himself goes over it, and, if it meets with his approval, he sends it to Congress in January. As one can imagine, the final version is a massive tome of more than one thousand pages.

Until 1974 the president's budget was the only one considered by Congress. In that year, however, Congress decided to take a more active and responsible role and established the Congressional Budget Office which is empowered to prepare a separate budget based on its conceptions of the economy and its priorities. Having their own budget gives Congress a basis for comparison, and it is hoped that with this new system the final budgets adopted in the future will be tighter and more in tune with what a majority of the taxpayers really want to see the government do and what they are willing to pay for.

Once Congress has adopted the budget, it then must adjust the tax laws, if necessary, to make sure that the revenue will be available to pay the government's bills. Taxes, however, are not the sole source of federal revenue, although they account for 74 percent. The other 26 percent comes from borrowing and other sources such as customs duties and the like. While the tax laws are being revised, the various appropriation committees are busy deciding which old programs will be refunded and which new ones the nation must have. It used to be that each congressional committee responsible for appropriations acted independently, and there was no way that a tally could be taken at a given moment to determine exactly how much of the annual budget had actually been expended, and all too often and too late it was discovered that the budget had been exceeded. The 1974 act setting up the Congressional Budget Office has ended that irresponsible way of doing business, and Congress is now policing itself. In May of each year it agrees to a tentative ceiling on spending. In September it reviews its spending to date to see how well it is doing and sets final figures for both spending and the amount of revenue that must be raised. After that no further appropriations can be made, and when October 1st arrives, the executive branch begins receiving funds appropriated for its approved programs which are then carried out.

In the Bureau of Management and Budget's other capacity, to improve the efficiency of the executive branch, the director advises the president on the reorganization of the executive functions. As he and his staff review the detailed budget requests from all parts of the government, they gain insight as to how the departments, bureaus, agencies, etc., are managed, and they are constantly searching for ways to improve them so that the government will deliver better services at lower cost to the American people. It is a difficult task because government has a way of expanding each time a new program is inaugurated. Government employees are civil servants, and are, therefore, protected by regulations originally established by the Civil Service Commission, the first independent government agency created by Congress in 1883. It is virtually impossible under the law to dismiss government employees simply because the Bureau of Management and Budget decides to abolish an agency or a bureau. It must find a way by which to streamline the government without resorting to wholesale firings, and about the only way a reduction in personnel can be achieved is by attrition. When a government employee reaches retirement age, he is not replaced and his job is abolished if it is no longer necessary.

Presidents try to achieve greater efficiency by reorganizing functions. For instance, President Carter, acting on the recommendation of the Bureau of Management and Budget, proposed the establishment of a new agency, merging the independent United States Information Agency and the Bureau of Educational and Cultural Affairs of the Department of State. Originally established in 1953, USIA's job is to support United States foreign policy objectives by maintaining information centers and libraries abroad and by broadcasts beamed to foreign countries over the Voice of America, among other things. The Bureau of Educational and Cultural Affairs is in charge of all exchanges of people between the United States and other nations, the purpose of which is to further understanding of the United States abroad and to foster good relations between Americans and citizens of other nations. This office also supervises student and teacher exchange programs, foreign tours by American specialists, and promotes the establishment of chairs in American studies in foreign universities. It also sponsors tours by entertainment and sporting groups such as the ping-pong team that went to the People's Republic of China a few years ago. Because the work of this office is so closely allied with that of USIA, it was eminently sensible to combine their functions under one director with four associate directors to assist him. Through coordination the interests of the United States are better served. The International Communication Agency came into being early in 1978 as neither house of Congress vetoed the president's proposal within sixty days after receiving it. Under President Reagan the original name of the agency was restored, and once again it is called the United States Information Agency.

The director of the Bureau of Management and Budget also reviews all suggestions coming from the component parts of the executive branch for new programs which would require legislation. If he thinks an idea worthwhile, he will recommend it to the president who, if he agrees, will include a request for it either in his annual message to Congress or in one of the many special messages he sends to the Capitol during the early months of the year. The close liaison between the director of management and budget and the White House is another in which the president is kept in touch with the vast machinery of the executive branch. The director is appointed by the president, confirmed by the Senate, and is one of the most influential men in Washington.

The purely advisory offices of the White House function generally in the same way, but each of their responsibilities is different and illustrative of the complexities and problems of modern American society. Since the Great Depression of the 1930s no administration has been unaware of the importance of gauging the state of the nation's economic health. The Council of Economic Advisers was first formally established by an act of Congress in 1946. Three members serve at one time on this council, and they are appointed by the president and confirmed by the Senate. The president appoints one of them as chairman. Their chief functions are to study the national economy, to evaluate the government's economic policies, and to advise the president on ways to stabilize as well as to advance national prosperity. It is they who make the eighteen-month projection as to the state of the nation's economy upon which the president bases his budget ceiling, and it is readily apparent that theirs is one of the most critical jobs in the country because so much depends on their judgment.

The overriding importance of economic affairs is also underscored by the fact that another presidential adviser is the Special Representative for Trade Negotiations. His office was first established by the Trade Expansion Act of 1962 which came about due to the changing economic patterns of the free world following the reconstruction of Europe and Japan after World War II. Western European and Japanese industrial development by the 1960s was such as to make them extremely competitive with the United States, and it became apparent that greater attention had to be paid to the nation's international trading position. The Trade Expansion Act of 1962 empowered the president to change certain tariff rates without congressional approval in order to increase trade between the United States and abroad. The post of special representative was created to negotiate such changes with America's trading partners, and under the Trade Act of 1974 he was given the rank of both an ambassador and a cabinet officer indicating the singular importance of his job. He now supervises and coordinates all trade agreements and is directly responsible to the president.

Another very critical service is performed by the National Security Council which dates from 1947, reflecting the international tensions and insecurities in the aftermath of the Second World War. The council members are the president (who does not always attend), the vice-president and the secretaries of State and Defense, the chairman of the Joint Chiefs of Staff, and the Director of the Central Intelligence Agency, and it is served by a staff headed by the president's national security adviser. Its task is to collect and to integrate all material, foreign, domestic, and military, relating to the nation's security. This clearinghouse enables all other departments and agencies of the government to act together more effectively, and the council with the correlated material at hand then advises the president on security matters. This information enables him to deal to the best of his ability with the vital problems of national preparedness.

Closely allied with the work of the National Security Council, although physically located about nine miles from the White House in nearby Virginia, is one of the most important agencies concerned with the nation's well-being, the Central Intelligence Agency. Before World War II the United States had no effective system of collecting and correlating intelligence. Whereas the British and other nations had had for many years a secret service devoted to the collecting and sorting of intelligence reports, the United States had simply relied on intelligence officers in each of the armed forces and in the foreign service of the Department of State. Without a clearing center there was much needless duplication and no coordination. During the Second World War it became apparent that the United States needed such a center, and the Office of Strategic Services was set up by the president under the wartime powers authorized to him by Congress. In the postwar years this temporary agency developed into a permanent one, Central Intelligence, or CIA as it is commonly called. The purpose of the agency is to collect all foreign intelligence information pertinent to the national security for the Intelligence Oversight Board where it is coordinated with information received from the State and Defense Departments, evaluated and passed on to the National Security Council. The chairman of the Intelligence Oversight Board is the director of the CIA who is appointed by the president and confirmed by the Senate. If the director of the CIA is a civilian, his deputy is always a military man, and vice versa. Because of the nature of its work, which depends on the utmost secrecy if the agency is to do its job, its budget is handled in a special manner. Were it a matter of public knowledge, much would be divulged about its work which would aid any potential enemies of the United States, thereby destroying its usefulness. Americans, as a people, are remarkably open, and many today find the operations of the agency offensive in our democracy, but it would be naive to believe that the nation without the CIA could protect itself in the world in which many other nations with alien political, social and economic systems are working against the interests of the United States.

Much as the National Security Council deals with the international threats to the United States, the Office of Policy Development focusses on problems within the nation. It works with the executive departments and agencies charged with responsibility for national affairs, and its members' task is to identify domestic problems and to propose solutions for the president's consideration.*

The two other advisory offices in the Executive Office are the Office of Science and Technology and the Council on Environmental Quality, and both were also created in response to developments of recent origin. The Office of Science and Technology, dating from a 1976 Act of Congress, is charged with advising the president and the secretaries of the departments on ways to implement the new developments in science and technology most effectively for the national welfare and security. The staff analyzes the effects of scientific and technological advances on national policies and tries to forecast major disruptions that might result. Automation, for instance, has a direct effect on the labor market, and the government must be prepared to meet the human problems which will follow when jobs are lost. The staff of this office also maintains close ties with scientists and engineers around the world, as well as in the United States. Thirty years ago no one could have possibly foreseen the need for this office, but with the speed with which scientific revolutions are occurring, it performs an indispensable service for the president. The Council on Environmental Quality became part of the Executive Office in 1969, and as its name suggests, has the job of advising the president on policies and programs by which the environment in which we all live can be improved. That

----

*One example of its concerns, for instance, is drug abuse, which in recent years has become a critical domestic problem. The Office of Drug Abuse Policy works with the presidential task force headed by the Vice President, whose mission is to coordinate all federal, state and community law enforcement agencies in order to combat the importation and sale of heroin, marijuana and cocaine. It also has mounted a major educational program to alert young people in particular to the extremely serious, often lethal, consequences of the drug habit. Mrs. Reagan has played an active role in this program.

there was a need for this council is a direct result of the sudden awareness a few years ago that Americans had so polluted their natural habitat that there was real danger to the survival of the ecological balance necessary for life. This high-level council, working very closely with the Environmental Protection Agency (see page 261), monitors changes in the environment, administers the process involved in the environmental impact statements required of industry, and keeps a close watch on energy research and development to see that it conforms to conservation standards. It also makes policy recommendations to the president and assists him in the preparation of the annual statement required by Congress on the quality of the environment. This vital task is carried out by three presidential appointees, one of whom is chairman, and they must be confirmed by the Senate. President Carter had thought to abolish this council, but there was so much opposition that he decided to continue it. That the public would react so strongly is heartening because it means that many Americans are finally really concerned more for the quality of their lives rather than simply for the quantity of material goods.

The newest addition of the Executive Office of the President is the Office of Administration which was an innovation of President Carter's continued by President Reagan. It actually is not an advisory group at all, but is concerned with the many administrative details of running the White House and the Executive Office. It handles the mail and all the personnel, payroll and accounting data, thus ending the overlapping of administrative functions which had existed before. It was Carter's way of streamlining White House and Executive Office management in order to deliver better and less costly government to the people and was suggested to him by the Bureau of Management and Budget.

This, then, is the White House and the Executive Office of the President, and one can be sure that neither George Washington nor Abraham Lincoln would recognize the office he once held. Although many Americans long for the old days when the White House was simply the residence of the First Family and the president was available to any and all who wished to call on him, the world is so complicated today that the president could not execute the responsibilities of his office without all the assistants and the councils to help him out. It is, in fact, quite extraordinary that one man can still keep up with all the reading he must do to be abreast of what is happening, meet with all the foreign and national leaders as well as with members of Congress and the cabinet, and still have time to digest all the information and come to policy decisions which affect not only the people of the United States, but of the world.

THE EXECUTIVE DEPARTMENTS

As WAS stated above, the thirteen secretaries in charge of the executive departments form the cabinet, and after the vice-president are the senior officials of the president's administration. They have great responsibility in that they must advise the president, administer all the programs pertinent to their area authorized by Congress, run their departments, each of which is enormous, and must be prepared to testify before Congress at any time they are asked. The secretaries are all appointed by the president and must be confirmed by the Senate, but they hold their office only at the president's pleasure, and should he choose to dismiss them, he can. If they remain in office for the president's term, and he is not reelected they leave office, and if a change occurs in the presidency during a term, the secretaries automatically offer their resignations to the new president, who may or may not accept them, depending upon his wish.

The secretaries all have undersecretaries and various assistant secretaries to help them with their work, and these positions are also political appointments. Below the assistant secretary level, however, each of the departments is manned by permanent government servants who do not change with the administrations. Because the responsibilities of the departments are so vast and so important to the life of the nation, the government would virtually grind to a halt if the entire personnel of a department were to be changed every four years. The civil service of the United States, however, was not established until late in the nineteenth century. When the government was small, it was the practice for each incoming administration to appoint its political supporters to almost all the jobs in the federal government, but after the Civil War it became apparent that this practice, known as the spoils system, was not the best for two main reasons. It was mentioned above that Abraham Lincoln could hardly do his job because of the number of people who came daily to see him. A great majority of those people were seeking federal jobs. By President Garfield's administration, the number of job seekers had reached astronomical proportions, and the nation was jolted into changing the system radically when he was assassinated by a man who had not received a job he felt he deserved. At the same time advances in technology such as the typewriter required certain skills, and it became obvious that there should be standards of performance demanded of federal employees whose salaries are paid by the public. Congress, therefore, in 1883 passed the Civil Service Act establishing a permanent civil service which was administered by the United States Civil Service Commission until 1976 and since then by the Office of Personnel Management and the Merit Systems Protection Board. Government servants are hired on the basis of proficiency, are promoted on merit, and their tenure is not subject to political change.

It is these civil servants who staff the departments and make it possible for the work of government to go on day after day regardless of the changes that take place at the top. At the present time there are well over two million civil servants, making the federal government the largest employer in the nation.

The Department of State

The State Department performs the oldest ongoing function of government in the history of this country, antedating, in fact, the Constitution. As early as 1775, before the signing of the Declaration of Independence, foreign affairs were desperately important to our revolutionary ancestors because they realized that without help from abroad they had little chance of gaining independence from Great Britain. In that year under the wise direction of the most traveled American,

Benjamin Franklin, the Committee of Secret Correspondence was established with the express purpose of presenting America's case to European nations. In 1777 with the Revolution well under way, its activities became overt and were directed by the Committee for Foreign Affairs of the Second Continental Congress. Benjamin Franklin, Thomas Jefferson, and John Adams were America's first ambassadors and were responsible for the treaty with France by which that nation agreed to help the American cause with financial, military and naval support. In 1781 when the Articles of Confederation were adopted, the committee became the Department of Foreign Affairs and was responsible for the peace treaty with Great Britain in 1783 by which American independence became a fact. At that point the United States opened diplomatic relations with other nations, leading to the deployment of about twenty-five Americans abroad, the beginning of America's foreign service. With the ratification of the Constitution, one of the first acts of Congress was to set up the Department of State, and from that day forward this department has handled all the foreign affairs of the nation for the president. The chief executive is responsible under the Constitution for the conduct of foreign affairs, but to think that with all his many duties he could attend to all the details involved in foreign relations would be ridiculous. The secretary of state, therefore, has the job of handling America's relations with other nations, and he and his advisers formulate policies which he then recommends to the president. It is, however, the president who is constitutionally responsible for the foreign policies of his administration.

The aim of foreign policy is to advance American ideals and to promote friendship with other nations in the world. Although foreign affairs have always been important, today with the United States in the role of a leading world power plus the many new factors which have come into being since 1945, they have become extraordinarily complicated. The uneasy peace following the war, the clash of opposing political, economic and social ideologies between the great nations of the world, and the explosion of new nations out of former colonial possessions across the earth have profoundly altered the conditions in which American foreign policy is made. United States membership in the United Nations and in more than fifty other international organizations has added still another dimension to foreign affairs. Economic and humanitarian considerations must now influence policy to a degree never before experienced. The economic requirements of the developing nations, for instance, are of top priority and vital to their political stability. The frightening population explosion and, as a consequence, the world crisis in food production are new problems which must be reckoned with if the United States, a land of plenty, is to maintain friendly and mutually satisfying relations with the rest of the world. And in recent years the dependency of the United States, the largest and most profligate consumer of energy in the world, on the importation of oil has created a problem of critical proportions, and has had a direct bearing on United States relations with the oil-producing nations of the Middle East, Africa and Latin America. Also, the advent of terrorism on an unprecedented scale—kidnappings and assassinations of foreign service personnel, the destruction of United States embassies, the hijackings of airplanes—has added another dimension to the responsibilities of the department. Lastly, the technological revolution in communications and the advent of the nuclear and space age have made international relations the single most important factor for the future of the world. The State Department has, therefore, an enormous task, and, to add to its burdens, the department must also review all domestic policies of other government departments and agencies and must try to correlate all their activities which could affect our relations with nations abroad. To accomplish this complex and vital task, the secretary of state has an extremely large department working both in Washington and all over the world.

From the original two-room office manned by the secretary and a few assistants in the building next to the White House on Pennsylvania Avenue, the State Department is now housed in several large office buildings containing many thousands of employees. The secretary must have a host of assistants, each of whom has a specific area of responsibility. The deputy secretary of state heads the list and is acting secretary when the secretary is out of the country, which he often is, attending the many international conferences which characterize modern diplomacy. He is also chairman of the Board of the Foreign Service and is responsible for the department's role in carrying out the mandates of the National Security Council. There are three undersecretaries: one concentrates on the political aspects of foreign policy, another on economic matters, and the third sees that the Security Assistance Program is carried out. A deputy undersecretary for management administers the department as well as supervising the work of the director general of the foreign service. Under the secretary are also the ambassadors-at-large. These men or women are generally very senior and experienced persons and are appointed by the president to handle any special tasks in the foreign field that he or the secretary assign. The counselor of the department is also part of the secretary's immediate staff, and his primary responsibility is to advise the secretary in all the complicated relations the United States has with Western Europe as well as with the Soviet Union and the Communist bloc in Eastern Europe. He also carries out any special assignment for the secretary such as representing the department in intergovernmental committees. Another important office is that of the policy planning staff. This committee, headed by a director, focusses on trying to identify long-range problems for the United States and to formulate alternative policies for the secretary's consideration. It is this office that gives overall direction to our foreign policy and prevents it from being determined solely in reaction to crisis.

Five assistant secretaries of state are each concerned with one of the regions into which the world is divided by the department: Africa, Europe, East Asia and the Pacific, the American Hemisphere, and the Near East and South Asia. They advise the secretary on policy toward their region and they supervise the work of the embassies in their area. They also work closely with other government departments, bureaus and agencies whose work involves them in things that could affect our foreign policy. Beneath the assistant secretaries are country directors who deal on a day-to-day basis with the American ambassadors abroad and are responsible for seeing that our foreign policy objectives are being carried out by all members of the embassy staff according to the department's directives.

In addition to the five assistant secretaries who oversee geographical divisions, there are ten bureaus which have responsibility for what are called functional areas, headed by officers with the rank of assistant secretary.

The Economic and Business Affairs Bureau is involved in trade promotion abroad and helps the secretary formulate economic policy. Its staff also works closely with the office of the Special Representative for Trade Negotiations in the Executive Office of the White House.

The inspector general of the foreign service and his staff are responsible for reviewing all foreign economic and military assistance programs to insure that they are run efficiently and conform to the established tenets of American foreign policy. Under his supervision, therefore, are the Agency for International Development, the Security Assistance Program, the Peace Corps*, the Food for Peace Program, the Overseas Private Investment Corporation* and the Inter-American Foundation.* Each of these groups carries out one of the many economic, social or military programs authorized by Congress by which the United States implements its overall aim of maintaining a stable and peaceful world.

The Bureau of Intelligence and Research is the department's "in-house" center for intelligence analysis which assists the secretary and his staff in the formulation of policies so that he can advise the president. This bureau also works closely with universities and other groups to encourage research into foreign affairs. Often an outside group brings a fresh approach and contributes innovative ideas for the department's consideration, and, in addition, the close contact between the department and the private sector promotes a greater understanding among Americans of the goals of American foreign policy. The Bureau of International Organizations develops

---

*Although the inspector general does have supervisory functions over these offices, they are not located in the Department of State at present. The Peace Corps is a component of ACTION (see p. 274); the other two are government corporations.

policies for the United States in all international groups and encourages support around the country for American participation in these organizations.

The Bureau of Public Affairs is concerned with explaining our foreign objectives to the American people at large and, in addition, relays public opinion on foreign policy back to the department's policy makers. This bureau prepares films, pamphlets, and the like for distribution to the people directly or through the media and arranges upon request briefings by foreign service officers and other department officials for interested groups of citizens. It also arranges to send speakers around the country who not only interpret the department's policies, but can answer any of the questions any particular American might have. This bureau also keeps close tabs on what other people around the world think of American actions, a service of value for the secretary and his staff. Public Affairs also is responsible for the publication of the *Diplomatic History of the United States* as well as administering the Freedom of Information Program for the department. This program, authorized by the Freedom of Information Act first passed in 1966 and amended in 1974, gives every American access to public documents unless they contain material which would endanger national security and is one of the most important ways in which citizens can know exactly what their government is up to.

The Bureau of Security and Consular Affairs is probably the best known to the general public, as it issues passports to Americans, authorizing them to travel outside the United States. The demand for passports each year exceeds three million, and the department maintains passport offices in all the major port cities in the United States as a convenience to the traveling public. All one has to do to get a passport is to have proof of citizenship, generally a birth certificate, three copies of a photo of standard size, and the money to pay the fee. The passport is a person's ticket to overseas travel and a guarantee that the United States government will protect its citizens' rights, provided that they have abided by the laws of the country they are visiting. In recent times because the problem of drug abuse is widespread, the State Department publishes a pamphlet especially aimed at young people who want to travel abroad in which all the laws of foreign countries relating to drugs are spelled out, and it is made extremely clear that the United States government can do nothing for an offender in certain countries where drug abuses are punished by long jail sentences. This pamphlet also offers extremely useful advice for travelers and is well worth the small fee charged for it. The Bureau of Security and Consular Affairs also grants entry visas to foreigners wishing to visit the United States. It is not, however, concerned with illegal entrants. They are the responsibility of the Immigration and Naturalization Service in the Department of Justice.

The Bureau of Politico-Military Affairs illustrates the interrelationship of foreign and defense policy. Both the State Department and the Defense Department must be concerned with security problems involved in nuclear and arms control and disarmament policies and in military assistance programs, and this bureau works with its counterpart in Defense to protect American interests in these fields.

A recently established bureau is that of Oceans and International Environmental and Scientific Affairs. It covers the fields of oceanic research, fisheries, population, nuclear technology, and the like which reflects the new horizons that must be considered by the Department of State. It is also responsible for American participation in international conferences devoted to global problems such as the Law of the Sea Conference which worked out an agreement as to how exploration and exploitation of the resources of the oceans can be carried out for the good of all nations. To date the United States has not ratified this treaty.

Protocol is the agreed upon rules of diplomatic conduct among civilized nations, and the chief of protocol* and her staff have one of the most important jobs in the government. The Office of Protocol covers a multitude of responsibilities. The chief and her staff handle the accreditation of foreign diplomats. When an ambassadorial appointment is made by another country to the United States, that country first sees if the

---

*The chief at present is a woman.

person in question is acceptable; if he is, before he can begin his official duties, he must present his credentials to the president. It is the job of Protocol to make all the arrangements entailed in this procedure. The bureau also is in charge of all diplomatic immunities and privileges which often involve the staff with local officials not only in Washington but in cities such as New York in which there are many hundreds of foreign diplomats. Traffic violations, disputes over zoning regulations and the like must be handled with the proverbial kid gloves in order not to cause a diplomatic incident. The Protocol Office is in charge of all visits of foreign heads of state or other high officials and runs all the necessary ceremonies in accordance with the accepted rules on conduct. When heads of state arrive, for instance, the president meets them officially in a very impressive ceremony on the White House lawn, weather permitting. An honor guard representing all the branches of the armed forces must be assembled, and the designated service band must know the anthem of the visitor's nation. Proper speeches must be prepared, and the right people must be assembled as an audience. Those who hold office must be ranked correctly. Usually in the evening following the arrival of the guest, a state dinner is held at the White House, and it is again the job of the Protocol Office to see that everyone is seated properly according to rank, and that the proper food is served. Many nations have dietary taboos, and it would be as much of a disaster for the United States if the wrong dish were served as it would be if the band played the wrong national anthem! Whenever the president goes abroad, again it is Protocol's job to make all the necessary arrangements and to adjust American practices to conform to those of the host country. It may seem to be a less important job when compared to the responsibilities of those in charge, say, of nuclear policy, but it must not be forgotten that relations between individuals are always basic to relations between nations, and if the Protocol Office makes a serious mistake, it can set off an international incident.

Another of the secretary's most important advisers is his legal counsel. He and his staff are responsible for all the legal aspects of the department's work which, as one can see, is a tremendous job. The legal counsel usually is close to the secretary and accompanies him when he goes to testify before congressional committees. His job is also to defend the secretary against any suit which might be brought against him involving his actions as secretary of state. When this occurs, the legal counsel may handle it in his office or he may hire outside counsel. In addition to the legal counsel himself, there are three deputies and sixteen assistants as well as a special member assigned to the International Law Commission. Each member of the staff must be an authority on American law, on international law and well versed in the diplomatic history of the United States. Again, as with the Office of Protocol, a mistake or a misinterpretation can have serious consequences for the secretary of state and for the nation.

Probably one of the most important and sensitive jobs is that of the assistant secretary in charge of congressional relations. Although the Constitution requires that the president be responsible for the foreign relations of the United States, it also gave Congress considerable voice in foreign affairs. Not only does the Constitution require that the Senate confirm all ambassadors, ministers and consuls and the political appointments to the Department of State and ratify treaties negotiated by the executive branch, but it empowers Congress to appropriate all the funds necessary for carrying out our foreign policies. It is of the utmost importance, therefore, that there be close contact between the Department of State and the congressmen who are concerned with international affairs. It is the job of this assistant secretary to keep Congress informed, and when the job is handled well, much discord between the two branches can be avoided. Had President Wilson, for instance, worked closely with the senators on the Foreign Relations Committee at the time of the Versailles Peace Treaty in 1919, it is possible that the Senate would have ratified it and the United States would have been a member of the League of Nations. Again, in the immediate postwar period in the 1940s, President Truman was able to gain Congressional approval for the revolutionary Marshall Plan by which the United States undertook to help in the reconstruction of Europe largely because he and his secretary of state included the leaders of the Congress in the decision-making process.

The work of the State Department could not be effective if it were not for the foreign service of the United States. The men and women of this corps are those who carry out the policies of the United States in 136 embassies, twelve missions, sixty-four consulates general, thirty-five consulates, three branch offices, and thirty-four consular agencies around the world, and it is they who send back to Washington the basic raw material out of which much of our foreign policy is made. The foreign service is the oldest career service of the United States, and its proud tradition is a result of the high caliber of individuals who over the years have been attracted to it. It is not easy to enter the foreign service. Applicants must be college graduates, usually with an advanced degree, and must pass rigorous examinations which test one's knowledge of language, history, economics, and political science as well as one's general aptitude and judgment. Those who qualify, after further training, begin on the lowest rung of the ladder as third secretaries, and from then on promotions are made on the basis of merit. Not all who enter the service make it to the top rank of ambassador as it is a highly selective service, and, in addition, it has long been the custom for presidents to appoint outsiders to ambassadorial posts. This practice is almost as old as the nation not only because presidents have wanted to reward political supporters, but because ambassadors are their personal representatives in foreign nations and presidents have often wanted close friends in that post. In certain instances political appointments have not been in the best interest of the country as the incumbent has not been the most qualified individual to serve as an ambassador, and one of President Carter's innovations was to appoint a panel of experienced persons representing different segments of American life to provide him with a list of qualified persons from which he proposed to select a number of ambassadors. He had been particularly concerned that the panel consider women and members of minority groups within the nation and not just the leaders who automatically come to mind. One might wonder why persons other than foreign service officers should ever be appointed to such sensitive positions. The best reason is that there are many very talented Americans in the private sector who bring to ambassadorships not only a wide range of knowledge and experience, but who, because they have not been conditioned by years of government service, bring a fresh approach to the complexities of foreign relations which can be valuable to the secretary of state and the president as they seek to determine the best policies for the nation to follow.

United States embassies exist in all countries with which we have diplomatic relations. They are located in the capital city, and the chancery, as the embassy office is called, and the residence of the ambassador are United States property. This fact is mentioned because it explains why, upon occasion, a foreign national who for some reason or other wants protection from his government comes to the embassy to seek asylum. The law of the host country does not apply within the embassy compound.* All business is conducted with the host government through the embassy staff which usually includes, as well as the ambassador, a minister who is the chief of mission in the ambassador's absence, and a first, second, and third secretary, political and economic counselors, military and press attaches, and representatives of other United States agencies, such as the United States Information Service and the Agency for International Development. All personnel of the embassy report to the ambassador and as a "country team," carry out his orders which he, in turn, receives from the president and the secretary of state. In other cities in the host country the United States is represented by consuls who handle any business the ambassador assigns and help Americans who may be in difficulty or who may need assistance in negotiating business affairs. The ambassador is empowered to speak for the United States at all times and to negotiate treaties. He or she is

---

*In Moscow over five years ago, family members of a Pentecostal sect sought asylum in the American Embassy. There they lived in the basement until in the early summer of 1983, the Soviet government finally granted them exit visas, and they were able to have U. S. protection and migrate to Israel.

responsible for maintaining cordial social relations with foreign nationals, official and unofficial.

If the United States decides to break off diplomatic relations with another country, the ambassador is recalled, and the embassy is shut down. Communications, however, are then handled through the good offices of another embassy. Such was the situation in Cuba where, until recently, the embassy of Switzerland acted as the liaison between the United States and the Cuban government. Because relations between the two countries have improved, they have exchanged representatives, but they are not ambassadors. Full diplomatic recognition has yet to be restored.

Ambassadors, like all presidential appointments, serve at the president's pleasure. All ambassadors, whether career or not, must resign their posts at the change of an administration. A career officer who is appointed to an ambassadorship may be replaced by a new president, but he retains his rank for life even if his next assignment keeps him in Washington. Ministers and the other foreign service officers do not resign, but continue to serve wherever assigned by the Department of State.

In addition to the foreign service and the divisions of the State Department described above, the Agency for International Development has been included within the overall jurisdiction of the department as a result of changing world conditions and problems. This agency was created in 1961 to carry out the Foreign Assistance Act passed by Congress in that year. AID directs all nonmilitary United States foreign assistance programs around the world. These programs in general take the form of economic and technical aid through loans and by development grants to less developed nations. With American technical and financial assistance it is hoped that these nations will be able to build essential industries, develop modern farming methods and promote health and educational facilities with which to establish viable political, social and economic systems. This kind of aid has become an essential element of United States foreign policy.

The Agency for Arms Control and Disarmament, although physically within the Department of State and in spite of the fact that its director works extremely closely with the secretary of state, is structurally not a part of the department. It is an independent agency created by a 1961 act of Congress, and its primary responsibility, as its name suggests, is to control the spread of nuclear weapons and to work toward disarmament among the nations of the world to a degree compatible with national security. The creation of the agency reflects the growing dangers to the world of the nuclear potential. The aim of the United States is to work toward world peace, and the control of armaments is extremely necessary to the attainment of that goal. Much of the work of the officers of this agency takes place in New York at the United Nations, in Geneva, Switzerland, and in Vienna, Austria, where for a period of years the United States and the Soviet Union as the principal nuclear powers have been trying to hammer out a mutually acceptable limitation of armaments. To date, the major accomplishments of the agency have been the treaty which banned the testing of nuclear weapons in the atmosphere signed in 1962 and the success of the first Strategic Arms Limitation Talks in limiting antiballistic missiles. SALT, as these talks were called, continued. In 1975 President Ford signed an interim agreement with the Russians at Vladivostok in the Soviet Union limiting the number of certain missiles and warplanes, and negotiations went on under President Carter to seek permanent arms controls which would preclude a catastrophic outbreak of nuclear war. Although the United States and the Soviet Union did reach an agreement which both parties initialed, this treaty was withdrawn by President Carter from consideration by the Senate because in the light of the Soviet invasion of Afghanistan, approval seemed highly unlikely. President Reagan, whose general attitude toward arms control is different from Carter's, began his term by renaming the negotiations START, Strategic Arms Reductions Talks. Under his term negotiations continue in Geneva over both the reduction of intermediate range missiles in Western Europe and intercontinental strategic weapons. The agency also conducts talks with the Russians aimed at reducing the armed forces of the North Atlantic Treaty Organization and the Warsaw Pact countries in Central Europe and works toward preventing the spread of nuclear weapons to nations which, to date, do not possess the technology to make them. It goes without saying that the responsibility of this agency is staggering. It must try for the sake of mankind to control nuclear proliferation, but it must be sure to guarantee the security of the United States which depends on being prepared to counter a nuclear attack.

Another quasi-independent division closely associated with state is the United States Mission to the United Nations in New York. The United States ambassador to this international organization not only heads the delegation, but is a member of the president's cabinet and as such holds equal rank with the secretary of state. Because the two, therefore, each have a voice in the formation of foreign policy, it is very important that they see eye to eye so that America's positions are consistent.

World War II marked the beginning of a new era for the United States because for the first time in its history the nation could no longer avoid world responsibility. The two oceans which had effectively separated the country from entanglement abroad could no longer act as such a barrier in the air age, and the American people have no alternative other than to assume a leadership role in order to maintain peace in the nuclear age. The role of the secretary of state has, therefore, become second only to that of the president, and the work of the Department of State is vital to the guarantee of the security of future generations.

The United States Treasury

Along with the Department of State at the beginning of the history of the United States under the Constitution in 1789, the Department of the Treasury was established. Originally, the Treasury was responsible simply for the management of the nation's finances. As the years have passed, however, the work of the Treasury has expanded to include four distinct functions. The secretary and his staff formulate financial, tax and fiscal policies. The Treasury is the financial agent for the federal government. It manufactures the nation's currency, both coin and paper, and it has wide law enforcement responsibilities. In organization and purpose, therefore, the Treasury differs from the Department of State. Whereas the State Department has the sole object of making and carrying out foreign policy for the president with its entire organization devoted to that task, because the Treasury has many different functions, it is organized as a confederation of various offices all under the direction of the secretary. Today the department has under it the Office of the Comptroller of the Currency, the Bureau of Engraving and Printing, the Fiscal Services, the United States Savings Bond Division, the Bureau of the Mint, the Internal Revenue Service, the United States Customs Service, the United States Secret Service, the Bureau of Alcohol, Tobacco and Firearms, and the Federal Law Enforcement Training Center. Each of these groups has its own head, but each is subordinate to the secretary.

In his role as manager of the country's finances, the secretary of the treasury has many responsibilities. He is the president's chief financial adviser and an important member of the cabinet. He, too, is a political appointee and holds office only as long as the president does or as long as the president wants him to. His job requires that he make policies designed to improve the management of the nation's revenue, and he plays an important role in determining tax policy. He also keeps all the public accounts and authorizes all the money that is issued from the Treasury to pay the nation's debts. Should Congress request any information relevant to his financial responsibilities, the secretary is obliged to comply. Also, each year he is required to present a report to Congress on the financial state of the nation. In addition, in recent years he has come to play an important role in the formulation of international financial policies. Not only does the secretary perform all these duties, but he is also on many other government and nongovernment boards, commissions, and councils. He is the chairman of the cabinet-level Economic Policy Group, the United States Governor of the International Bank for Reconstruction and Development (the World Bank), the International Monetary Fund, the Inter-American Development Bank, the Asian Development Bank, and the African Development Bank. He is the chairman of the National Advisory Council on International Monetary and Financial Problems as well as the honorary treasurer of the American National Red Cross, the chairman of the Library of Congress Trust Fund Board, and a member of the establishment of the Smithsonian Institution. To name all his other board memberships would require a page. Suffice it to say that his presence is required on the many different boards and commissions in Washington whose business relates to the government's finances in some way.

To help him with these varied responsibilities, the secretary has a deputy, two undersecretaries, the treasurer of the United States, nine assistant secretaries, a general counsel plus their assistants as well as the heads of the divisions under the Treasury. The deputy is the alter ego of the secretary and assists him in all his administrative and policy decisions. He also is acting secretary in the secretary's absence. One undersecretary is in charge of monetary affairs which include both domestic and international financial matters, and he is responsible among other things for the management of the public debt. The treasurer of the United States, customarily a woman, whose signature is on all the currency, works in his office. The other undersecretary handles all tax and economic affairs which include tariff administration, law enforcement, legislative and administration liaison work, the currency, public affairs, and the revenue-sharing program, a recent innovation whereby the federal government returns money to the states for their internal use. The assistant secretaries each have responsibility for one of the divisions under the undersecretaries. In addition, the secretary's general counsel handles all the legal work of the department. Although the number of responsibilities of the department has required the creation of many positions, it is the secretary alone, however, who is the president's chief adviser for financial policy, and his position as the chief expert on financial matters makes his opinion weigh heavily among the secretaries of the other departments.

As money is clearly the most important subject in the Treasury, it is not surprising that several of the Treasury's subdivisions concern themselves exclusively with its creation and its use. The Office of the Comptroller of the Currency, the Fiscal Services, the Bureau of Engraving and Printing, and the United States Mint all have to do directly with aspects of the nation's complicated financial life. One of the important changes made when the Constitution was adopted was the introduction of only one kind of currency for the whole United States. In 1792, in order to make that currency, the United States Mint was established, and in 1873 Congress changed its name to the Bureau of the Mint. Since its inception all the coins in use in the country have been made by the Mint and by the Mint alone. The Mint, since 1873, also strikes all medals for the government to be presented for acts of valor in time of war or for meritorious service to the nation. It also will strike coins and medals for other countries which do not have the facilities to do so themselves. It also is in charge of all the gold and silver bullion owned by the United States and is responsible for its disbursement to the proper places. It also serves as a research center for the government by compiling and analyzing statistical data pertinent to gold, silver and currency in the world at large. The Mint is run by a director in Washington, but is assisted by subordinates in the seven field offices in various parts of the United States. There are two functioning mints, one in Philadelphia, the other in Denver, and the Old Mint in San Francisco. There is an assay office in San Francisco whose function is to weigh and assess the monetary value of gold or silver that individuals, such as prospectors or jewelers, wish to sell. In addition, the nation's supply of gold is secreted in the bullion depository in Fort Knox, Kentucky, and its silver is in the depository at West Point, New York, both of which are under the control of the director of the Mint and are protected by the United States Army. When the United States must pay its international debts, many of which must be paid in gold, it is the director of the Mint who arranges for the transfer of the actual gold from Fort Knox for delivery abroad. Needless to say, when such transfers occur, they are performed in great secrecy. In addition, the director of the Mint administers all the federal regulations concerning the mining of gold and silver in the nation and its uses.

The Bureau of Engraving and Printing, also administered by a director, makes all the paper currency for use in the United States. This operation also involves many security precautions to preclude the easy counterfeiting of our currency. Since paper money was first authorized during the Civil War, only one company has supplied the paper for the currency to the bureau, and it is manufactured from a secret formula known only to a handful of trusted employees of the paper mill. The actual printing takes place in a building in Washington, and the people involved in making our dollars must undergo stringent security measures. The public is welcome to watch the making of our money, but visitors are only allowed to view the operation at a distance. It is extremely tantalizing to see millions of dollars rolling off the presses, but, in fact, they are not legal currency at that moment. Every bill has its own serial number printed on it, and until that number has been recorded by the Federal Reserve, the bill is, in effect, play money. It is the Federal Reserve that distributes new currency to its member banks, thus putting it in circulation. The Federal Reserve also collects worn-out paper currency which is destroyed in Washington by the Bureau of Engraving and Printing. There used to be a furnace with a tall chimney adjacent to the building in which the money is printed where old bills were burned, but since people have become concerned with smoke pollution, it has been removed as a concession to environmentalists. Besides this very important job of making the millions of dollars that Americans use every day, the bureau also prints other government paper documents, such as bonds, bills, treasury checks, revenue, customs postage and savings stamps as well as all the White House and State Department invitations.

Much that contributes to the nation's stable financial life has to do with banking. The Office of the Comptroller of the Currency, which was created in 1863 when Congress first authorized the national banking system, has to do entirely with the regulation of the national banks across the country as well as the banks in the District of Columbia. The establishment of a new one, an addition or a branch to an existing one, or the liquidation of such a bank can only be effected with the approval of the comptroller. His office also regulates the investments and the accounts of the national banks, and once a year the comptroller is required by law to examine the financial condition of each of the national banks in the states and in the District of Columbia. This time-consuming task is handled by over two thousand bank examiners who work for the comptroller and examine over 4,500 banks each year. Although the comptroller's office is in the Treasury, the comptroller is actually independent in that by law he reports to Congress rather than to the secretary and his office is funded by assessments on the national banks. The logic of this status is to insure an apolitical approach on the part of the comptroller as he supervises the national banks of the United States.

Another important division of the Treasury is that of the fiscal services. In 1940 a reorganization of the Treasury established this office which directs many treasury operations regarding revenue. An assistant secretary heads the services under the supervision of the undersecretary for monetary affairs. The work is divided between two main bureaus, the Bureau of Government Financial Operations and the Bureau of Public Debt. The Bureau of Government Financial Operations is, in turn, subdivided into other bureaus which handle the myriad of details involved in the fiscal affairs of the government. In general, it is the bookkeeping department. It is responsible for the accounting and reporting of all the monetary assets and liabilities of the Treasury, and it must prepare periodic reports as to the state of the budget and the financial status of the United States. It disburses the over two million checks to government personnel each payday, the federal payments to beneficiaries of the many social programs authorized by Congress, administers the Federal Payroll Savings Plan by which those wishing to automatically purchase United States savings bonds every pay period, and it also has the task of adjudicating claims against the United States for lost checks and reimbursing those who actually are owed the money. It is sometimes a difficult job because there are many who would, unfortunately, attempt to cheat the government by claiming that they had not received their check. In addition, it has the job of handling mutilated currency, and it oversees the destruction of worn-out currency by the Federal Reserve Banks, making sure that the serial numbers are removed from the current lists. The Bureau of the Public Debt is responsible for publicizing the sale of all government securities and maintaining the lists of accredited owners of these securities. It sees that the proper interest accrues and that the purchasers of government bonds receive their checks. The work of the fiscal services is extremely exacting, and it is vital to the honest management of the public's money. For those who do this work, the advent of the computer was a life saver, and today, instead of hundreds of clerks with green eyeshades bending over account books, gigantic computers in seconds handle the million details involved in the bookkeeping of the United States government.

Also under the Treasury and directly responsible to the secretary are other divisions whose jobs are concerned with the collecting of United States revenue and the enforcement of laws regulating that collection. Their functions in those aspects make it logical that they should be under the Treasury. They are the Internal Revenue Service, the United States Savings Bond Division, the Customs Service, the Secret Service and the Bureau of Alcohol, Tobacco and Firearms.

Of all the revenue collection agencies none is as well known as the Internal Revenue Service. This bureau is headed by a commissioner appointed by the president and confirmed by the Senate. His job is to see that all taxes providing for internal revenue are duly collected all over the United States. No one who owes taxes is immune from paying them, and the commissioner has the responsibility of seeing that everyone from the president of the United States on down abides by the law. The commissioner is in Washington, but his bureau is decentralized and divided into seven geographical regions each supervised by a regional commissioner. The regions are subdivided again into sixty districts, and it is to these district offices that the individual taxpayer pays his bill. The Internal Revenue Service does everything in its power to make paying taxes as easy and as pleasant as possible. Anyone who has trouble filling out the complicated forms may go to any Internal Revenue Office and get free help. The forms are all provided by the government and are usually distributed shortly after the New Year to the taxpayers, and if by chance one loses it, copies may be attained at various places, including the post offices. The service takes the attitude that Americans are a law-abiding people and that the majority will pay what they owe to support their government, but to those who try to avoid paying their taxes, the service is not lenient. Tax forms are processed very carefully. This auditing used to be handled individually by the many employees of the service, but increasingly in recent years the returns are subjected to the infallible, impersonal scrutiny of the computer. This modern marvel has speeded up the auditing process and has resulted in far more accurate tax returns. When delinquents are discovered, the service immediately goes into action. If the tax is to be paid, it is then promptly collected. In certain cases the service takes criminal action in order to collect what is legitimately owed to the government. This careful auditing has another purpose, however. Occasionally too much tax is paid. In that case, the surplus is refunded to the taxpayer. The United States is an enormous country, and the job of collecting taxes could be difficult, as it is in many other nations, but most Americans are aware of the fact that their own representatives in the United States Congress are those who set the amount of tax money that must be collected to pay for all the services that citizens want, and, therefore, have an extremely good record of honest tax payments.

The United States Savings Bond Division is another section of the Treasury that adds to the revenue of the nation, but in a different way from Internal Revenue. Whereas everyone who has a certain level of income is required by law to pay taxes, only those who wish to, do business with the Savings Bond Division. The government offers several kinds of bonds and savings stamps for sale. In return for cash, the purchaser receives a bond, which is a promissory note. In a certain number of years the purchaser cashes in his bond and receives not only his full purchase price, but interest as well. The government has used his money and has paid for the privilege. This program offers citizens a way of helping their government while helping themselves at the same time. The savings bond system that is presently in use was originally designed during the Second World War to meet the immediate need on the part of the government, but it worked so well that it has been continued in the postwar years, and offers every American a chance to invest in his nation.

Anyone entering the United States from abroad by boat, airplane or car has reason to know about the United States Customs Service, a subdivision of the Treasury. Even before landing or docking, a person returning from a trip must make out a statement declaring what articles he is bringing in with him to the United States from abroad. Everyone returning from abroad is permitted to bring in a certain amount of foreign goods duty free, but anything over that amount must be taxed. This law is for the protection of American merchandise. The declaration of goods is presented to the customs inspectors immediately upon entering the United States. They check the statement and then open and look through all the luggage to see that no contraband items are being smuggled in. Not only are passengers and cargo on the commercial overseas carriers subjected to this inspection, but all yachtsmen and pilots of private aircraft as well. If there is no duty due, the individual passes through, but if a tax is collectible, one pays it immediately and then is free to enter the country. Although this procedure may be a nuisance to the individual, it is an important and necessary precaution. Not only do the laws of the country demand that duty be paid on the importation of foreign goods over a certain dollar value, but they also forbid the bringing in of many harmful items such as narcotics, plants that may be infected or foods that may be contaminated or do not meet American health standards. The customs officials, therefore, act not only as tax collectors, but also as law enforcement and detection agents, working closely with other government departments and agencies. With the Drug Enforcement Administration in the Department of Justice and in coordination with foreign governments, they seek to prevent the illegal traffic in narcotics. They work to enforce patent and copyright regulations established by our government for the protection of American inventors and writers. They inspect foreign imports of materials to see that their labeling complies with the standards set by the Federal Trade

Commission. In conjunction with the United States Coast Guard, a division of the Department of Transportation, they help enforce laws against polluting American waters by ships discharging refuse or oil, and they also see that foreign automobiles coming into the United States meet the safety and emission standards required by Congress. In addition, as customs officers have the task of patrolling the borders between the United States and Canada and Mexico, they work for the State Department by checking visas of foreigners and passports of Americans traveling to certain foreign countries. They also check exports for the Nuclear Regulatory Commission to make sure that no atomic materials leave without the proper license or permit.

The customs office seems to have varied duties. Originally its purpose was only to collect duties on imports and exports for the Treasury, and that job makes its location in the Treasury logical because the money collected is part of the revenue of the United States. The subsidiary duties of the Customs Service all stem from the fact that the officers of this service are those who are on the scene at all times. If each task required a different individual to carry it out, the number of federal employees at each port of entry and on the borders would be staggering. To handle the task efficiently and economically, the Customs Service has taken over these additional duties for the government offices concerned. This many-dutied subdivision of the Treasury is headed by a commissioner of customs who is appoined by the secretary of the treasury. The central office is in Washington, and there the commissioner administers all the laws pertaining to the importing and taxing of foreign goods for the secretary of the treasury. The main body of the service, however, is all along the borders of the country and in all the seaports and airports where twenty-four hours a day customs officers maintain a watch for the Treasury.

Closely associated with the work of the Internal Revenue and the Customs Services is that of the Bureau of Alcohol, Tobacco and Firearms. This division used to be part of the Internal Revenue Service, but in 1972 the amount of work involved in enforcing federal laws relating to these subjects became so demanding as to warrant the establishment of a separate service. The bureau, headed by a director, is centered in Washington, but like Customs and Internal Revenue, the majority of its staff is stationed all over the nation. The bureau has two major functions, enforcement and regulation. As an enforcement agency it suppresses criminal activities. "Bootlegging" is the illegal manufacture, distribution and sale of alcohol, and the bureau's agents have the job of tracking down illegal stills and putting their owners out of business. In American folklore, bootlegging has always been associated with backwoods mountaineers, but, in fact, much of this illegal activity takes place in large cities. Not only are the manufacturers of moonshine, as illegal alcohol is called, breaking the revenue laws, but usually they are also not conforming to the standards required for alcoholic beverages, and those who consume their product are often severely physically impaired and in some cases lose their lives. Unfortunately, in recent times firearms and explosives have become a serious problem to the safety of many law-abiding Americans. There are laws regulating the sale and use of these items, but criminals are not interested in purchasing guns and explosives through proper channels as they do not expect to use them for legitimate purposes. The agents of the bureau, therefore, have the responsibility of suppressing this traffic. Also of recent origin in the United States is the problem of illegal gambling operations by major crime syndicates, and it is the Bureau of Alcohol, Tobacco and Firearms that has the responsibility of stopping these operations. In its regulatory capacity, the bureau has the job of collecting all the revenue due to the government from the federal excise taxes imposed on the tobacco industry and the legitimate manufacturers of alcoholic beverages. This bureau works very closely with state and local officials in carrying out its responsibilities which are designed to protect Americans from physical dangers, from fraudulent practices and to see that legitimate businesses pay their taxes.

Another well-known division under the Treasury is the Secret Service. Probably most Americans associate the Secret Service almost entirely with the job of protecting the president and vice president of the United States and therefore wonder why it is in the Treasury. In fact, its original and primary job had nothing to do with the safeguarding of high officials, but was totally concerned with protecting the American people against the counterfeiting of their money and all other government securities and documents. For this reason it was placed in the Treasury in 1860 when the service was established, and because it still has this extremely important responsibility, it has remained there. A majority of the staff are engaged in tracking down counterfeiters and bringing them to justice. Its other responsibility, that of protecting the president and vice president and their families as well as others who are from time to time granted this protection by Congress, only came to the Secret Service after three presidential assassinations had tragically proved it necessary. It is a sad commentary on a country that prides itself on its law-abiding character, but there is no question that there are those who wish harm to the First Family and others in government service, and they must be protected. The Secret Service guards the president at all hours day and night wherever he is at home or abroad, and it can be an extremely dangerous job. In 1950, for instance, when an attempt was made on President Truman's life, an agent lost his life while protecting him. At all times it is a very difficult assignment. Presidents of the United States are politicians as well as chief executives of the nation, and it is hard for them to be sealed from the public whom they serve. Yet every time they are exposed to large crowds, they run a terrible risk, and the Secret Service would be much happier if its charges remained out of the limelight a little more, but that is impossible in a democracy. All the service can hope for is cooperation from the White House so that plans to safeguard the president can be made well in advance of a personal appearance. When President Carter made his historic decision to walk from the Capitol to the White House after his inauguration, he notified the Secret Service of his plan, and they had plenty of time to make the route down Pennsylvania Avenue as secure as possible. Every rooftop had agents watching the crowd; every person entering a building along the route had to be cleared; and hundreds of agents as well as plainclothes policemen circulated in the crowds. When the president, his wife, and their family reached the White House safe and sound, there must have been a collective sigh of relief from the Secret Service, who could never forget that in spite of all its precautions President Kennedy was assassinated and President Ford shot at twice. Unfortunately, shortly after taking office, President Reagan, his press secretary, a Secret Service officer, and a District of Columbia policeman were shot outside of a Washington hotel. All the Secret Service can do is its very best to be on guard.

The last division over which the secretary of the treasury has jurisdiction is the Federal Law Enforcement Training Center, and its formation is very different from those described above. In 1970 during the period of intense domestic disruptions, caused in large part by widespread opposition to the Vietnam War, the government became concerned about the effectiveness of federal law enforcement and the quality of training available for those who served as law enforcers. Because the Treasury already had many enforcement duties, it was logical to inaugurate under its auspices a training center for all federal employees engaged in law enforcement. The center, which was established by an executive order by the secretary of the treasury, first began operations in Georgia in an unused naval air station and was then moved to a location near Washington, D.C. The center serves ten executive departments which have law enforcement responsibilities, and its purpose is to coordinate all aspects of law enforcement from the initial recruiting to advanced and specialized training. It offers a wide variety of courses at various levels and trains its students with the most modern equipment available. The goal is to have as effective a force as possible and to cut the cost to the taxpayer by centralizing all law enforcement training for the federal government.

The secretary of the treasury assumes a lot of extremely varied responsibilities when he takes office. His principal job, however, is the same as Alexander Hamilton's, the first secretary who served George Washington. He is primarily responsible for advising the president on how to make the United States a financially secure nation.

The Department of Defense

Perhaps the single most important reason that the American form of government has worked so well over the years is its flexibility and ability to adapt to changing circumstances. The best proof of that statement is to be found in the history of the Department of Defense. The Department of Defense was established in 1949. Scientific and technological developments in the field of weapons had outdated the traditional way of defending the country, and new methods and systems had to be devised for the best protection of the nation in the nuclear and missile age.

Originally, the defense of the United States was the responsibility of the War Department and the Navy Department, which included the United States Marine Corps. These departments were run by secretaries who by constitutional dictate had to be civilians. The professional military men worked with the civilians, but were always subordinate to them. The Constitution sets up a civilian government with the president of the country the commander in chief of the armed services, and in the service departments civilian control has always been essential to our democracy.

Until the twentieth century these two separate departments were solely responsible for the defense of the United States. The invention and development of the airplane was the first event to cause changes in the military setup. When the airplane was adapted to military use, the War Department built up its own air corps as did the Navy and the Marine Corps. World War II so emphasized the importance of aircraft in warfare that following the war it became apparent that there should be a separate service. Thus the Air Force was established on equal status with the Navy and the Army.

Modern warfare has become so complex and the need for coordinated defense policies so compelling that shortly after World War II Congress had to give consideration to the idea of abolishing the separate service departments and establishing a central defense organization in their place. In 1947 a step was taken in this direction, and the National Security Act created the National Military Establishment. In 1949, subsequent to amendments to the 1947 act, the Defense Department was initially established, headed by a secretary of defense. Under him were the secretaries of the army, navy and the air force who, although they had lost their cabinet seats, were still responsible for the separate administration of the three services.

In 1952 and again in 1958, primarily because of the advent of the space age with its rockets, guided missiles and satellites, further reorganization was necessary. Experience had also proved that the 1949 act did not give the secretary sufficient authority to run the department efficiently. Although the National Security Act and its amendments had ostensibly established one department for all defense, it actually had only superimposed a new office consisting of the secretary of defense, an undersecretary, and assistant secretaries over the secretaries of the army, the navy, and the air force. The act had made the secretary of defense the president's chief adviser on military and defense policies, but it did not, however, grant him unquestioned authority over the three service departments to carry out efficiently his role as coordinator and overall director of the defense establishment. Specific restrictions on his authority seriously weakened his position. The act, for instance, expressly forbade the secretary to transfer, resign, abolish or consolidate any combatant or other functions assigned to the services. The secretary could only formulate policy, but did not have the undisputed authority to carry it out if the service secretaries disagreed with him. His authority could also be challenged by the fact that the three service secretaries could, if they felt strongly enough, bypass the secretary entirely, although he was a member of the cabinet, and go directly to the president or to Congress. The secretary's role was also made difficult because the services had been traditionally separate, and keen rivalry marked their relations from the West Point–Annapolis football level straight up to the top commanding officers.

The secretaries of the Army and the Navy Departments had been the civilian heads of the services for well over a hundred years. It was not surprising that this first reorganization of the defense system only took the first steps toward the coordination of the services and left much of the old pattern unchanged. Therefore, to make the department more efficient and to clarify the position of the secretary, in 1958 Congress passed the Department of Defense Reorganization Act. By this act the secretary was given the authority to coordinate the military departments of the Army, the Navy (including the United States Marine Corps) and the Air Force, thereby eliminating unnecessary duplication and providing more economical administration of the nation's defense. The act, however, specifically forbids the merger of the services, and each branch of the military is still headed by a secretary and is organized independently of the others.

The present Department of Defense, housed in the famous Pentagon Building across the Potomac River from the White House, consists of the Office of the Secretary of Defense, the Organization of the Joint Chiefs of Staff and the three military departments. The secretary of defense, two deputy secretaries, nine assistant secretaries, the general counsel, and a great number of assistants, both civilian and military, make up the Office of the Secretary. The secretary himself is the president's chief civilian adviser on all military matters, and the deputy secretaries are responsible for supervising and coordinating all activities of the department. The assistant secretaries each head a special branch and advise the secretary about his area of responsibility. One is in charge of the financial administration of the department. Another is responsible for health matters, which include a section devoted to drug and alcohol abuse prevention, a particularly important area in that a great number of servicemen are young and in need of guidance. A third covers installations and logistics which involves housing, procurement, environment and safety, and energy, among other things. Two assistant secretaries are responsible for intelligence matters, one domestic, the other international, and they both work closely with other agencies in this field—the CIA, the State Department and the National Security Council. Another is in charge of legislative affairs and maintains close relations with members of Congress concerned with military matters. The eighth heads the section responsible for program analysis and evaluation where cost effectiveness studies are made to insure that the public is getting an adequate return for its money. A weapon, a ship or a plane must be of proven value to warrant the tremendous sums it costs. The ninth assistant secretary handles all the public affairs of the department and is the spokesman for the secretary, and the general counsel is in charge of all the endless legal work. In addition to these assistants there is also the director of Defense Research and Engineering who works in the secretary's office. He and his staff conduct research into all sorts of new fields and evaluate the results as to their usefulness to the defense of the United States. Although most of the research has to do with weaponry, and the like, the scientists are also interested in finding ways to improve the life of the men and women in the armed forces. One particular piece of research during the Vietnam War led not only to the saving of a great deal of money, but also to the boosting of the morale of the American fighting forces. Lettuce is a particularly perishable as well as bulky item, and it costs a great deal to ship long distances. In addition, the rate of spoilage was very high. Through the Office of Defense Research and Engineering a method was found by which lettuce could be dehydrated and consequently shipped in bulk by air without spoilage, then reconstituted upon arrival. United States servicemen, hungry for fresh salad, were able to eat lettuce regularly.

These officials in the secretary's office are all civilians. The professional military, however, is quite obviously essential to the formulation of defense policy and to its being effectively implemented. The principal military advisers to the president, the secretary of defense and the National Security Council are the Joint Chiefs of Staff. This staff is appointed by the president and confirmed by the Senate and consists of the chairman of the Joint Chiefs of Staff; the chief of staff, United States Army; the chief of naval operations; the chief of Staff, United States Air Force, and the commandant of the Marine Corps. The latter, although he sits regularly with the others, only enters the discussion as a coequal when Marine Corps affairs are under review. The Joint Chiefs are the senior military commanders of the United States defense establishment, and they are the vital link in the chain of command that goes from the president to the secretary of defense to the commanders of each of the armed services. They are also the liaison between the directors of the Defense Communication Agency, the Defense Intelligence Agency, and the Defense Mapping Agency and the secretary. These agencies deal with highly specialized areas pertinent to the defense of the nation. The Defense Mapping Agency, for instance, is responsible for making all the maps, the marine charts and geodetic surveys necessary for the armed services. In addition, it operates two schools of map making, one in the Panama Canal Zone for Latin American defense officials whose countries want to become self-sufficient in this field, and the other at Fort Belvoir in Virginia for United States military personnel.

Under the umbrella of the secretary of defense are the three military services, each with its secretary and his assistants. The Army is responsible for all the land forces. The majority of its officers are trained at the Military Academy at West Point, New York, but men from the ranks can rise to become officers, and, in addition, the Reserve Officer Training Corps program which operates in many universities and colleges across the nation supplies officers also. The army at present is manned by volunteers. Conscription, or the draft, has never been very popular in the United States, and until the eve of World War II was only instituted during war crises. At that point Selective Service, however, became necessary and due to the uneasy years after the war had to be continued until a short time ago. Under that system eighteen-year-old boys received a number, and if that number were drawn in a national lottery, they entered the army for a specific length of time. Today only those who so choose enter the service. Although one automatically associates the army with fighting, it has other functions which it has traditionally performed. The Army Corps of Engineers, for instance, has always had responsibility for protecting the nation's environment. It builds dams, maintains waterways, and works on flood control and beach erosion. In addition, the Army works closely with the National Civil Defense Program and aids state and local governments in times of natural disasters. In such cases its medical units help to transport the injured to hospitals and the military police assist local law enforcement officials. The Navy is, of course, responsible for the nation's defense on the seas, but it, too, has the additional responsibility of maintaining the freedom of the seas during peace time. In earlier days this meant preventing piracy on the high seas. Naval officers are trained at the Naval Academy at Annapolis, Maryland, but other college students can enroll in naval ROTC units similar to those run by the Army, and men can also rise from the ranks. Seamen and noncommissioned officers are recruited and today's navy is staffed by women as well as men. A recent decision has permitted women to serve aboard naval vessels, but only in noncombatant circumstances. The United States Marine Corps is a separate service, but is under the secretary of the navy. It recruits its own personnel and trains them at Parris Island, South Carolina. The United States Coast Guard in peace time is under the Department of Transportation, but in case of war becomes part of the Navy. Aside from patrolling the seas, the Navy also has important other duties concerned with oceanographic research and in recent years in the search for offshore oil. The United States Air Force is the youngest of the three services, but its age in no way lessens its importance to the nation's defense in this space age. It really is the first line of defense because of the speed with which it can be mobilized and put into action. In addition to its combat role, the Air Force is also responsible for transporting members of the armed forces and materiel anywhere in the world where they are needed. Its officers receive their basic aeronautical training at the Air Force Academy in Colorado Springs, Colorado, and flight training at various bases around the country. One of the most exciting and hazardous opportunities for young fliers is testing the many experimental planes designed by Air Force and private aerospace engineers, and many of these pilots were among the original astronauts. In addition to its other functions, the Air Force has the honor of flying the president when he travels, and Air Force One is the pride of the service. It is always under the command of one of the most senior and distinguished pilots.

The Defense Department is a vast and complicated organization charged with providing for the security of the two hundred and sixteen million Americans. In addition, through alliances with other nations such as NATO, it cooperates with foreign military establishments and coordinates military plans for the defense of Western Europe. The secretary presides over more than two million men and women in the United States armed forces and over another million civilian employees. His budget represents about a quarter of the national budget, and he must spend it as carefully as he knows how to provide the best possible defense for the American people. This is not an easy task because scientific and technological developments are constantly being made and the secretary must decide which new types of weapons, ships, and planes, all extremely costly, to order to meet future needs which are always difficult to determine. And, at the same time he must also try to keep the cost consonant with his budget. His job is made even more difficult because he is required by law to be a civilian, but he is dealing with highly sophisticated technical matters of a military nature. To the best of his ability, he must advise the president, who in the last analysis must make the final decisions. The secretary really needs to have the wisdom of Solomon.

The Department of Justice

The Department of Justice is the legal branch of the United States government, and it can be compared to a very large law firm except for the fact that its clients are all the citizens of the nation. It exists to serve the people by enforcing federal law, by guarding the Constitution, and by protecting the rights of the American people as described in that document. Under its direction are many bureaus and divisions, each concerned with one of the many facets of enforcing federal laws and seeing that justice is carried out across the land. Because this department is charged with such an important responsibility, it is imperative that everyone from the attorney general to the youngest and most inexperienced lawyer on the staff be of impeccable integrity so that the citizens whom the department serves can be confident that they are indeed receiving just treatment. The fact that the attorney general, his deputy and the many assistants are political appointees puts the burden on the president to choose persons primarily for their legal expertise and integrity rather than for their political support. Because, during the Watergate scandal, the integrity of the department was questioned, President Ford went far to restore the nation's confidence in Justice by his immediate appointment of a legal scholar as attorney general. Since then, many of the leading members of the American bar and political scientists as well have urged that the attorney general be a nonpolitical appointment. It is more likely after Watergate, which included the conviction of a former attorney general, that those holding that position now and in the future will lean over backwards to insure impartial justice for the American people.

The Department of Justice, like many of the executive departments, has grown tremendously over the years, and its responsibilities have been greatly enlarged since the first attorney general was sworn in in 1789 to advise the president on all legal matters. At that time the attorney general had no department under him. He simply advised the president when consulted, sat with the cabinet, and enforced federal law with the help of a few assistants. Surprisingly enough, this system continued until 1870, although the nation had grown from the original thirteen states on the eastern seaboard into many more which stretched across the continent to the Pacific Ocean, and the legal business of the federal government had expanded accordingly. It was only in that year, however, that Congress deemed it necessary to establish the Department of Justice. The attorney general heads the department and he is secretary of justice, despite his different title. He now has thousands of lawyers, investigators and agents working for him in Washington and across the nation carrying out the laws and protecting Americans.

The Department of Justice has many major tasks as the federal law enforcement agency. It supplies the lawyers who represent the United States government in all cases to which it is a party in the federal courts. It runs all the federal prisons; it handles all appeals to the president for pardons for federal crimes and all requests for parole from federal prisoners. It is responsible for the discovery of violations of federal laws and the investigations of those violations. And, of course, the attorney general with the help of his subordinates is the president's adviser on all legal problems confronting the executive branch. The department also gives legal aid to any of the other departments or agencies if asked and has the responsibility of defending officers of the executive branch should suits be brought against them. In such cases, however, outside counsel can be hired by the department if for any reason the attorney general feels that it would be in the best interest of the defendant to do so. To carry out these many different assignments, the Department of Justice is organized into subdivisions, each entrusted with one of the aspects of providing justice to the American people.

The attorney general is, of course, the chief law enforcement officer in the United States. He is primarily concerned with advising the president and other cabinet officers if they request his help. In cases of exceptional seriousness he argues the government's case before the Supreme Court.*

As chief law enforcement officer, the attorney general is also responsible for insuring that the department provides the fairest system of justice and that its employees meet the highest standards of performance. To those ends two new offices have been created, the directors of which report directly to the attorney general. The Office of Policy and Planning has the job of devising ways to improve the quality, fairness and effectiveness of federal justice, particularly in the area of criminal justice. If the attorney general adopts the suggestions made by this office, he sees that they are carried out by all the United States attorneys across the nation, and, should they require new legislation, he then proposes it to the appropriate com-

---

*It should be noted, however, that one of the most important cases to come before the Supreme Court in the nation's history was not argued by the attorney general. During the Watergate affair Congress had created the post of special prosecutor in the Department of Justice to handle all the allegations arising from the initial break-in into the Democratic party's headquarters, and it was he who argued for the United States government in *The United States* v. *Richard Nixon.*

mittees in Congress. The Office of Professional Responsibility is charged with seeing that standards of performance are adhered to by the lawyers and other employees of the department. It looks into charges of misconduct, and if there appears to have been a violation of the law, the office advises the attorney general who will then refer the case to the appropriate investigative agency. The attorney general is assisted by the deputy attorney general, who administers the department and stands in for the attorney general if necessary.

Because of the increased amount of work assigned to the Department of Justice in recent years, a new position, that of counselor to the attorney general, has been created. He and the deputy attorney general divide the responsibilities in accordance with the attorney general's wishes. It is of paramount importance that the Justice Department carry out its work promptly, efficiently and with integrity, and the creation of a new senior position was designed to meet that requirement. The associate attorney general supervises all the heads of the department's subdivisions.

The number four man in the department is the solicitor general of the United States. His primary task with the help of his staff is to represent the United States in the Supreme Court. For a lawyer this is one of the most coveted jobs in the whole nation and is generally viewed as the acme of one's career. The solicitor general has the sole authority both to decide which cases the United States will appeal from the district courts to the circuit courts of appeal and which cases the government will ask the Supreme Court to review. He supervises the preparation of all the briefs in the cases he takes to the Supreme Court and personally argues before the high court, usually resplendent in a cutaway.

A great deal of the work of the department is carried out by the legal counsel. He serves not only as the counsel for the Justice Department, but he also with his staff prepares all the formal opinions of the attorney general and assists him with his cabinet responsibilities. The counsel also must review the legality of all the executive orders and proclamations. He resolves substantive disagreements beween departments or agencies of the executive branch over legal matters, and handles the department's work relating to treaties, international agreements and executive agreements.

The office of the attorney general also includes the Office of Legislative Affairs, headed by an assistant attorney general. He and his staff are the liaisons between the department and Congress and make recommendations concerning legislation which is pending that relates to their own department or that originated in any one of the other twelve. This assistant and his staff spend a good bit of time on Capitol Hill and play an important role in the making of federal laws.

Another senior official, the pardon attorney, has the very specific task of reviewing all the requests for pardons which come to the president from federal offenders. He then makes recommendations to the attorney general, who then advises the president, but it is the president who makes the final decision because he has the sole authority under the Constitution to grant pardons. Closely related to the subject of pardons is the issue of paroles. The American system of justice requires that a person convicted of a crime serve a sentence in prison. For most crimes the sentences vary according to the severity of the crime and the inclination of the sentencing judge. There is no law, however, that forces a prisoner to serve his full sentence, and it is customary for a person who has cooperated and been an exemplary inmate to leave the prison on parole. The United States Parole Commission is in the Department of Justice, and it is made up of nine presidential appointees who review all cases in which parole is being considered. This review is handled by a commission rather than by one person because the decision as to whether or not to free a prisoner is very important to the public at large. If the parole is granted, the commission is then responsible for the supervision of the parolee until the expiration of his sentence. The commission reports directly to the attorney general or to his deputy.

As is the case in all the departments, an assistant attorney general is responsible for the management of the department and for its financial affairs. In addition to his managerial responsibilities, he has the job of running the Justice Data Center, which is a computer operation, and the Publications Services Facility of the department.

Since the founding of the United States the number of subjects covered by federal statutes has obviously increased by geometric progression. As the Department of Justice is responsible for providing the means for enforcing all federal laws, it must have sufficient personnel and an efficient organization to carry out this task. Each subject covered by federal law is the exclusive responsibility of a division within the department. At present there are six: Antitrust, Civil, Civil Rights, Criminal, Land and Natural Resources, and Tax.

The Antitrust Division has the primary responsibility of enforcing federal laws against monopolies in restraint of trade, the first of which was the Sherman Antitrust Act of 1890. The division has both investigative and prosecuting authority. It first detects violations and then institutes legal proceedings against the offender to stop them. Some antitrust cases involve criminal activity, and if the offender is found guilty by the court, he is subject to fines and imprisonment. Others are called civil suits, and the object of the prosecution is to stop the monopolistic practice by having the court issue an injunction which is a court order. This division works closely with the Federal Trade Commission which protects the public against monopolistic practices as defined by the Clayton Act, the Federal Trade Commission Act and others. There is an overlapping of responsibility between the Antitrust Division and the Federal Trade Commission which produces dual safeguards against illegal monopolies or restraints of trade. The number of cases appears to be sufficiently large to keep both offices busy. The two offices work together toward the same general end, and, in fact, if a case brought by the Federal Trade Commission should go to the Supreme Court, the Antitrust Division is required to assist with the preparation of the government's brief and to participate in the argument. The Antitrust Division has more responsibilities than could be deduced from its name. It protects consumers, for instance, by prosecuting cases which may have originated either in the Food and Drug Administration or the Federal Trade Commission and involve practices on the part of industry which deceive or harm the public. It also reviews many policies of government agencies such as the Nuclear Regulatory Agency to see that fair competition with the private sector is maintained. It really is the federal watchdog designed to protect the American free enterprise system and to prevent unfair practices or illegal restraints of trade from occurring.

The Civil Division covers an enormous area because it handles all the suits brought against the United States government and by the United States government, and it is empowered to bring cases in all federal district courts, the United States courts of appeals, the United States Court of Claims, state courts and courts in foreign countries. The kind of cases it deals with covers a wide range. It defends all federal officers against suits brought against them in the course of their official government duties, and it handles all litigation involving admiralty and shipping, fraud, customs, negligence, patents, copyrights and trademarks, alien property, and many more. This is one of the largest and busiest divisions within the department and often in cases being argued in foreign courts must rely on foreign counsel in addition to the many lawyers already employed.

The Civil Rights Division, in contrast to the Civil Division, has very specific responsibility for a particular subject. It was created in 1957 by Congress to enforce the initial laws forbidding discrimination in the United States against Americans on account of race, color, sex, religion or national origin. As Congress has extended the authority of the federal government over the area of civil rights, so has the responsibility of this division been enlarged. It is directly charged with the enforcement of all the civil rights laws, the right to vote, the right to trial with an impartial jury, the right to education without discrimination, the right to use all public accommodations freely, the right to fair practices of employment and the right to open housing. The Civil Rights Division investigates complaints by citizens who claim they have been denied their rights. In the case of voting rights, federal examiners are appointed to oversee local elections to guarantee that all who may vote under law are, in fact, able to register and cast their ballot. The assistant attorney general in charge of this division has the authority to initiate suits in federal courts in cases where civil rights have been abused. In addition to the legal work, he and his staff work very closely with the Community Relations Service which is an important part of the Justice Department and operates directly under the attorney general. This service originated in the Department of Commerce, but was moved to the Department of Justice because its work is so closely related and intertwined with that of the Civil Rights Division, and it made sense to have them under common leadership. The Community Relations Service seeks to erase problems of racial origin before they erupt and, therefore, require legal action. The officers assigned to this service work with communities all across the land through the communications media, helping them to understand the civil rights laws and to identify sources of racial friction. If need be, the service provides on-the-scene mediators who try as objective outsiders to bring the two sides to a dispute together and by so doing prevent an outbreak of violence. This service, therefore, has a positive approach to the correcting of the wrongs of society and to creating an America in which all citizens, in fact, enjoy their constitutional privileges. It is to be hoped that because of the Community Relations Service the Civil Rights Division will in the course of time find that it has fewer and fewer cases to prosecute.

The Criminal Division handles the enforcement of all the criminal laws passed by Congress except those that are the special responsibility of other divisions such as Antitrust, Civil Rights and Tax. These laws cover a multitude of crimes: bank robbery and other violations, illegal gambling, airplane hijacking, kidnapping, extortion, labor racketeering, cheating the government, election fraud, perjury, obstruction of justice, counterfeiting and forgery, interstate car and securities theft, illegal traffic in firearms, explosives, narcotics, and pornography, interception of private communications, mail fraud, bribery of public officials, crimes on the high seas, fishing violations in United States territorial waters, to name a few. In addition, the division is responsible for international extradition proceedings and for coordinating all activities aimed at smashing organized crime syndicates. To that end the division is authorized by statute to maintain special "strike forces" in the big cities where organized crime is most prevalent. It also handles all internal security matters, including terrorist activities, treason, espionage and sedition. This enormous workload is carried out by the over ninety United States attorneys who operate in communities in the fifty states and all United States possessions. They and the assistant United States attorneys are the federal prosecutors who are appointed by the president and confirmed by the Senate. They also handle trials and hearings of civil suits in which the United States is a party.

The Land and Natural Resources Division is becoming more widely known at present because one of its responsibilities is to deal with Indian tribes who in the past few years have taken to bringing suits against the United States government claiming that treaties which guaranteed their ancestral lands have been violated. The division not only defends the United States in such suits, but it also defends Indian tribes against encroachments of their property and their rights to hunting, fishing, and water areas. In addition to this rather curious two-sided responsibility for the Indians, this division also deals with matters involving the government's acquisition and disposition of land and natural resources and suits involving environmental issues such as the control of air, water and noise pollution, as well as the preservation of wetlands and other natural resources. Although the Land Division has been in existence for a good many years, its responsibilities have been greatly increased by the recent inclusion of natural resources in its jurisdiction which is a reflection of the growing national attention to the despoliation of our environment. This division works closely with the Environmental Protection Agency in carrying out its functions.

The sixth division is devoted to litigation involved in tax collection, and its primary client is the Internal Revenue Service. Actually there are very few Americans who deliberately evade their taxes, but those few are promptly prosecuted by the tax lawyers in the Department of Justice or by the United States attorneys' offices. The bulk of the Tax Division's work arises from disputes in civil suits over the meaning of the tax laws. If a taxpayer interprets the law differently from Internal Revenue and is challenged by the service, he must pay what it says he owes. He then, however, may sue the government for a refund if he feels that he is right and the government wrong. The Tax Division will then defend the Internal Revenue Service in court. The Tax Division, through tax prosecution, also aids in the war against crime. Al Capone, for instance, a well-known gangster in the 1930s, managed to slip through the fingers of various other law enforcement officers, but was finally caught for not paying his income tax.

Each of these divisions of the Department of Justice is headed by an assistant attorney general who is appointed by the president and confirmed by the Senate. Working for each of these assistant attorney generals are lawyers who are specialists in the subject matter of their division. These attorneys are the ones who bring the lawsuits in the name of the United States against violators of federal statutes, and they prepare the cases and argue them in federal courts. It is important to note that these lawyers are in no position of favor before the bench just because they represent the United States of America. If they cannot prove their case to the court, they lose. When the Justice Department loses a case, it can be appealed only if the solicitor general in consultation with the division's assistant attorney general decides to do so.

The attorney general, in addition to his responsibility for seeing that his department carries out its prosecuting duties, supervises six bureaus, each with a specific function relating to the general area of law enforcement. They are: the Federal Bureau of Investigation, the Bureau of Prisons, the United States Marshals Service, the Immigration and Naturalization Service, the Drug Enforcement Administration, and the Justice System Improvement Act Agencies.

One of the most important aspects of the task of carrying out the laws of the country is the detection of violations of those laws. That is the job of the Federal Bureau of Investigation, the FBI. The FBI is one of the best known of all the government's operations. It is essentially a large investigative agency, and its activities cover all violations of federal laws except for those specifically assigned to other departments. Counterfeiting, for example, is the responsibility of the Secret Service in the Treasury. The job of the FBI is a big one. It must detect crimes; it must track down the criminal; it must find evidence and locate witnesses. It makes absolutely no judgment, however, as to the guilt of the individual involved. That is the duty of the courts. The specially trained agents who work for the FBI protect Americans against the crimes of espionage, sabotage, treason, and kidnapping, to name a few.

As the name suggests, the FBI only enters a case when a federal law has been violated. Crimes committed within state borders are the responsibility of local authorities, except those of espionage and sabotage which are always the responsibility of the federal bureau. To accomplish its task, the FBI has agents all over the United States who operate out of field or branch offices. The central office in Washington administers the entire organization, keeps the criminal files, and does all the laboratory work connected with crime detection. All the latest devices are used, and the speed with which the FBI can work is one of the best safeguards of Americans against widespread crime. During World War II, particularly, the work of the FBI agents in detecting and foiling espionage and sabotage plots was impressive.

The Bureau of Prisons serves Americans by undertaking the custody of criminals convicted in federal courts. The bureau is in charge of all the federal penitentiaries and is responsible for the care of those incarcerated for the duration of their sentences. In recent years the whole approach to criminals has undergone radical change, and the Bureau of Prisons reflects these changes in the management of those in its custody. It used to be that persons convicted of crimes were all placed in prisons regardless of the type of crime they had committed and were all treated not much better than penned animals. Today prison officials are aware both of the need to segregate hardened criminals from those who have committed less heinous crimes and the importance of rehabilitation for all prisoners. Therefore, the federal prison system today maintains maximum, medium and minimum security institutions. Federal judges sentence a convicted person to the type of prison suited to his crime and his personal character. A hardened criminal who is a danger to society will be placed in a maximum security prison, while a person who is either a first offender or has committed what is called a "white collar" crime, stealing securities, for instance, and who does not threaten anyone's physical well-being will normally go to a minimum security institution. All prisons today have rehabilitation services, including psychiatric and other counseling. Classes are available so that those driven to crime partly because of lack of education can learn while serving their sentences. Not only are vocational courses offered, but academic subjects on all levels are taught so that high school diplomas can be earned as well as in some cases college degrees. In addition, the bureau runs a government-owned, self-supporting corporation, the Federal Prison Industries, Inc. Prisoners are able to work for wages in these industries, and the products they make are sold to federal agencies. Their time in prison, therefore, is spent profitably, and they have a little money when they leave. Health is given much more consideration, and not only are clinics and infirmaries within all prisons for those who are ill, but athletics as a preventative measure are an important part of an inmate's day. In the less than maximum security facilities, prisoners in some cases are allowed to be with their families for a period of time. In addition to the regular prisons, the bureau also has inaugurated community treatment centers, or halfway houses, which allow a prisoner a chance to make an easier transition between prison life and the free society on the outside. That prisons are essential for the protection of society, no one can dispute, but today the predominant emphasis is on rehabilitation of persons who have committed crimes.

Working very closely with the Criminal Division of the Department of Justice, the United States attorneys, and the judiciary are the members of the United States Marshals Service. This service originated in the administration of George Washington and is well known largely because of the exposure it has had through television's innumerable western dramas. Wyatt Earp, for instance, was a United States marshal. The responsibilities of the United States marshals have increased enormously since the early days because of the complexities of modern life, and Wyatt Earp would hardly recognize the job he held which was mainly concerned with establishing law and order in the western territories. Today the United States marshals play a vital role in the United States system of justice. They are responsible for the physical security of judges, lawyers, juries, witnesses, etc., in all federal courts. They are responsible for the physical security as well of all witnesses to organized crime and their families outside of the courtroom. They also are responsible for juries when they are sequestered during a trial and they must see that no juror has any access to any information that might prejudice his impartiality, such as newspapers, radio or television news programs. The marshals serve all the subpoenas issued by federal judges demanding the presence of an individual at a trial. Sometimes this task can be very difficult as occasionally a person does not want to receive the subpoena and makes every attempt to hide. The marshal must locate the person and often has to resort to odd subterfuges to deliver the subpoena. They are also in charge of prisoners during trials and must see that they arrive in court and return to jail at the close of the session. If a person on trial is not incarcerated in jail during the trial, the marshals are still responsible for seeing that they appear in court as expected. After a conviction they are responsible for delivering the prisoner to the assigned federal prison. During a trial they are also responsible for all pieces of evidence that will be introduced by the prosecutor. In addition to serving the courts, the United States marshals serve the attorney general in any way he demands. In times of civil disorder, for instance, they are called upon to restore law and order. The importance of the United States marshals is reflected in the fact that they are presidential appointees, and they can be proud of a service that dates from the founding of the nation.

Another major division of the Department of Justice is the Bureau of Immigration and Naturalization. This bureau, originally established in 1891, used to be in the Department of Labor, but in 1940 it was transferred to Justice. The history of this bureau is of particular interest in that it reflects a fundamental change in American policy. Until the late nineteenth century there were no immigration laws in the United States. As everyone knows, the country was populated from the beginning by immigrants who came to seek a new life in a new land. In the early days of our country there was little need for any restrictions on immigration. There was plenty of land and many jobs for all comers. As the western frontiers were pushed back and the population increased, however, it occured to some that, if unrestricted immigration continued indefinitely, the country would become overpopulated and the means of making a living would become threatened. In addition, with the growth of cities with overcrowding and lack of sanitation facilities, health became a problem, and many people felt that it was necessary to prevent people from abroad who were ill from bringing their diseases to the United States. For these reasons Congress passed the first laws restricting immigration before the turn of the twentieth century. These laws were limited to prohibiting persons with certain diseases such as tuberculosis from immigrating, but in the 1920s far more restrictive laws were passed, designed not only to curb the numbers of immigrants to protect American jobs, but to allow only those from certain countries to enter the United States. The quota system was established and favored the northern European countries over the central and southern. Orientals were denied immigration visas altogether. Although these laws were designed to protect the heavily Anglo-Saxon, protestant cast of American society, they also undeniably were put on the books to protect the interests of the American working man, and for that reason the first Immigration Bureau charged with the implementation of the laws was placed in the Department of Labor. Changing world conditions and the emergence of different political philosophies in the mid-twentieth century led to a change in the nature of American policy toward immigration. In the World War II decade it was not only a question of how many new citizens the United States could absorb, but also, and most importantly, a question of what kind of immigrant and what ideas did he hold. With the world in a state of uneasy division between the free and the Communist countries the United States looked at each immigrant more carefully. No one who did not believe wholeheartedly in democracy was welcome. For these reasons the Bureau of Immigration and Naturalization was moved to the Department of Justice which is responsible for the internal security of the nation. Its officers, however, still work closely with the Department of Labor because in the 1960s United States immigration policy was broadened to include not only those who had relatives in the United States but also those who possessed skills needed by this country.

The Immigration Bureau carries out all the work involved in admitting legal immigrants to this country. Immigration officers are at all the ports of entry and process aliens immediately upon their arrival. Because persons wishing to migrate legally must have applied for visas from the American embassy in their native country before embarking for the United States, the immigration officers actually only check the papers to make sure they are in order and that the individual does have a place to go and a means of support, both of which are required by law. Although the process is generally handled very efficiently and smoothly, occasionally, however, things go wrong. Recently, an immigrant was returned to his country of origin because his sponsor, in this case, his brother, had gone to meet the wrong airplane, and the immigration officers had followed the rules which specifically forbid the entry of a person without a sponsor. The story had a happy ending, however, because an alert reporter picked up the story, and the ensuing publicity resulted in having the president himself authorize the return of the would-be immigrant with the cost of his flight being met by the United States government!

The bureau not only greets new arrivals at the ports of entry, but continues its responsibility for them until they become naturalized citizens. The naturalization section of the bureau provides all the information necessary for an alien to become an American. This information is distributed through the public school systems of the country, and Americanization schools teach English and prepare aliens for the test on the American government that they must pass before they are eligible to become naturalized citizens. They are given plenty of time in which to learn the language and the ways of the country because an alien must live in the United States for five years before he may take the oath of allegiance by which he becomes an American. Before naturalization, all aliens, as well as American citizens, are required to obey the law. If an alien fails to abide by the law, the Bureau of Immigration and Naturalization must institute deportation proceedings. Under United States law a hearing is required at which the alien has the chance to argue any extenuating circumstances that might affect his case. If he is deemed deportable, however, immigration officers must arrange for his departure immediately.

The biggest problem that the bureau must deal with which has exploded into serious proportions in recent years is that of aliens who slip into the United States illegally. Agents of the bureau patrol the borders of the nation continuously to prevent illegal entry, coordinating their work with customs officers. They work also with the Coast Guard to prevent illegal entry from the oceans. Because the areas to be covered are so vast and because there are so many people determined to enter the United States to improve their lives, but who do not have sponsors, the immigration officers are simply unable to catch them all at the borders or the coasts. Furthermore, once they are in the country, they seem to melt away, particularly in the big cities, and evade the Immigration Bureau's most diligent efforts to find them. The number of illegal aliens presently in the United States is staggering, and many of them who have been here for years are virtually indistinguishable from native Americans, making them impossible to identify. Because the problem actually defies solution by deportation, there is talk today of declaring an amnesty for illegal aliens who have been here for a certain number of years or who have families. Such a solution would bring an end to the constant fear in which many people are living, and in addition, would conform with the traditional picture of the United States as a haven for the oppressed peoples of the world. At this point when around the globe the issue of human rights is a burning one, it would enhance the image of the United States abroad immeasurably.

One of the most serious problems that has confronted the United States in recent years is the frightening growth in the illicit traffic in narcotics. Narcotics are drugs such as heroin and opium which, though perfectly safe when used in medicines, are extremely dangerous when circulated freely. The uncontrolled use of narcotics leads to addiction which can result either in insanity or death. Unfortunately, the problem of narcotics is not a purely domestic one. Opium and heroin are extracts from certain kinds of poppies which grow in abundance mainly in the Middle and Far East, and cocaine comes in great quantities from Latin America. The traffic in these drugs, therefore, is of international dimensions. The United States law forbids the importation of these drugs except under strict licensing controls for use in medicine where they are beneficial, but it is extremely difficult to prevent smuggling for many reasons. One is the nature of the substance involved. When the gum of the poppy is treated chemically, it is reduced to a powder which is easily secreted on a person, in his luggage or in otherwise innocent cargo. In addition, to suppress the trade, the United States must seek the cooperation of foreign governments. In countries such as Turkey, poppies are a major cash crop and farmers are dependent on them for their livelihood. Although the Turkish and other governments obviously do not overtly support illicit trade, they are hard put to stop poppy cultivation because of economic considerations. For a period the United States through the Agency for International Development tried to get foreign farmers to plant food crops such as wheat instead of poppies, but for many reasons the program was not successful. Also, the narcotics trade is, unfortunately, very profitable, and crime syndicates have organized the traffic on an international scale which again mitigates against the United States being able to suppress it almost single-handedly.

The federal law, however, demands that the trade be stopped and those engaged in it apprehended. The Drug Enforcement Administration in the Department of Justice is charged with the responsibility of carrying out these laws. Drug enforcement agents work closely with all state and local law enforcement agencies and with Interpol, the international police force, abroad. In addition to tracking down and arresting those engaged in illicit drug traffic, the Drug Enforcement Administration is responsible for making the public aware of the dangers of narcotics through a variety of programs. Under President Reagan this arm of the Justice Department has gained greater national prominence in that, as was mentioned above, the White House is determined to put an end to this insidious traffic.

As the law stands now, marijuana is included on the list of illegal drugs, and, therefore, its cultivation and use are of concern to the Drug Enforcement Administration. As the plant is a common weed and grows almost everywhere in the United States, suppressing marijuana traffic is almost impossible. There is considerable debate, however, over whether marijuana is, in fact, a dangerous drug, and if the conclusion is that it is not, federal laws will be changed. Until they are, marijuana is illegal, and its possession is a federal offense. Because it is illegal, those who use it run the risk of being known to the pushers of hard drugs who generally lose no opportunity of enticing a marijuana smoker into trying heroin, which is addictive and extremely costly. Addicts account for a great deal of crime in the United States because they must have money to support their addiction. This is another compelling reason for the suppression of the narcotics traffic. Above all, however, the loss of human productivity and of life as well is tragic, and all Americans would do well to support the work of the Drug Enforcement Administration as it is entirely in their own interest to do so.

Although the United States is a nation in which respect for law has been a widely accepted principle, there have always been elements in its society who have acted in defiance of the law. Until recently these elements were essentially a minority capable of being controlled by law enforcement agencies using traditional methods. In the 1960s the nation witnessed such a shocking upsurge in lawlessness and violence that Congress reacted by enacting the Omnibus Crime Control and Safe Streets Law. Among other things this act included an experimental agency called the Law Enforcement Assistance Administration. This administration was placed under the jurisdiction of the attorney general and its object was to help states strengthen and improve their law enforcement and criminal justice. It did so by funding innovative programs proposed by the states, the amount of the grants being in proportion to the population of the state. Federal grants supported all sorts of law enforcement projects, some to buy new equipment for police forces, some to underwrite the cost of further education for law enforcement officers, some to provide funds for the victims of crimes. In 1974 the Law Enforcement Assistance Administration's responsibilities were enlarged by the Juvenile Justice Act to include juvenile justice and prevention of delinquency. It was a sad commentary on the breakdown of many of the nation's traditional values in the 1960s and '70s that made this act necessary. Until that time juvenile delinquency when it occurred had been coped with by local communities.

In 1979 Congress evaluated the results of its anti-crime laws and decided to rewrite them in order to strengthen the programs which had been successful. The result was the passage of the Justice System Improvement Act which established three new agencies in place of the experimental Law Enforcement Assistance Administration to aid the Justice Department and the states in their fight against crime.

Essentially these agencies provide research and statistics for local law enforcement groups as well as federal grants for programs designed to curb crime and delinquency. Most importantly, perhaps, they seek to encourage citizen participation in crime prevention. The Office of Juvenile Justice and Delinquency Prevention was left unchanged, and it enhances its efforts to establish uniform standards for juvenile justice across the nation and to work out programs to prevent young people from becoming delinquent.

The Department of Justice, then, encompasses many varied activities. The attorney general and all who work for him have enormous responsibilities in enforcing the nation's laws and in protecting law-abiding Americans from criminals. In the course of carrying out their duties, they also have tremendous power as they have the full thrust of the United States government behind them, but it is important to remember that as they exercise that power, they, too, are under the law as is every citizen. They may not abuse the trust that is placed in them to carry out their responsibilities wisely and justly.

The Department of the Interior

Of all the executive departments the Department of the Interior has changed the most in its more than one hundred years of history. Established by an act of Congress in 1849, Interior was originally the housekeeper for the United States government. All matters having to do with the interior of the nation were dealt with by this department. It became a center for many bureaus and offices such as the Pension Office, the Commissioner of Public Buildings, the Patent Office and the Census Bureau, unrelated to one another but not really fitting under any of the other executive departments. As the federal government grew, and the creation of new departments and independent agencies was necessary, the nature of Interior changed also. Today the department is primarily the custodian of the nation's natural resources. It still is, however, a department whose responsibilities cover seemingly unrelated offices. Although its main function is to make the most of the natural wealth of the country for better peacetime living and for preparedness in case of war, Interior still has some of its old responsibilities to look after. Therefore, to understand the makeup of Interior, it is best to divide its functions into three major fields: the administration of Indian affairs, the direction of all the United States territories and trusts abroad, and the custodianship of the nation's natural resources.

Between the adoption of the Constitution and 1824, the federal government gave little thought to the problems of the American Indians. Ever since the days of the earliest settlers, although treaties guaranteeing certain lands and rights to the Indians were made, the native Americans were, in fact, simply pushed off the land that the white men wanted.* This pattern

---

*Until very recently the treaties made by the government and accepted in good faith by the Indians were disregarded. It came as a tremendous shock, therefore, to the citizens of Maine and Massachusetts when the Passamaquoddy, the Penobscot, the Micmac, and the Mashpee Tribes demanded that the states return their lands that had been guaranteed by a treaty ratified by Congress in 1790. The Maine Indians won this case and were granted not only the land but an enormous sum of money as well. The Maspees lost. The Court determined that they had ceased being a tribe in the legal sense and had, therefore, no right to sue.

repeated itself from 1609 to the early nineteenth century.

In 1803 Thomas Jefferson's purchase of the Louisiana Territory from Napoleon added an enormous piece of land to the United States. In the years that followed a great western migration took place, and by 1824 it was obvious that something had to be done about the original inhabitants of the land, the Indians. In that year the first Bureau of Indian Affairs was created and placed under the direction of the War Department. The army had the responsibility of protecting the white settlers in the early days of the West, and it was logical that Indian relations should be carried out by the military. In 1849, however, the Bureau of Indian Affairs was transferred to the newly created Department of the Interior, and its responsibilities were enlarged when Alaska was purchased in 1867 from the Russians to include the Alaskan natives.

The purpose of the bureau is to act like a friendly uncle to the Indians and the Alaskans. It supervises the many reservations on which the remaining tribes live. The aim of the bureau is twofold: to help the Indians and Alaskans to adjust their social, economic and political lives to the conditions of the twentieth century, and to assist them to achieve independence from the government. Until the termination of government assistance is possible, the bureau is the trustee for the lands and wealth belonging to the Indians and the Alaskans, and its agents help the owners to realize the most they can from their possessions. In the field of education the bureau is also very active. The government operates schools which not only teach English and American government, but the native languages and customs as well. There is a strong emphasis on the Indian and Alaskan culture with the aim of inculcating ethnic pride as well as of enriching the diverse American culture by preserving the native American heritages. In addition, economic aid is provided by the government. The thrust of the bureau is toward preparing the Indians and the Alaskans for full participation in the affairs of the United States and toward ending their second-class citizenship.

The Bureau of Indian Affairs is centered in Washington, and its commissioner is responsible to the secretary of the interior. Most of its work, however, is accomplished in the field, where there are more than sixty Indian projects across the continental United States and in Alaska. The Washington office serves in an administrative and policy-making capacity. The commissioner is also responsible for presenting the budget of the bureau to Congress which appropriates the money with which to run Indian and Alaskan native affairs.

The Department of the Interior is also responsible for the administration of the territories which belong to the United States and the trust areas which are under the guardianship of the United States. The territories include the Virgin Islands in the Caribbean and the Pacific islands of Guam, American Samoa, and the Trust Territory of the Pacific Ocean, including the Northern Mariana Islands. The residents of the Virgin Islands and Guam are represented in the United States House of Representatives by a nonvoting delegate elected every two years which makes them similar to the citizens of the District of Columbia. These nonvoting delegates sit on the congressional committees whose business is pertinent to their affairs, and their job is to present the opinions of their constituents. American Samoans, however, are not represented in Congress although they send a representative to the Office of Territorial Affairs in the Department of the Interior. The major concern of this office is to assist the governors of the territories who are appointed by the president and to encourage the social, economic and political development of the residents of the islands. The defense of these territories is the responsibility of the United States Department of Defense. The trust territories, which consist of the Caroline, Marshall and Mariana Islands in the Pacific, are legacies of the Second World War. After the defeat of Japan, under whose control they were, they were turned over to the United Nations which, in turn, in 1947 gave them to the United States to administer in trust for the international body. Since 1947, therefore, the United States has been responsible for the well-being of these islands and has been working with their inhabitants toward a termination of the trust status. The people of the Marianas have taken the first step toward self-government by having voted in January 1978, to become a commonwealth in political association with the United States, which is the status of Puerto Rico. To that end they have adopted a constitutional government with a bicameral legislature and have elected a governor and a lieutenant governor. As the trust will not formally end until the mid-1980s, the Marianas are in a transitional period in which the residents are not yet United States citizens. When the trust does end, they will be full-fledged United States citizens, as are the Puerto Ricans, entitled to the privileges of citizenship and subject to all federal laws. At that time, again like Puerto Rico, the Marianas will have their own agency in Washington and will no longer be under the jurisdiction of the Department of Interior. The Caroline and Marshall Islanders are in the process of negotiating their future political status with United States officials, and, therefore, the islands are still trust territories for which the United States must continue to report to the United Nations.

The third and the largest responsibility of Interior is made up of many parts, all having to do with the natural resources of the United States. The aim of the department is to manage, conserve and develop every natural resource of the nation to the greatest degree possible. The natural wealth of the country includes so many things that to achieve the purpose there are practically as many offices and bureaus as there are natural resources. Land, mines, oil, gas, water, fish and wildlife, reclamation are each the concern of a section of Interior.

It may seem surprising, but until the latter half of the nineteenth century the government had only scant knowledge of what the natural resources of the nation actually were, and what information it had was derived from descriptions written by explorers such as Lewis and Clark and reports made by army engineers in the course of their service in the West. In 1879 Congress decided that the government should provide for a careful and accurate assessment of the nation's natural wealth, and therefore, created the Geological Survey in the Department of the Interior. This office, in the words of the act establishing it, was to provide "the classification of the public lands and the examination of the geological structure, mineral resources, and products of the national domain." That is precisely what the Geological Survey does, and, in addition, it makes maps of the topography of the land. It covers so many areas that it can be called the key office and provides much of the information upon which the other bureaus and offices charged with responsibility for the management and conservation of our natural resources depend.

The other offices deal with land, water, minerals, fish and wildlife, and recreation, and their major purpose is to conserve and protect our natural wealth and our environment for generations to come. The Bureau of Land Management is responsible for over four hundred and fifty million acres of public land mostly in the Far West and Alaska, plus three hundred and ten million additional acres in which the government owns the mineral rights, and the submerged lands of the outer continental shelf. The resources that the bureau manages and in certain cases leases to private companies include timber, minerals, livestock forage, and geothermal energy. It is also concerned with recreation areas and with preserving open spaces for the enjoyment of Americans who love the outdoors. In addition, the herds of wild horses that roam the empty spaces in the West are under the jurisdiction of the Office of Land Management and during the severe drought of 1977, its agents in helicopters rounded up these animals, first to provide them with water and second to offer them for adoption so that they would not die in the searing heat of the desert. The office also maintains all public land records and is responsible for the survey of property owned by the federal government.

Water is one of the most precious resources of the United States and is of great concern to Interior today because for all too many years we have wasted and polluted it, not realizing that it was possible that we could run out of clean, pure water which, needless to say, is essential to life. Several sections of Interior work on various aspects of the conservation and uses of the nation's water supply. The Bureau of Reclamation works throughout the nation improving methods of irrigation, particularly in the arid regions of the Southwest and West, and studies ways of controlling floods. The Office of Water Research and Technology works primarily with universities and other research centers to train water scientists and engineers so that existing problems involving water resources can be solved and future ones prevented from occurring. This research center is also trying to find economically feasible ways by which salt and brackish water can be made fresh.

The Bureau of Mines does research on ways to improve mine safety and to find ways to increase production without hurting the environment. It is also concerned with the potentials of recycling mineral resources to add to the nation's supply, and it explores techniques by which to use low-grade ores to preclude the necessity of importing costly foreign minerals. The bureau is also concerned with pollution and damage done to the land from strip mining. In this respect it administers some of the laws which require that any damage to the surface done by mining must be repaired.

The United States Fish and Wildlife Service performs one of the most important and rewarding jobs in the entire federal government. It is devoted to the protection and preservation of all forms of wildlife—fish, animals, and birds—not only for the enjoyment of the American people, but for their ecological value which has been appreciated only in recent years. It manages all programs concerning fish, animals and birds everywhere in the United States, and maintains over three hundred and fifty wildlife refuges, research stations, laboratories, and about a hundred fish hatcheries. It is responsible for enforcing all laws concerning wildlife preservation, and it works out and enforces the international agreements regarding migratory birds and animals. The service is particularly concerned today with the problems of pollution and works closely with other government agencies and departments to clean up the environment and to prevent further pollution. When projects such as nuclear power plants are being considered, the wildlife people study the plans to see if fish and shellfish would be harmed by the heating of the water in bays where the plant would discharge the water it uses to cool the reactor. Recently, when hearings were held in New Hampshire to determine whether a nuclear plant would be built, the service testified that, in fact, sealife liked the warmer water and lobsters and other shellfish and fish were not harmed as had been thought. The service is also called upon to testify as to the ecological effects that channel dredging, dam construction, and other projects involving man's tampering with nature will have on wildlife, and their opinions are given careful weight. The service is also responsible for publishing the Endangered Species lists and actively works to control natural habitats so that nearly extinct species, such as the whooping crane, can propagate. Americans who love nature and want to see the many North American wildlife species preserved for future generations to enjoy have much to thank the Fish and Wildlife Service for.

The other service in Interior that exists primarily to give Americans pleasure is the National Park Service. Anyone who has ever visited a national park or a historical place of interest is aware of the work of this service. Not only is it responsible for the creation and maintenance of the national parks through the country, but it also provides educational and historical information for anyone interested. Much of the nation's natural lore is explained by the well-trained staff who run the parks. Also they have done a superb job in presenting American history in a clear and interesting fashion at the many battlefields and other places of historical interest in the United States.

Administering the enormous Department of the Interior is the secretary and his assistants. The secretary himself is a member of the cabinet, appointed by the president and confirmed by the Senate. Because so many of the natural resources under the jurisdiction of the Interior Department are in the West, it has become traditional that the secretary come from that region of the country. His office is staffed by the undersecretary, who is the deputy to the secretary, seven assistant secretaries, and a solicitor. Each of the assistant secretaries is responsible for one or more of the many bureaus within the department. All subordinates report to the secretary whose primary task it is to inform and advise the president on the many subjects covered by the Department of the Interior. Without this housekeeper and watchdog over the resources of this wonderfully rich land, much that we as citizens take for granted would be destroyed or wasted, and the nation would be immeasurably poorer for it.

The Department of Agriculture

Agriculture is one of the oldest and most fundamental of man's activities. It is basically the science of growing crops and raising livestock, but at the present time it is also deeply concerned with and involved in conservation work. Without agriculture it is obvious that no human life could be sustained, and in today's world with its exploding population agriculture has become even more important than ever. In the United States a vast majority of the population now lives in cities or in suburban communities, and it is entirely dependent on a small number of farmers and ranchers to provide food and clothing. In addition, in recent decades the United States, which has traditionally exported agricultural products in large quantities to Europe, has become one of the foremost suppliers of food to peoples in almost every corner of the earth. Food, in fact, has become a major factor in international relations, and the importance of the American farmer cannot be underestimated. The Department of Agriculture is, then, one of the key departments of the federal government which touches every American's life every day and the lives of countless foreigners as well.

1862 was a historic year for American agriculture. In that year in the midst of the Civil War, the Union Congress passed three acts which signalled the government's awareness of the importance of agriculture to the well-being of the nation. The Homestead Act enabled Americans to farm 160 acres of federal land in the West and to gain title after five years of continuous residence and work. The Morrill Act gave federal land to endow colleges devoted to the scientific study of agriculture, and the third established a Department of Agriculture in Washington. This department was initially very small and was headed by a commissioner who did not have cabinet rank. By 1889, however, the role of agriculture in the nation's economy was so major that Congress enlarged its responsibilities and made it the eighth executive department with the secretary of agriculture a member of the president's cabinet. President Franklin Roosevelt's New Deal in the 1930s, however, brought about the most radical expansion in the role of the

Department of Agriculture. The Great Depression of those years, which coincided with the nation's worst and most prolonged drought to that date, spelled disaster for the American farmer, and the federal government had to intervene in agricultural affairs to a degree that had never before been contemplated.

Today the secretary of agriculture with the deputy secretary, two undersecretaries, and seven assistant secretaries preside over a wide range of programs and activities both in the United States and abroad. One undersecretary is in charge of international affairs and community programs; the other administers small community and rural development. An assistant secretary is in charge of all administrative affairs and the others head the six major divisions responsible for the mission of the department which is to serve the farmer, to protect the consumer, to improve the nutrition and health standards of low-income Americans, to improve the standard of living of rural America, to insure future agricultural production capacity, to expand American export markets, to manage philanthropic food programs abroad, and to conduct research, scientific and technological, in all areas of agriculture.

The department serves the farmer in many different ways. One of the most important, which dates from the New Deal, is designed to secure his income. Before the administration of Franklin Roosevelt, the federal government, other than to establish the Department of Agriculture, had enacted few programs to assist the American farmer whose economic position due to many factors had been steadily deteriorating since the end of the nineteenth century. In the years after the Civil War the whole complexion of American farming had changed radically. In the pre–Civil War era, with the exception of the plantation South, farming was a diversified business and pretty much a family-run operation. This type of farming was particularly suited to the kind of land in the East and in the old Northwest. After the Civil War, however, a great migration took place to the central plains and the Far West, and the farmers there found that the land was different and more conducive to one-crop farming or to the raising of livestock.

In addition, the increased demand for grain and meat both in the United States and abroad further enticed farmers to a single cash crop planted on a large scale and encouraged ranchers to put all their energies into raising sheep or cattle. The Industrial Revolution which had swept America in the postwar years also played its part through the production of mechanized farm equipment which enabled the farmer to cultivate large areas. Unfortunately, the cost of the machinery to the farmer was great, and the fact that he was producing so much more led to overproduction, and, therefore, a fall in prices. As his expenses mounted, his income was reduced, and to add to his woes, cyclical droughts hit the United States and took their toll of both farmers' and ranchers' incomes. Between the 1890s and 1914, the year that World War I broke out, farm income had been steadily decreasing and there was an alarming increase in tenant farming. World War I, however, so improved the farmer's lot because of the greatly increased demand for food and other agricultural commodities that he was encouraged to expand his acreage and, unfortunately, went into debt to do so. With the drop in demand at the end of the war, the farmer found himself in very straitened circumstances, but the federal government did little to help him as a majority of the nation, tired of the expansion of federal authority which had been necessary during the war, preferred to see the government curtail its activities rather than take on new obligations. During the 1920s, although the general economy appeared strong, the agricultural segment was falling far behind. When the Great Depression hit, accompanied by adverse weather conditions, a vast number of the nation's farmers and ranchers, as was mentioned above, were bankrupted and literally lost their means of making a living. Because of the importance of agriculture to the nation's survival, President Roosevelt had no choice other than to inaugurate revolutionary new federal farm programs, and it is somewhat ironic that the American farmer, traditionally the most independent member of American society, has become not only one of the most heavily regulated, but more dependent on the federal government for his security than almost anyone else.

Roosevelt's programs, which to a large extent are still in existence, introduced a system of federal price supports for agricultural products. To guarantee the farmer an adequate and fair income, the government sets a target price for each regulated commodity: wheat, corn, cotton, peanuts, tobacco, rice, milk, soybeans, grain sorghums, wool, mohair, honey, barley, oats, tung nuts, rye and crude pine gum. If the open-market price equals or exceeds the government level, all well and good. If, however, the free-market price falls below the established level, the government steps in and buys enough of the product to pull the price back up. The farmer to qualify for this program must, however, have complied with the regulations determining how many acres he can cultivate. The acreage is determined by a two-thirds vote in a referendum of the producers of the given commodity who are participating members of the federal program, and if a farmer defies the decision and plants more than he should, he must pay a penalty. The object of this program is to enable the farmer to count on a steady income which is important not only because he deserves security, but also because he is a consumer, and when he buys, he is helping to keep the industrial producers of the nation healthy. Furthermore, through this innovative program the government has managed to keep agricultural production more in line with demand by controlling the acreage under cultivation. If overproduction seems likely the farmer is encouraged to keep some of his fields idle. The land is always available in what is called the Soil Bank and can quickly be brought back into cultivation if shortages threaten or demand suddenly increases. Until recently the farmer was paid not to plant. Under President Reagan a new plan has been inaugurated. Because of the enormous agricultural surpluses stored in government warehouses, instead of paying cash to the farmer to keep his land idle, the government pays him in kind. He may either sell what he receives or use it for seed. This experiment is designed to cut back the surpluses of agricultural produce which costs the government a great deal to store, to save the government the cash outlay to the farmer, and at the same time to provide him with income. The program is voluntary, and so far the response has been overwhelming. The Department of Agriculture administers these programs through the Agricultural Stabilization and Conservation Service under the subdivision of International Affairs and Commodity Programs.

Also under this service is the Resources Conservation Program. Under this program the government will share the cost up to 75 percent with farmers who are willing to engage in necessary long-range environmental improvement and conservation measures. The Forestry Incentives Program will help meet the cost of planting trees and maintaining timber stands to private owners. The Water Bank Program subsidizes owners of wetlands who are willing to preserve them for migratory bird nesting and breeding or to improve and conserve inland waterways, and the Experimental Rural Clean Water Program is designed to control pollution from agricultural lands, thereby improving the quality of the water that the farmer and his family drink. These three are recently enacted programs and reflect the national concern over environmental and ecological matters. In addition, the Agricultural Stabilization and Conservation Service provides certain emergency assistance to farmers who are in designated disaster areas following a natural calamity and who are participants in federal agricultural programs.

The money necessary for these programs is the responsibility of the Commodity Credit Corporation which was first established in 1933 as an independent corporation, but in 1939 was reorganized under a federal charter and moved to the Department of Agriculture. It is a corporation run by a board of directors who are appointed by the president and confirmed by the Senate with the secretary of agriculture an ex officio member and chairman. It is capitalized at $100 million and is authorized by Congress to borrow up to $20 billion in order to meet its obligations. The corporation disposes of the commodities it buys in various ways. It may transfer them to other governmental agencies. It may sell them abroad, or it may donate them to countries to alleviate famine.

Of great importance to the nation's economy and to its foreign policy are the department's international responsibilities of which there are three: to increase the export of American farm products, to feed the world's hungry with American surpluses, and to encourage agricultural development in the poorer countries through technology. The Foreign Agricultural Service is responsible for increasing exports and managing the philanthropic programs. To increase our markets abroad, the service has agricultural counselors, attachés, and trade officers stationed in over 100 countries, whose job it is to promote American products and to negotiate agreements with foreign governments. They also work closely with international organizations such as the Food and Agricultural Organization of the United Nations, and the information they gather on world markets is made available to the public and is invaluable to farmers and the department in planning production. In addition, within the United States the service encourages greater export of farm products through the Commodity Corporation Exports Credit Guarantee Program. This program provides guarantees to private exporters selling to customers abroad on credit. Without this federal guarantee many in the private sector would not want to risk a credit sale. American sales, therefore, are increased as the risk of non-payment is removed. The efficacy of the Foreign Agricultural Service is proved by the fact that American agricultural exports totalled over $40 million in 1982.

In the philanthropic area the service manages the Food For Peace Program, originally enacted in 1966 and amended several times since, in conjunction with the Commodity Credit Corporation. The aim of the program is to improve the economies and health standards of underdeveloped countries through American farm surpluses. The United States government offers low-interest, long-term credit arrangements to a country which then purchases American surpluses. Payments to the country are made in dollars, and the proceeds from the ensuing sales are then invested in agricultural improvements within the country. In the case of a less developed country hit by a natural disaster, such as drought or flood, the surplus is simply given outright. The Food For Peace Program has been very successful and is a valuable aid to United States foreign policy by proving to the less developed countries the sincere concern of the United States for human welfare, and it has made a significant contribution to peace.

The Office of International Cooperation and Development

is also responsible for the United States' efforts to encourage agricultural development in the underdeveloped world. To this end it supports exchange programs and research projects and facilitates and encourages private investment abroad by American agribusiness. It works with international organization as well as with American universities and Land Grant colleges to bring scientific and technological know-how to the people in the less developed countries in order to combat the hunger and malnutrition which affect an altogether too large proportion of the human race. This effort to improve the lives of people is of major importance in creating a better image of the United States, a land of plenty, among the less fortunate in the world.

The Small Community and Rural Development section of the Agriculture Department is divided into four units: the Farmers Home Administration, the Office of Rural Development Policy, the Rural Electrification Administration, and the Federal Crop Insurance Corporation, each of which is dedicated to improving the standard of living for America's smaller farmers and lower-income groups who live in rural areas. The Farmers Home Administration makes loans of various kinds available to those to whom normal borrowing channels are closed. Loans are made for home and land improvements, for seed, equipment, fertilizer, and livestock. The individual applying for assistance does not have to deal with an endless bureaucracy, as there are 2,200 local county offices which dispense the funds. This particular program is very democratic in that a committee of three reviews all applications and by law two of the three must be local farmers. This guarantees a fair and probably a sympathetic evaluation as the applicant will be well known to the committee. This office is also particularly concerned with encouraging young people to exercise their imagination and to establish small businesses either at home or in their communities. Normally a person under twenty-one has a hard time borrowing even a small amount of money, and the Youth Projects Loans made through the Farmers Home Administration have resulted in the launching of many an enterprising young person on a successful business career. Loans are also available for emergency purposes to those struck by natural disasters, to communities such as Indian tribes, and for housing in rural areas for low-income groups and senior citizens. The terms of these loans are easy: the interest rates are low and the time period for repayment is generally long.

Whereas the Farmers Home Administration is a field operation, the Rural Development Service is located in Washington, and it is responsible to the secretary for evolving a rural development program for the nation. It works very closely with the other executive departments and agencies concerned with rural America to coordinate all their activities. Its emphasis is on community development, and its programs are directly aimed at towns of about 10,000 people, although some apply to small cities of 50,000. It assists communities through leadership development programs which teach citizens to plan for their towns effectively, and it conducts research into rural problems and makes its findings available to all concerned. It also evaluates the nation's progress toward the goals of improving rural living established by the secretary and the president.

The Rural Electrification Administration dates from the New Deal era, and its original mission was to bring electricity to rural America by financing power stations and lines. In 1949 it was authorized to introduce and improve telephone service as well. The Rural Electrification Administration has done as much as any government agency to revolutionize the life of America's farm and rural population by bringing the wonders of electricity to its doors. All the daily chores were miraculously made easier and life became less of a drudgery. Milking machines and separators lightened the farmer's load, and vacuum cleaners, washing machines, irons and refrigerators radically improved his wife's housekeeping duties. Telephone service not only brings the pleasures of a daily gossip, but, more importantly, often can mean the difference between life and death in emergencies. Radio and television bring the isolated farm family into the mainstream of American life and, again, not only give pleasure, but bring information on weather which is vital to a farmer or rancher in that advance warning of severe weather conditions can often enable him to save his crops and livestock, and in case of hurricanes, tornadoes and floods, his and his family's lives. To date, about one thousand rural electric and telephone facilities have been installed under the Rural Electrification Administration. It does not build not does it own these facilities, however, but makes them possible through the loans it is authorized by statute to make to private companies.

The fourth unit under Small Community and Rural Development section is the Federal Crop Insurance Corporation. This corporation, originally part of the New Deal, provides insurance to the nation's farmers so that they are protected against loss of income due to natural disasters such as plant disease, insect infestation, or adverse weather conditions. Over the years it has more than proved its worth, and it has played a major role in the stabilization of farm income. In 1980 Congress amended the act to expand coverage and to put more emphasis on the private sector in the delivery system. Today twenty-eight crops grown in forty-nine states can be insured. Corn and soybeans, the nation's two largest crops, can be insured up to 98 percent of their anticipated value, and wheat, cotton, grain sorghum, rice, barley, and oats, up to 82 percent. Farmers have flexibility in their coverage and can buy what insurance they want at low cost with the government paying up to 30 percent. Originally the government provided the insurance, but under President Reagan, who favors more involvement by the private sector, the government contracts policies with insurance companies. The corporation is also testing an experimental program, the Prevented Planting Program. This program guarantees the farmer an income even if he is unable to plant his land at all due, for instance, to too much rain. It is an innovative way of assuring the farmer's financial security in the face of circumstances completely beyond his control.

The Marketing and Inspection Service division of the department is one of the busiest and most important to the American people. It has the dual responsibility for supervising the marketing of the nation's agricultural produce and for safeguarding the health of the consumer. An assistant secretary is in charge of this office which includes the following services: Federal Cooperative, Agricultural Marketing, Animal and Plant Health Inspection, Federal Grain Inspection, Packers and Stockyards and Food Safety and Inspection. The Federal Cooperative Service basically provides advice to those who own small farms and who would benefit financially by joining a cooperative. Those interested can call on the service for help in setting up a cooperative, managing it and marketing its produce. The service is constantly engaged in research aimed at improving the performance of cooperatives and it publishes its findings in a monthly magazine available to members of cooperatives across the nation. The Agricultural Marketing Service has diverse responsibilities, all in general directed at providing efficient delivery of agricultural produce to markets across the nation. It collects and makes available all market news which is invaluable for the orderly distribution and sale of farm products. It also protects consumers and others engaged in the food industry from deceptive practices such as the deceitful labeling of seeds, and it also licenses warehouses and inspects them to see that they meet government standards. In addition, it acts like the Patent Office in that it protects the farmer who develops a new hybrid by granting him the exclusive right to his innovation for seventeen years. This guarantee of exclusivity encourages advances in agriculture which benefit Americans by providing better products for their consumption. The service will also inspect and grade a myriad of different agricultural products—live cattle, swine, sheep, rabbits, poultry, eggs, vegetables, fruits, tobacco, cotton, mohair, to name but a few. This inspection is not mandatory, and farmers must pay a fee for the service. They do so willingly, however, because assured quality control results in greater consumer confidence and therefore increased sales. The Animal and Plant Health Service protects and improves the health of animals and plants for the benefit of the consumer and for humane reasons as well as far as animals are concerned. This service handles the task of controlling and eradicating animal and plant pests and diseases which can endanger livestock and horticulture. This work involves the service with the Canadian and Mexican governments as well as with state agricultural units in order to coordinate programs. Quarantine is required for plants and animals being imported, and agriculture agents work along with the customs officers in all the major ports of entry in the continental United States, and in Hawaii, Alaska, the Virgin Islands, Puerto Rico, Nassau and Bermuda. They are also stationed in many foreign nations such as the Netherlands, France, and Japan where they inspect and certify flower bulbs before they are shipped to the United States. This service in recent years has been concerned with the use of certain pesticides and monitors their effect on wild animals, plants, insects, fish, and humans to see if they are harmful. In line with their responsibility for animal health, the service maintains a large veterinary force which, in addition to protecting Americans against diseased animals, is responsible for the humane treatment of animals in interstate commerce. Federal veterinarians, for instance, enforce the Horse Inspection Act of 1970 which forbids the "soring"* of horses shipped across state lines for horse shows, and they supervise and enforce federal regulations concerning the transportation, sale and handling of dogs, cats, circus and zoo animals.

Many Americans who deplore the ever-increasing size of the federal government do not perhaps stop to analyze the reasons for the expansion. In most cases a new responsibility is thrust upon the federal government because either the states or the private sector cannot solve a general problem or they have failed to provide acceptable services. A case in point is the Federal Grain Inspection Service of the Marketing Services, which was set up in late 1976. The government had to assume this responsibility because of the scandalous cheating that had occurred in the grading and weighing of grain being exported abroad by private companies which badly damaged

---

*"Soring" is a particularly inhumane practice which applies specifically to Tennessee walking horses. These show horses walk in a special way—raising their forelegs abnormally high and thereby throwing their weight on their hind legs. Unfortunately, it is possible to achieve this gait more easily and quickly by either hurting the front legs or by placing weights on the front hooves which forces the horse to raise his forelegs unnaturally than by training the horse gradually over a period of time.

our relations with the foreign nations which had in good faith negotiated the purchases. Congress had no choice but to insure integrity in United States grain sales by legislating standards and authorizing the Department of Agriculture to carry them out. The Federal Grain Inspection Service, therefore, has the responsibility of seeing that government standards are met uniformly across the nation. All large exporters of grain now are required to register with the Department of Agriculture, and the staff of the inspection service, which is located across the nation, inspects and grades the grain and checks the weight and the quality as grain for export is loaded aboard ships. The service can authorize state units to inspect and weigh, but they are subjected to an intensive review before receiving clearance. The act also covers grain for domestic consumption, but it, too, must be inspected and weighed by either the service, state units or designated private companies who have met government requirements. In addition, if either a buyer or seller disputes the inspector's report, he may appeal first at the local level and then to Washington if he is still dissatisfied. The establishment of this new office is a clear example of the government meeting its responsibilities toward protecting the public against fraudulent practices as well as guaranteeing the integrity of the United States in its commercial dealings with foreign nations.

Another unit under the Marketing Services is the Packers and Stockyards Administration. Its job is to see that farmers and ranchers get true market value for their meat and poultry and their byproducts. It establishes rules of fair procedures to maintain free and competitive markets, and its aim is like that of the Federal Trade Commission in regard to business, to prevent unfair practices which would lead to monopoly or to discrimination against individuals as they sell their livestock. Agents of this service superivse stockyards, meat packing companies and poultry processors to make sure that they are abiding by the regulations. They also check scales for accuracy and see that stated weights are indeed what they say they are. As there are 2,000 public stockyards, 3,000 private livestock buying yards, and about 5,500 meat-packers, 400 poultry dealers, and 15,000 livestock commission firms and dealers, the service has an extremely large staff which works out of field offices almost everywhere in the nation.

The job of protecting the consumer against unwholesome food is the task of the Food Safety and Inspection Service. It carries out both the mandatory and voluntary inspection of agricultural products. All eggs, sold in interstate commerce or abroad for example, whether fresh, dried or frozen, must by federal law be graded and inspected. In addition, although not actually required by law, over three hundred other products are inspected and graded and bear the government's stamp. Major food processors do not mind paying the fee for this service because the government's approval enhances the salability of their products at the store as the American housewife is extremely quality minded. All meat and poultry and their byproducts must also be graded and inspected by law. In order to insure wholesomeness, the inspection process begins for interstate products before the animal or bird is slaughtered and continues through until the final stage of preparation has been reached. Abattoirs, where the slaughter takes place, are also subject to government scrutiny. Not only can the housewife be sure of the quality of the meats and poultry she serves, but the nation's pets are protected as well, as all meats put into pet food must be inspected as carefully as that destined for human consumption.

In 1969 a reorganization of the Agriculture Department brought into being the Food and Consumer Services. Its principal function is to administer all the federal food assistance programs. Federal concern with the nutrition of the nation's lower income families is new. Until very recently no one was aware of how many people, old and young, in this rich land were badly undernourished partly because they could not afford the high price of quality food and partly because they did not understand the importance of a balanced diet. The Food and Nutrition Service was inaugurated to provide the nation's needy people with more and better food. The Food Stamp Program is under this service. The government distributes through local welfare agencies food stamps to those who qualify. The recipients then use the stamps to purchase food in stores that participate in the program, and the government reimburses the merchants at the face value of the stamps. Needy Americans, therefore, are able to buy more and better food than they would have if they had to pay with their own cash. The Food and Nutrition Service also administers other federal food assistance programs mainly for children, expectant mothers and the elderly. Surplus food, milk, turkeys, and the like is made available to schools, day-care centers, summer camps and institutions which help the aged. Government funds, in addition, pay for school lunches and in some cases breakfasts for those who cannot afford them or do not get them at home. The Office of Food and Consumer Services is also responsible for research on human nutrition, and its Office of Consumer Advice is the place to which Americans can turn if they have problems. Health is a very important concern to government because a nation whose citizens are ill or undernourished will not be strong, and, furthermore, to a nation like the United States, it is a matter of principle that its citizens be provided with a decent standard of living.

The Department of Science and Education is concerned with precisely those areas. The Agricultural Research Service conducts scientific research to find ways to produce better plants and animals, to control pests and diseases without the use of dangerous chemicals, and to improve all aspects of our environment. The Cooperative State Research Service grants funds to state agriculture experimental stations which are located in the fifty states, Puerto Rico, the Virgin Islands, and the District of Columbia, and, in general, coordinates all research projects, private and public. The Extension Service brings department experts into communities as well as right into the homes of Americans desiring their services to show and explain the latest techniques and equipment that are available. Home economists conduct educational programs for homemakers in child rearing, nutrition and cooking, clothing, budget management, and consumer protection. Other agents work with young people exploring career opportunities and developing leadership skills mainly through the 4-H clubs, and in recent years the department has included low-income and minority groups in the urban areas in its programs with the specific object of teaching better nutritional habits.

Another important division of Agriculture is that of Natural Resources and Environment. Under its jurisdiction are the Forest Service, established in 1905, the Soil Conservation Service, and the National Agricultural Library. The Forest Service's aim is to preserve and improve America's forests which are vital to our ecology, important to our national economy and afford tremendous recreational pleasure. One hundred and fifty-four national forests and nineteen national grassland areas are under its jurisdiction, and the service manages these lands to insure the greatest good to the greatest number of Americans. When forest fires occur, the service not only fights them, but immediately reseeds the burnt-out area to prevent erosion as well as to replace the trees. Forest fires destroy a priceless national resource, and the Forest Service has done a magnificent public relations job, making Americans aware of how terrible the consequences of the careless tossing of a match or of not dousing the coals of a camp fire can be. Smokey, the famous bear victim of a forest fire who died after a long life in the National Zoo in Washington, is the symbol that looks down from posters across the nation reminding Americans to be very careful of our forest heritage. The Forest Service also decides on timbering policies in the national forests and reserves some from lumbering entirely. It also trains young people, mostly from the inner cities of the nation, in the science of forestry and conservation through its operation of seventeen Job Corps Civilian Conservation Centers. This program had its origin during the Great Depression when many an unemployed and disillusioned American boy from the urban areas was offered a wonderful experience by working in the Civilian Conservation Corps inaugurated by President Franklin Roosevelt, and the idea was resurrected by President Johnson in his War on Poverty in the 1960s. The Forest Service is also responsible for all kinds of research programs which will insure that future generations will have the many beautiful forests to enjoy that have always been a feature of the American landscape.

The Soil Conservation Service was founded also in the 1930s largely as a result of the tragic misuse of land that had produced the dustbowl in the central states of the nation. Ignorant of conservation measures, farmers had for many years been displacing the deep-rooted prairie grasses with short-rooted crops which resulted in erosion on such a scale as to turn the once rich land into a desert. The service operates across the nation teaching farmers and ranchers methods by which they can utilize the land without causing erosion. It also works at water conservation projects and on flood control in cooperation with other federal agencies.

The National Agricultural Library is unique. It contains one million, five hundred thousand volumes and is one of the largest collections of material on agriculture in the world. Located in Beltsville, Maryland, the library's resources are available to federal employees, students at the land grant colleges and to anyone else who is interested. It loans out reference material for use across the nation and around the world.

The seventh subdivision of the department is devoted entirely to the economic aspects of agriculture, both foreign and domestic. This section is headed by an assistant secretary and under his jurisdiction are the Economic Research Service, the Statistical Reporting Service, the Economic Analysis Staff, the Office of Energy, and the World Agricultural Outlook Board. The Economic Research Service is the center for all economic intelligence related in any way to agriculture, and it serves a myriad of different public and private agencies. The Statistical Reporting Service covers all data concerning the production, prices and supply of American commodities and makes them available so that efficient planning of the agricultural segment of the economy can be made. Of recent origin, the Energy Office concerns itself with the efficient use of energy in the agricultural field and coordinates the department's energy policies with the Department of Energy and the other federal agencies concerned with conservation. The World Agricultural Outlook Board literally reviews agricultural data on a global scale and works closely with not only other domestic agencies but with international organizations and foreign governments. It provides reliable information on potential agricultural yields and on weather and climate conditions which affect agriculture, and its forecasts are invaluable for effective planning around the world as well as in the United States. Not surprisingly, the work of this division has been made immeasurably easier with the advent of the computer.

Lastly, the Department of Agriculture runs a unique school, the United States Department of Agriculture Graduate School. This institution, located in Washington, was established in 1921, and although it does not give a degree, its purpose is to improve federal agricultural services by offering educational opportunities to federal employees. Interested students may either attend the school or enroll in the correspondence courses it offers. Those who teach are government employees, but they are not paid for their time. They either take leave without pay or use their vacation time, which attests to the dedication of many people involved in agricultural work. Students pay a fee, which makes the school self-supporting, and the department does not include it in its budget. The school is run by a director and a general administrative board appointed by the secretary of agriculture.

That the Department of Agriculture is intimately involved with the daily life of Americans is obvious. It is difficult to catalogue its every service, but in Washington and in every county in the nation there are employees of the department ready to help any person with problems that are of concern to the Department of Agriculture. Housewives who are interested in better nutrition or who are having trouble getting rid of household pests can get help from the department as readily as the owner of an enormous farm who is interested in global marketing conditions. If the department's local agent cannot help for some reason, the department in Washington has a vast number of useful pamphlets for sale for very little on practically any subject, which can be received by mail. The concern of the Department of Agriculture since its inception has been to enable Americans to live better lives and in recent years to assist others who are less fortunate at home or abroad to improve their standard of living as well. The secretary has a challenging and rewarding job as do his many assistants in Washington and across the nation.

The Department of Commerce

Commerce includes all business and trading activities. The Department of Commerce, which was set up as an independent department in 1913, is the executive department under the president responsible for all the vast commercial affairs of the United States. Its overall purpose is to advance the economic and technological development of the United States within the free, competitive system which is the hallmark of our economic philosophy. In order to carry out its mission, Commerce is responsible for a great many different aspects of the nation's commercial life. The department encourages, promotes and develops domestic and foreign trade, and to this end, it provides information and advice to any American business as well as to international concerns. It is responsible for the decennial census mandated by the Constitution, and it is the source of all statistical data pertaining to the nation's economic and social affairs. It supervises the Bureau of Standards and issues patents and trademarks. Commerce also directs scientific studies of the oceans and the earth's environment and is responsible for telecommunications policies. It also encourages travel to the United States by tourists from abroad, and promotes American trade overseas. Lastly, in recent years when the national attention has been directed to the severe problems of the underdeveloped areas of the United States, the decay of the inner cities and increasing unemployment particularly among ethnic minorities, the department has assumed the responsibility for assisting to solve them. The department, then, is actually a confederation of many different offices and bureaus all in one way or another related to the carrying out of the mission of the department, but often completely unrelated to each other.

The secretary of commerce supervises the department and

advises the president on all matters pertaining to the nation's industrial and commercial affairs and its position in international trade. He is assisted by the deputy secretary who is his alter ego, two undersecretaries, one for travel and tourism, the other for international trade, eight assistant secretaries, and the directors and administrators of the bureaus within the department. In addition, the general counsel is in charge of all legal matters and coordinates all legislative proposals emanating from the department, and the inspector general's job is to see that the department is managed efficiently. As much of Commerce's work, like that of the Department of Agriculture, is in the field, there are many offices of the department across the country. Their staffs maintain close contact with state and local officials, individual businessmen and industrial leaders, and their job is to report to Washington on all matters which affect the department's programs.

Of all the responsibilities that are assigned to the Department of Commerce probably the best known to most Americans is the work of the Bureau of the Census. It is the most valuable source of information about every aspect of American life, and it is by far the biggest fact-finding agency in the entire federal government. All the other government offices, federal, state and local, as well as private concerns, universities, research groups and just plain curious individuals rely on this bureau to provide them with accurate statistics relating to all facets of our national life. Originally, census taking was established by the Constitution for the purpose of counting the population for the apportionment of seats in the House of Representatives. The number of senators is fixed at two, but the number of representatives each state is entitled to is determined according to its population. The Bureau of the Census, therefore, provides every ten years an accurate and official count of the people in the United States. From these figures the number of representatives to be elected from the states to the Congress of the United States are computed, and the seats are then apportioned among the states according to their respective populations. The states then determine the number and the boundaries of districts from which representatives will be elected. Today the apportionment of representatives, however, is not quite the question of simple arithmetic that it once was. Recently the Supreme Court decided that congressional districts must be fairly drawn, and to ensure that they are, the Court ruled that it had to agree to any redistricting within a state that occurred because of a change in population. The 1980 census recorded substantial shifts in population away from the Northeast to the South and the Southwest, causing several states to have to adjust their congressional districts to reflect the changes in their population. These new plans must be submitted to the Court for approval before the next congressional elections. The reason behind the Court's action was to put an end to the practice of gerrymandering. Gerrymandering means that districts are drawn for political purposes, to exclude or include a particular voting group. As this is a discriminatory practice, it is unconstitutional.

Although census taking has existed since 1790, the Bureau of the Census only became a separate and permanent office by an act of Congress in 1902. This was necessary because over the years its functions had expanded to cover a great deal more than just a population count. Today almost every subject imaginable is covered by the census. How many farmers are there? How many businesses and what kinds? How many babies are born every second? How many people die? How many people immigrate to the United States every year? How many emigrate? How many mothers work? How many children have some sort of employment? How many people own their homes? How many rent? There is hardly a statistical question that cannot be accurately answered by the bureau, and the information it provides can be very helpful to planners. To give an example: If a clothing manufacturer knows that there are more people in their twenties and thirties, for instance, than in other age brackets, he will tailor his production to meet this greater demand. Though the population count is taken only every ten years, many other surveys are constantly going on, and the bureau is always busy. Census forms often come in the mail, but data is collected by many employees who walk from door to door asking questions, and it is a citizen's duty to answer honestly.

The material collected is assembled and sent to the central office in Suitland, Maryland, just outside of Washington, D.C., where it is evaluated and made available to any interested person. In recent years the development of the computer has greatly facilitated the work of the bureau and has permitted the storage of fantastic amounts of information for future generations to mull over. It should be stressed, however, that all information that is collected from individuals is confidential and is available only in statistical form.

The Census Bureau is not the only agency concerned with gathering information for the public. The National Technical Information Service, a part of the Commerce Department, collects every bit of information there is on scientific and technical subjects and, unlike the Census, sells it to the public. This service is unique among federal offices in that by act of Congress it must be self-supporting. Not a penny of taxpayers' money is spent on this office, and, like any private business, it covers its expenses by its sales. Its inventory is enormous, consisting of well over one million titles. These are available in full or in summary form and can be purchased in book form or microfiche. To keep the public abreast of developments, the service publishes weekly newsletters and a biweekly journal. The latter is primarily designed for use by librarians and universities who require comprehensive reports. The service also welcomes those who are interested in the latest technical reports to use its Bibliographic Data Base on line, which is maintained by nongovernment organizations under contract with the office. Not only is this service invaluable to specialists working in scientific and technical fields, but for doctoral candidates who must find new and unexplored subjects for their dissertations. By using this service, they can find out very quickly what subjects have been researched.

The work of the National Bureau of Standards and the Patent and Trademark Office is also probably familiar to most Americans. The National Bureau of Standards' primary goal is to promote the nation's scientific and technological advances and to make all advances effectively applicable for public use. The bureau is responsible for the developing and maintaining of national standards of measurement of physical quantities such as length, mass, time, temperature, etc. Have you ever wondered why an inch is an inch? It is because the bureau has determined that it is. This bureau also does all the research and development work in the physical sciences for the federal government. In conjunction with this work the bureau is a testing laboratory for all sorts of different materials and in recent years has taken on the job of establishing standards for all the new electronic wonders such as data-processing machines and computers. The bureau also works with other nations to establish agreed upon standard systems of measurement for international use. The bureau's services are available to the states and to private institutions as well as to individuals. If, for instance, a regular fever thermometer seems inaccurate, the Bureau of Standards will check it for free if the owner sends it to its headquarters just outside of Washington in Maryland. In this way much of its scientific research becomes known and disseminated throughout the country and is of immediate value to each American.

The Patent and Trademark Office was created originally as the Patent Office in 1790 in order to administer the patent laws which Congress enacted under Article I of the Constitution. Since then it has been under several departments, first in the Department of State; then in 1849 it was transferred to the Department of the Interior; in 1925 the Department of Commerce took it in, and there it has remained under the title of Patent and Trademark Office. The primary function of the office is to issue patents for inventions and to register trademarks. There are three kinds of patents which are issued. One kind is for designs and may be granted for three and one-half, seven, or fourteen years. In that period, the inventor has exclusive rights to his idea. The second is for plant or process patents and runs for seventeen years, as does the third, utility patents. Over 70,000 patents are issued annually, attesting to the great imaginative skills of the American people. The office registers about 31,000 original trademarks each year, and renews about 6,000. A person seeking to gain the exclusive use of a sign, symbol or picture by which to identify his product or service may get it for twenty years with renewal rights. The Patent and Trademark Office also maintains all the records pertaining to patents and trademarks and maintains a search room where interested people can look and see if their idea has already been patented or if their trademark has already been used. The office also handles all United States government efforts to cooperate with other countries on patent and trademark policies. The staff must decide on all questions of priority of invention and the patentability of each invention brought to the office. If it denies a patent, the inventor may appeal his case to the United States Court of Customs and Patent Appeals which is authorized to review the decision of the Patent and Trademark Office. Until recently the Patent and Trademark Office was housed in one of the most beautiful buildings in Washington which today houses the National Portrait Gallery and the Museum of American Art, both under the Smithsonian Institution. In a great room under a vaulted ceiling visitors could see every conceivable model of an invention. It was a veritable paradise for those with imagination. Many of the models were successful, therefore patented, and put into production to make life easier, but many were absurd and left to collect dust and to tickle the sense of humor of the curious. The Smithsonian now has custody of these models.

A recent government reorganization created the National Oceanic and Atmospheric Administration which brought together for efficiency purposes different services which had been scattered under other jurisdictions. This administration is now made up of the National Weather Service, the National Ocean Survey, the National Fisheries Service, the Environmental Data Service data centers, and the Environmental Research Laboratories. An administrator is in charge and is directly responsible to the secretary of commerce. The best known and most appreciated service this office renders to the ordinary person is the daily weather forecast. At first glance it may seem strange to find the Weather Service in the Department of Commerce, but, in fact, weather is extremely important to maritime transportation as well as vital in many other ways to the nation's commercial and agricultural life. The first weather service was established in 1870 under the Signal Corps of the Army. Later, a weather bureau was set up in the Department of Agriculture, and it took over the work of the Signal Corps. In 1940 the service was relocated in the Department of Commerce, and there it has remained. The forecasting of the weather is *the* business of the service. What used to be an inexact science based pretty much on hunch and a finger held into the wind is now extremely precise. Using highly sophisticated instruments on the land, the sea, and in satellites which spin far above the earth, forecasters can determine weather patterns with great accuracy. They collect information from all over the United States and its possessions, plot the winds and temperatures, and then alert the public via newspapers, telephone, radio and television. Storm flood warnings are of particular importance as they mean the difference between life and death for residents and travelers in the path of the storm as well as preventing the destruction of property. During a hurricane the service is constantly on the air monitoring the course of the storm, giving the public plenty of time to beach boats, shore up their homes, and evacuate if necessary. Weather forecasts are also invaluable to farmers and ranchers as advance notice of adverse conditions can save their crops and livestock. The weathermen, in addition to their service to Americans, contribute much to the piecing together of global patterns and work with international weather scientists of other nations. They now can forecast long-range patterns based on shifting winds and temperatures which provide much data on prolonged droughts, for instance, and enable governments to plan to meet these conditions. Although most ordinary people use the weatherman every morning in order to decide whether or not to carry an umbrella, to air-traffic controllers, businessmen, farmers, and ranchers these reports are vital, and we could not do without this service.

The National Oceanic and Atmospheric Administration also includes today what used to be called the Coast and Geodetic Survey, one of the oldest research offices in the government. As early as 1807 this office was established to study the coast of the United States, and in 1878 its work was expanded to include geodesy. Geodesy is the field of applied mathematics by which exact points in the world and exact sizes and shapes of the earth's surface are determined. No accurate maps can be made without geodetic science. In 1925 the office took over all research into the problems of earthquakes and monitors earthquake occurrences all around the globe, and with the advent of the airplane, the survey was given the task of compiling and publishing the aeronautical charts for the civil airways. In 1947 Congress further expanded the survey by authorizing it to conduct research into all geophysical sciences. Today, in addition to charting all our local waters, lakes and rivers, these scientists study all aspects of the oceans. They predict tides and currents and carry out research into all the living matter in the seas. They also are concerned with ocean fish and the protection of marine mammal life, and to this end they work toward ending the pollution of the seas. Coastal lands and the protection of shellfish which abound in these shallow waters are a responsibility of this office as well, and in this area the federal government and the coastal states work together. This office also administers the National Sea Grant Program which supports oceanic research institutions such as the one at Woods Hole, Massachusetts.

Since the advent of the space age, this administration includes research into the atmosphere. It maintains a system of satellites which provide information on the environment. Not only the weathermen use this data, but other scientists as well, American and foreign, who are trying to understand the mysteries of the earth and its atmosphere for the purpose of improving man's utilization of his environment.

Advances in the last few years in the field of telecommunications have brought another responsibility to Commerce. When President Carter came to the White House in 1977, the Office of Telecommunications Policy was part of the Executive Office, his predecessors having thought that such an important new field should be closely monitored by the president's staff. Carter, however, decided that this office did not belong in the Executive Office, and under his reorganization the Telecommunications Policy Office was dismantled, and its functions taken over by Commerce. At present the

National Telecommunications and Information Administration's main task is to make policy in order to encourage the growth of the industry and to regulate its development. It does research as well and gives evaluations of systems of engineering and advice on electromagnetic wave transmissions, the efficient use of the spectrum, and on telecommunication applications. It serves both the federal government and the private sector.

Because of its importance to the nation's economy, as well as to our image abroad, the recently created United States Travel and Tourism Administration is headed by an undersecretary of the department. Around the world today tourism is big business, but it has been primarily the Americans who have been the inveterate travelers, spending millions of dollars in foreign lands. In the 1960s the United States government became seriously concerned with an adverse balance of payments problem. The United States was spending more money abroad than was being spent by foreigners within her borders. One of the many ways by which the government attempted to solve this financial problem was to establish the United States Travel and Tourism Administration. Its task is to entice tourists by publicizing the United States abroad. The administration has six field offices abroad, in London, Paris, Frankfurt, Tokyo, Toronto and Mexico City, which advertise the beauties and wonders of the United States by means of colorful posters, brochures and films. The Americans who staff these offices are knowledgeable and attractive people who act as tourist agents and help to plan pleasant trips. The service also works with American hotel and motel chains, transportation companies—air, rail and bus—and local chambers of commerce to encourage them to offer packaged tours at moderate rates and campaigns among the American people at large to insure that foreign visitors will have a warm welcome. Many of the staff of the administration are hired because of their proficiency in a foreign language. They can, therefore, greet visitors who do not speak English and make them feel at home. Tourists to the United States not only contribute to some degree to the solution of the economic problems of the balance of payments, but by coming to the United States broaden their knowledge of the American people and through understanding contribute to international goodwill.

A strong international trade position is key to American prosperity, and in the last decade it has become increasingly difficult for the United States to maintain a competitive edge in world trade. This is so mainly because of the remarkable recovery of Western Europe and Japan since World War II, made possible largely because of American aid. These nations have become direct competitors in the areas of American industrial strength—steel, automobiles, agricultural products, textiles, to name a few—not only because their products are of high quality, but because their lower wage scales and their policies of government subsidies to private industry enable them to undersell American goods in both our domestic and world markets. To respond to this challenge is one of the major tasks of the Department of Commerce. In 1982, a reorganization of the department gave responsibility for all trade policy, domestic and foreign, to the International Trade Administration, headed by one of the undersecretaries. His job is to coordinate the work of the four subdivisions of the Administration, the Office for International Economic Policy, the Office for Trade Administration, the Office for Trade Development, and the United States and Foreign Commercial Services, each headed by an assistant secretary.

The assistant secretary for International Economic Policy is responsible for devising programs for increasing United States trade across the world in Europe, the Americas, East Asia and the Pacific, Africa and the Near East and South Asia. The assistant secretary for Trade Administration handles import and export issues, including dealing with foreign boycotts and administering the "anti-dumping" law recently enacted by Congress. This law became necessary because, as stated above, some governments subsidize their major industries which are then able to export their products to the United States at a considerably lower price than the unsubsidized American industries can match. Agreements between the United States and foreign governments have been negotiated whereby, if foreign goods are "dumped" in the United states market, the United States can raise the tariff on the imports, thereby protecting American sales. It is the responsibility of the Trade Administration to determine if foreign imports are in violation of the law. The office is also responsible for carrying out other United States statutes concerning quotas on particular items such as watches and all other import restrictions. Although the United States is in favor of free trade as opposed to protectionism, the whole subject of international trade is extremely complex as each nation quite sensibly works to sell more than it buys. The International Economic Administration has the difficult task of supporting free trade in general, but at the same time responding to the problems of American industries which are hurt by cheap foreign imports.

The job of the assistant secretary in charge of Trade Development is just that. He works to strengthen the United States trade position by keeping domestic industries informed about investment opportunities abroad and by encouraging them to widen their export trade. He also organizes United States trade missions abroad and plans American participation in international trade fairs.

Much of the work of the International Economic Administration is carried out by the staffs of the United States and Foreign Commercial Services, headed by a director general who reports to the undersecretary. In the United States there are forty-seven offices of the Commercial Service located across the country, and it is their staffs who communicate directly with American businessmen. Abroad, the foreign commercial staff administers 120 offices in sixty-seven countries. These offices work at promoting American trade with foreign nations. Both the domestic and the foreign staff report to Washington, and their input is invaluable to the formation of trade policies which are designed to strengthen our economic position.

If the United States is to be in a strong economic position abroad, it goes without saying that the domestic economy should be strong as well. As was mentioned above, in recent years it has become apparent that not all Americans share equally in the nation's abundance, and to remedy that situation Congress in the 1960s enacted legislation to improve the economy of the underdeveloped parts of the country, to attack inner-city blight and to help minority groups achieve financial independence. The Department of Commerce has the responsibility of carrying out these programs and does so through the Economic Development Administration and the Office of Minority Business Development Agency. An assistant secretary is in charge of the Economic Development Administration. He and his staff carry out the provisions of the Public Works and Economic Development Act of 1965 and its amendments. Their job is to devise means by which economically depressed areas, rural and urban, can be upgraded by the creation of new and permanent jobs through public facilities and private enterprise. The assistant secretary is responsible for designating the areas eligible for this program, and members of his staff work with the communities, helping them to plan for their economic development. The administration is authorized to make public work grants and loans for industrial and commercial facilities and to provide working capital. One example of such a project took place a few years ago in Barnstable, Massachusetts. The town needed a new police station badly, but could not afford to build one. It appealed, therefore, to the Economic Development Administration for aid. Once the administration had decided that Barnstable was eligible for the program, the townspeople voted the project at their town meeting, and the police station was built with a combination of federal, state and local funds. It must be added that whenever federal money is to be provided for projects such as this one, all federal laws such as those guaranteeing equal employment opportunities must be complied with. Before the funds are actually made available, the staff of the Economic Development Administration must be satisfied that all requirements are met.

The overall purpose of the Minority Development Agency is to encourage and support those members of minority groups who so desire to be able to open a business and to run it successfully. The agency gives indirect support, however, in that it works with state and local groups, public and private, who are directly involved with helping minorities to achieve financial independence. The agency provides financial support as well as advice and will defray all or part of the cost of demonstration projects, the purposes of which are to help teach business management. The local organizations come to this agency if they wish assistance. It, in addition, coordinates all work in this area between the federal agencies involved and develops a national policy.

Finally, two other bureaus in Commerce, the Bureau of Economic Analysis and the Bureau of Industrial Economics, provides data to both the public and private sectors on the overall state of the nation's economy without which efficient planning would be impossible. The Bureau of Economic Analysis, established in 1953, prepares monthly a quantitative view of the nation's economy, basing its analysis on the production, distribution, and use of the nation's total output. It ascertains the gross national product (GNP) which is the sum total of all the goods and services produced by Americans. The GNP is a basic factor in determining the state of the nation's economy. If it is up, we know times are good, employment is high, and production booming. If it is down, the reverse is true. The bureau also tries to forecast the economic trend, and its services are fundamental to the Council of Economic Advisers to the president, to all the executive departments, to the Congress, to the stock markets and to all industries of the United States as well as to every American. The Bureau of Industrial Economics is of more recent origin. It was set up in 1980 at a time when the nation's economy was in recession. What this bureau does is to provide more detailed information on all factors both domestic and foreign that have impact on the industrial life of the nation. It conducts studies on such subjects as worldwide economic trends, the availability of funds for capital formation in the United States, the implications of major federal policy decisions, the impact of federal regulations, and energy conservation trends, and all its research is available to the private as well as the public sector. The hope is that all this data assembled through the resources of the federal government for the nation's industrialists will assist them in planning their future production effectively and by so doing will hasten the end of the current recession and put the country's industrial capacity back into full production.

The secretary of commerce has, then, a very challenging job in overseeing a department which has many varied responsibilities. Its primary purpose is to promote a healthy economic life for the nation by offering diverse services by which American business and commercial life can prosper. In recent years its functions have been greatly expanded to include responsibilities for maintaining and strengthening our position in international trade, a difficult task in an increasingly competitive world, but of vital importance to the economic security of the United States.

The Department of Labor

Labor is one of the executive departments whose existence is particularly illustrative of the growth of the nation and of the changing pattern of life in the United States in the last ninety years or so. Until the mid-nineteenth century the United States was a predominantly agricultural land. Though cities, of course, existed, the majority of the population was self-supporting in the rural areas, and most industries were of the home type. With the onset of the Industrial Revolution in this country, however, the way of life for many Americans changed abruptly. With the rise of the factory system a new class of person came into being, the wage earner, the person living in a city and totally dependent on employment in a factory, for example, for survival. For many years this working class was ignored by the government. They were not given special consideration by anyone, nor did anyone outside of a handful of humanitarians care about the conditions in which these people worked. In the early days of America's industrial growth there was little the working man could do individually to improve his lot. If he demanded shorter hours and higher wages, he was simply fired by his employer who had no difficulty replacing him in that the population of the United States was increasing rapidly due to immigration in the post–

Civil War era. The obvious answer for labor was to band together and to present a united front to management, and by
the 1880s the successful founding of the first labor unions
began to focus attention on the problems of industrial workers. In 1884 Congress responded to this new situation by
creating the Bureau of Labor in the Department of the Interior. As its workload rapidly expanded, it was removed from
Interior and set up as an independent agency without executive rank. By the turn of the century, however, the industrial
development of the United States was such that Congress
created the Department of Commerce and Labor, but by 1913
the American labor movement had become so important that
a further reorganization was necessary, and in 1913 the Department of Labor was established, becoming the ninth of the
cabinet posts.

The purpose of the Labor Department is to promote the
welfare of all the wage earners of the United States. To accomplish this broad assignment, the department is responsible
for the administration of federal statutes passed by Congress
relating to labor, for the improvement of the working conditions of the laborer and the advancement of all opportunities
for employment. In recent years great emphasis has been
placed on finding ways by which the nation can utilize the
abilities of hitherto underutilized groups—blacks, Spanish
Americans, the elderly, the underprivileged, youth, and the
handicapped. Like the other executive departments, the
Labor Department is subdivided into many different offices
and bureaus, each with a specific responsibility related to the
department's overall mission. Heading the organization is the
secretary of labor, appointed by the president and confirmed
by the Senate.

In his office and under his immediate supervision are the
Wage Appeals Board which decides important or unusual
cases arising from federal laws concerning wages, the inspector general's office, responsible for the management of the
department, and the Women's Bureau. The location of the
Women's Bureau in the office of the secretary attests to the
importance attached to the women's liberation movement of
recent years which has focussed attention on the second-class

status of working women. The undersecretary advises him on
all activities of the department which are carried out by the
ten regional offices located in the major cities of the country.
A deputy undersecretary is responsible for legislative affairs
which entails close contact with Congress in presenting proposals for legislation the department deems necessary. Another deputy undersecretary is responsible for international
affairs. His job involves formulating international economic
policy, participating in trade negotiations with other nations,
and overseeing the labor attachés who serve in our embassies
abroad. He also supervises those who represent the United
States in the Manpower and Social Affairs Committee of the
Organization for Economic Cooperation and Development in
Paris, at the meetings of the General Agreement on Tariffs
and Trade, and the International Labor Organization. He
works closely with the State Department, the United States
Information Agency, and the Agency for International Development. A third undersecretary is in charge of the Office
of Employment Standards. The solicitor of the department
has a job similar to that of a senior partner of a big law firm in
that he has a large staff of attorneys under him in Washington and in the sixteen field offices. Together they handle the
litigation for the department which arises under all the
federal statutes dealing with labor and all the appellate work.
Seven assistant secretaries and a commissioner head the subdivisions of the department and are responsible to the secretary for the areas under their supervision. One assistant
secretary manages the administrative affairs of the department. The others are responsible for policy, for veterans'
employment, for employment and training, for occupational
safety and health, for labor-management relations and for
mine safety and health. Also, the commissioner is responsible
for all labor statistics.

Probably the Employment and Training Administration is the
best known to the general public because it directly affects so
many Americans for a combination of reasons. One, since the
1960s the nation has become aware of the many citizens in the
nation who are virtually unemployable because they lack skills,
and, two, in the 1970s unemployment due to recession has

soared. The responsibility of this office, therefore, is now intimately related to serious social and economic problems which the federal government is committed to solve. Originally, this division was created in the 1950s and was called the Manpower Administration because its purpose was to mobilize America's working force in case of national emergency in response to the uneasy state of the world at that time. Today, however, as its new name suggests, the Employment and Training Administration's major emphasis is on the development of policies and programs to enable the nation to utilize fully all its human resources.

Two subdivisions of the Employment and Training Administration, the Office of Employment Security and the Office of Comprehensive Employment Training, carry out this major and complex responsibility. The Employment Security section helps American workers in three ways. For those without work it oversees the Federal-State Unemployment Compensation Program. This program was part of the Social Security Act of 1935. It seems hard to believe today when unemployment insurance is taken for granted that throughout our history until the New Deal an individual who lost his job through no fault of his own was totally without income until, if he was fortunate, he found another job. It took the Great Depression during which unemployment reached unprecedented heights to open the nation's eyes to the necessity of providing insurance for those out of work. The program enacted by Congress operates through the states. Employers contribute to a fund which is then dispensed through state unemployment offices to those who have applied and have been certified as eligible. The unemployment benefits are available for a given period of time which is usually extended by Congress in times of severe recession. The point of the program is to tide a worker over a bad time, not to provide him with a permanent income.

Americans are directly assisted in finding work through the United States Employment Service, another responsibility of the Employment Security Office. USES, which also dates from the Great Depression, has 2,500 offices across the nation and the territories. It provides services for Americans seeking work which include counseling, job development and placement for many special categories of people. Veterans by statute are given priority in job placement, and disabled veterans, preference over the able-bodied. USES sees that this policy is carried out by the local public employment offices. Migrant workers are helped to get year-round employment where possible, and USES is responsible for making sure that federal standards are met by the employers of migrant labor. Other clients of the service are the young, the elderly, the handicapped, and recipients of the Aid to Families with Dependent Children program and food stamps. In addition, the service is responsible for the certification of aliens who want to immigrate legally to the United States. They must be certified by USES to prove that they are employable in a field where they will not take a job away from a citizen. The Work Incentive Program is also under the jurisdiction of USES. This program, administered jointly by the Department of Labor and the Department of Health and Human Services, was authorized by Congress in the 1967 and 1971 amendments to the social security laws, and it is only applicable to those able to work who receive federal help under the AFDC program. Those in this category who want to work are placed in jobs and, if they need training in order to hold a job, they receive the necessary skills before they are placed. The program is actually carried out by local welfare offices, and the work opportunities are generally in the areas of public agencies or non-profit private organizations which serve a public purpose. In conjunction with the Internal Revenue Service, the Employment Service administers the federal program which allows tax credits to employers who are willing to hire special categories of workers such as the severely handicapped or disadvantaged young people who in ordinary circumstances find it hard to get jobs. Last, the service is the source of all information concerning the job market. Through computers, available jobs and the persons with the skills to perform them can be matched. If, for instance, carpenters are out of work in the North of the nation due to winter weather or a slump in the construction industry, they may learn from the Employment Service that there are plenty of jobs in the South. If they are willing to move, they can avoid being idle. Up-to-date statistics on employment opportunities are also important to many varied groups. Vocational educators, for instance, if they know that a particular kind of work has been made obsolete due to technological advances will cease training students to perform this function and instead will train them to handle the new technology. The United States Employment Service, therefore, provides invaluable assistance to the employer, the educator, and the unemployed, and thereby contributes to a healthy economy which benefits the entire nation.

In recent years the Office of Employment Security has been given an additional task, that of assisting Americans whose jobs have been adversely affected by foreign imports. The shoe industry, for example, has been hard hit by the flood of cheap shoes from Taiwan and Korea where wage scales are considerably below those in the United States. The industry has had, as a consequence of shrinking sales, to lay off many employees. The Office of Trade Adjustment Assistance was established in 1974 to deal with this special kind of unemployment, and it is responsible for certifying that workers laid off in these circumstances are eligible for federal assistance.

The Comprehensive Employment and Training Office is the other major subdivision of the Employment and Training Administration. Its mission is to develop and administer training programs for the nation's most disadvantaged citizens with the purpose of helping them to become self-sufficient and contributors to the nation's economy. This program was first enacted in the early 1970s as an attempt to curtail the growing number of Americans on welfare. It made better sense to spend the taxpayers' money on training people who could work if they had the necessary skills than to support them on welfare. The office supervises three specific training programs enacted by Congress, the Job Training Partnership, the Senior Citizen Community Service, and Apprenticeship and Training. The Job Training Partnership program, enacted in 1983, replaced the earlier Comprehensive Training and Employment Act. Through this program the federal government makes block grants to the states which they then use to provide a wide range of training programs to the economically disadvantaged with particular emphasis on youth, young adults, dislocated workers, and others who face serious barriers, such as language, to employment. Still continued under the present legislation is the Job Corps. This program was an innovation of the 1960s during President Johnson's War on Poverty and has been one of the more successful of the many approaches to the problems of poverty and despair which engulf so many young people in the inner cities and in the disadvantaged rural areas of the nation. The Job Corps offers a unique residential training program for young people. Students may stay in the program for two years. They live in one of the 106 centers located in thirty-three states, the District of Columbia, and Puerto Rico where they are taught academic subjects, vocational and leadership skills as well as the meaning of citizenship. The 1983 Act requires much greater participation by the private sector in the training programs and also requires that 70 percent of the grants made to the states by the federal government be spent for actual training and only 30 percent for administration. The original CETA attached few strings to the expenditure of the federal funds, and upon reviewing the program, Congress felt that too many dollars had gone to administrative costs and that the training programs were too heavily oriented to government needs and not to the more productive private sector. In addition, the philosophy of the Reagan Administration is that the private sector not only should accept greater responsibility for social and economic programs, but that it can do a better job than government by offering training in a wider range of fields leading to permanent employment and upward mobility in the job market.

The Senior Community Service program is designed to help those over fifty-five and who have low incomes to feel useful and to be productive members of their communities. Federal funds are allocated to the states on the basis of the proportion of their population in this category and to public agencies and private non-profit organizations. The money is used to provide part-time work in community service projects. This program reflects the increasing awareness of and concern for the nation's senior citizens, and it has been eminently successful in bringing back into the marketplace many skilled persons who can share their experience, make a little income to ease their retirement, and, above all, to feel that there is still a place for them in society.

The Apprenticeship and Training section dates from the New Deal days of the 1930s. It has long been the practice for industries to have apprenticeship programs for those entering the job market, and when labor unions came into being, they also established such programs, partly to maintain a level of skill in their field, but also to control their membership in the days before equal opportunity was guaranteed by federal law. Apprentices could, however, be exploited, and the federal government, in order to protect them, established standards relating to the welfare of these young people. The Apprenticeship and Training section sees that these standards are, in fact, carried out and that equal opportunity laws are enforced. It also helps employers and labor to work together to expand apprenticeship programs in industrial training. It is very important to ensure that the nation has a continuous supply of skilled workers entering the labor market to meet the demands or our technological age.

Three other offices are also under the Employment and Training Administration, two of which are devoted to financial management and the administration of the regional offices. The third, the Office of Planning and Policy Development, is the "think tank" of the administration. It reviews all data and formulates new policies for the secretary. It is also an information center for all the areas covered by the office and sees that it is disseminated to the public.

The Labor-Management Services Administration is administered by the assistant secretary for Labor-Management Relations. This administration is responsible for all labor-management affairs, and the assistant secretary/administrator is the secretary's chief adviser on activities on the labor front in general and specifically on developments in major labor-management disputes in industries such as steel or transportation which could affect the entire nation's economic life adversely. This division is necessary because of the federal laws which establish rules and procedures for the conduct of relations between employers and employees.

It was mentioned above that the recognition of labor as an important and separate segment of the national economy led to the establishment of the Department of Labor in 1913. In 1914 Congress passed the Clayton Anti-Trust Act which the foremost labor leader of the day, Samuel Gompers, called the Magna Carta of labor in that for the first time it guaranteed certain protections to labor unions. It forbade, among other things, the use of court injunctions to prevent strikes. In 1935 the National Labor Relations Act (the Wagner Act) was passed and because it defined specific rights for labor such as the right of collective bargaining, it was immediately called the Bill of Rights of labor. Since then, in reaction to certain abuses on the part of labor unions, more legislation has been required to define further the rights of management and the rights of individual workers, to curtail the misuse of labor pension and welfare funds and to secure the rights of veterans. The Labor-Management Services Administration is charged with the responsibility for seeing that the provisions of these laws are carried out, and, in addition, it has the responsibility for executing a presidential order authorizing it to supervise the relations between federal employees and the government department or agency which employs them. In general, the administration provides assistance in collective bargaining and in advising state and local governments on labor relations, but the bulk of its work is in carrying out the federal laws and the executive order.

Veterans' reemployment rights are specifically defined in the United States code, and their inclusion became necessary because all too often persons who had served their country found upon their return to civilian life that they had lost many of the benefits, such as seniority, that would have accrued to them had they not joined the armed forces. Now when a veteran leaves the service, the Labor-Management Services Administration sees that he is informed of his rights as defined by law. It then assists the individual to get his seniority reestablished to receive the wages that he should have as well as his pension and welfare benefits. In case of a serious dispute, the administration can refer the case to the Department of Justice which will bring a suit. In 1974 Congress had to pass the Employee Retirement Income Security Act because certain union officials had mismanaged the pension and welfare funds for which they were responsible. Now, by this statute, all such pension and welfare plans must be filed with the Labor-Management Services Administration, employees must be given simply stated explanations of their rights under the plans, and the union official responsible for the funds must be bonded, and he must submit annually a financial report to the administration. The law forces fiduciary integrity which is imperative in that these officials are handling other people's money in trust. Similarly, because of flagrant abuses of the democratic process, Congress found it necessary to enact the Labor-Management Reporting and Disclosure Act which compels unions to file with the administration their constitutions, their bylaws and their financial reports. In addition, the law establishes procedures for the election of union officials, for the administration of trusts and the handling of union funds and defines precisely the rights of union members. It is unfortunate that these laws were necessary, but before they were enacted, in many instances the rights of union members were grossly violated, and the way in which their money was handled was anything but honest. The government had to legislate to protect the worker.

In recent years many federal employees have become unionized, and a presidential order in recognition of this fact gave the Labor-Management Services Administration the job of supervising the relations between the government and these unions. The assistant secretary/administrator has the authority to decide in case of a dispute which union is the proper one to bargain for its members. He supervises union elections and must receive the same financial information from the federal employees' unions that is required of the private ones, and it is he who decides if complaints of unfair labor practices are valid and whether they can be arbitrated. In all phases of the administration's work its staff seeks voluntary compliance with the statutory rules and procedures.

In addition, the administration also does research into labor matters and evaluates rules and procedures in order to advise the secretary as to how to improve the efficiency and effectiveness of the administration. It also works closely with state and local governments to assist them with labor and management problems such as how labor and industry can meet new conditions caused by economic and technological developments. It also assists special boards and commissions appointed by the president to deal with specific emergencies in labor-management situations which have national import.

The Employment Standards Administration has the responsibility for seeing that federal standards relating to the minimum wage, overtime, equal pay, and nondiscriminatory practices are followed. The work of the administration is handled by the Wage and Hour Division, the Federal Contract Compliance Programs, and the Office of Workers' Compensation Programs. The Wage and Hour administrator has more to do than simply seeing that the minimum wage laws are followed. He and his staff administer federal programs aimed at improving low-wage income, preventing the loss of employment for students and handicapped people, stopping discrimination in employment on the basis of sex or age, curtailing long hours to safeguard workers' health and protecting the health and safety of migrant workers. This office also sees that the wage rates on government contracted projects are what they should be. The Federal Contract Compliance Programs also sees that in government funded projects no discrimination in hiring takes place, and it has responsibility for the government's affirmative action programs in the hiring of the handicapped and Vietnam War veterans. The Office of Workers' Compensation Programs handles the work involved in carrying out federal statutes which relate to specific categories of workers: federal employees, longshoremen, harbor workers and others engaged in work in United States coastal waters, and coal miners (or their survivors) suffering from black lung and other respiratory diseases. These people are entitled to compensation from the government if they lose their jobs because of injury or because they are laid off due to cutbacks in the industry. This office also works with the states on standards and benefits in their compensation laws with the intent of equalizing compensation across the country. Most of the work of these offices described above is done in the field through regional offices, and Washington is the coordinator and the central point for the information which is collected in the field.

In 1970 Congress gave the Department of Labor the new responsibility for safeguarding the American industrial worker from man-made occupational hazards. By that year it had become apparent that in addition to the traditional hazards of industrial employment, advances, particularly in the field of chemistry, and their application to industry had introduced many new substances into manufacturing which are highly toxic to humans. The Occupational Safety and Health Act, therefore, was passed to protect Americans, and the Occupational Safety and Health Administration was set up to implement the law. The administration sets standards with which the employers specified by the act must comply for their employees' safety and health, and it investigates to see that regulations concerning these standards are carried out. In cases where compliance has not been forthcoming, the administration is authorized to issue citations and to propose penalties. This administration in the Department of Labor cooperates with three other agencies concerned with safety and health, the Environmental Protection Agency, the Food and Drug Administration, and the Consumer Product Safety Commission. They exchange information and share personnel so that needless duplication of effort is eliminated. The Occupational Safety and Health Administration has regional offices out of which most of its staff operates. This administration and the others concerned with the conditions in which people work hopefully will preclude a repetition of the tragedies which resulted from the exposure of workers to the deadly chemical Kepone a short time ago in a plant on the James River in Virginia.

Mining is one of the oldest occupations in the United States and certainly one of the most hazardous as over the course of our history mine disasters have taken a fearful toll of human lives. Not until the twentieth century did the federal government begin to recognize its responsibility, and it did so in a piecemeal fashion. Until 1977 there were scattered about the federal government many different offices each with a different area of responsibility either for the health of miners or the conditions under which they worked. In 1977 Congress consolidated all the various pieces under the Mine Safety and Health Administration and placed it in the Department of Labor. This administration develops and enforces federally mandated safety and health standards and has the power to assess penalties if they are not complied with. It also has the task of investigating accidents and uses what it learns from its investigation to further improve safety techniques. It works very closely with the states in which mines are located, and together the two levels of government devise training programs for miners to help them avoid accidents that can be prevented. The administration also coordinates its work with the Department of the Interior and the Department of Health and Human Services. Mining, unfortunately, is still hazardous and difficult, but it is a far safer occupation today than it was in the past, and with more knowledge available on how to limit hazards such as black lung disease, the health of the miners is better also.

One of the problems veterans can face when they leave the armed services is finding work, particularly if they entered the service at a young age as was the case with many who served in Vietnam. This problem can be especially devastating if a person has been disabled, and it is only right that the government for which he fought should give him help. Between 1974 and 1980 Congress recognized its responsibility and enacted five major laws providing special help for all veterans, but mandating specifically that the disabled should be given preferential treatment. These laws are carried out by the Veteran's Employment Service which offers through its field offices counseling, job training, and assists with job placement. It works through the United States Employment Service, but it monitors USES practices carefully to make sure that the veterans and particularly the disabled are given priority in job placement. It should be noted that this preferential treatment is the only legal exception to the equal-rights

laws that specifically prevent preferential treatment for anyone else. No one can disagree, however, with the policy of
giving Vietnam veterans, particularly those who are handicapped, preference in that it is one of the few ways the nation
has of thanking them for their sacrifice.

The Bureau of Labor Statistics is well known to those who
follow the vagaries of the nation's economy. Each month the
commissioner in charge of this office releases the latest unemployment figures, adjusted for the season. If unemployment is
down a fraction, it can be an indication of an upturn in the
economy. On the other hand, however, the commissioner of
the bureau is careful to compute the number of unemployed
who are actively seeking work, and if the unemployment rate
drops, it can be discouraging news because many who were
looking for work may have quit out of despair. Also on a
monthly basis the bureau issues the latest price index which
measures the rate of inflation, a major problem in the last few
years. A drop in the percentage is a heartening statistic to
everyone who watches his budget. The bureau also keeps
track of the number of jobs available, the hours of work performed, living conditions, technological developments,
labor-management relations, and a myriad of other data all
related to labor economics. The press release is only a summary, and all the detailed analysis is available to the public in
written form. This bureau is one of the key sources of statistics, and its work is vital to all those from the president on
down who are responsible for the health of the national
economy.

Because of the enormous area of responsibility that the
Labor Department handles, there are a great many disputes
which arise. In order to preclude the necessity for each problem to have to be decided by a court, there are administrative
law judges in the department who hear certain classes of cases.
After hearing all the evidence on both sides, they recommend
a disposition to the secretary or the assistant secretary most
directly concerned with the subject matter. In this way a great
deal of time and money is saved, and, in general, the judges'
recommendations end the problem. There is also an Employees' Compensation Appeals Board which hears appeals

from the rulings on questions of workers' compensation. Once this board decides a case, it is final and is not subject to court review, whereas cases disposed of by the administrative law judges can be appealed to a court if the disgruntled loser so desires.

One thing about the Department of Labor that must be made clear is that it is essentially a labor-law enforcement agency as well as a source of information on all aspects of labor in the United States. Although members of the department often work closely with the labor unions of the country, they are in no way connected with them. Labor unions are private organizations made up of wage earners, while the Department of Labor is a government agency set up to serve the wage earners through government policy and planning.

The Department of Health and Human Services

As has been mentioned, government reorganizations take place constantly, and the Department of Health and Human Services came into being in 1979 through such a reorganization. In that year Congress agreed to a proposal of President Carter's that a separate Department of Education be established. With education removed from the then existing Department of Health, Education and Welfare, Congress renamed it the Department of Health and Human Services. This department, more than any other of the executive departments, is the one whose sole concern is the welfare of the American people, and it touches the lives of all of the two hundred and twenty million of them daily.

The main divisions of the department are the Office of Human Development Services, the Public Health Service, the Social Security Administration, the Health Care Financing Administration and the Office of Child Support Enforcement.

The department administers all federal social and health programs and because its responsibilities are so diverse, vast, and in some cases overlapping, to get its work done requires careful organization. Basically, there are two levels, the Office of the Secretary and, what is called in government jargon, the principal operating components—of which there are five. These components are the agencies which already existed before the creation of the old Health, Education and Welfare Department way back in 1953 and several which have evolved since then in response to social and economic problems of more recent origin.

Under the secretary's immediate supervision are the undersecretary, the inspector general, the Office for Civil Rights, the Office of Consumers Affairs, five assistant secretaries in charge of legislation, public affairs, planning and evaluation, personnel administration, management and budget, and the general counsel. The undersecretary, who stands in for the secretary in his absence, is specifically responsible for the coordination of regional activities and federal-state relations. The inspector general is the watchdog of the department in that he and his staff make audits for the secretary and Congress and constantly investigate all department programs to prevent fraud and to see that they are administered efficiently and economically. He also makes recommendations to the secretary on ways to improve performance. The Office of Civil Rights carries out all the laws which forbid discrimination in federally funded programs in health and in government contracted projects. The Office of Consumer Affairs provides the special assistant to the president on consumer affairs with staff, advises the secretary on ways of making consumer protection more effective, and coordinates federal programs in this area. The assistant secretaries' titles indicate their responsibilities, and the general counsel handles all the legal work for the Department of Community Service. The Office of Human Development was recently set up within the department in recognition of the fact that there are many groups within American society who need special help in order to realize their fullest potential. The office, therefore, is concerned with children, youth, the elderly, the physically and mentally handicapped, native Americans (Indians, Alaskans and Hawaiians), and disadvantaged people living in rural America. Each of these groups is the responsibility of a special office. The Administration on Aging administers the federal programs and grants designed to help the nation's senior citizens. The National Nutrition Program for the Elderly provides low-cost meals, for instance, and federal funds help state agencies provide other services for older people. The office also conducts research into the problems of the aged. The mission of the Administration for Children, Youth and Families is to promote the sound development of the young upon whom the future of the nation depends. It develops and carries out programs designed to strengthen the family structure and to protect children's interests. The National Center on Child Abuse and Neglect, a part of this division, for example, is an advocate for children's rights and advises the secretary on their needs, and the Youth Development Office's principal thrust is to help young people to become useful and well-adjusted citizens. It works with youth-oriented services on the state and local level to enhance opportunities for the development of young peoples' talents. It is particularly concerned with runaways and acts as a coordinator of all federal programs related to this problem.

Although the deaf and the blind have received attention for many years, only recently has the government become involved with the broad spectrum of problems of those Americans who have handicaps, either mental or physical, and in working to alleviate them. The Administration on Developmental Disabilities is responsible for conducting research into ways by which the government can help those afflicted to become self-sufficient. The Administration provides financial grants to state and local agencies to support their services and to underwrite research on ways to prevent mental retardation from occurring in the first place. The primary concern of the Administration for Native Americans is to promote their social and physical welfare. Together with the Bureau of Indian Affairs in the Department of the Interior, the Administration works to foster self-determination by assisting with social and economic development programs. It recommends policies to the assistant secretary in charge of the administration who, in turn, advises the secretary. The long-range goal of this division, like that of the Bureau of Indian Affairs, is to see all native Americans self-sufficient and on a par with other Americans.

The Public Health Service, which is the oldest of HHS's responsibilities, has had an interesting history. Established originally in 1798, its first and only function was to authorize marine hospitals for American seamen. As medical knowledge has advanced, however, it has become obvious that good health is as important to a nation as a good economy, and it is only right that the United States government through the Public Health Service should protect and improve the health of all Americans. To do this, the service provides opportunities for medical research, financial assistance to educational institutions for the health profession, helps to train the public in health measures, provides medical and hospital care for those authorized to receive such care out of public funds, and protects Americans against impure and unsafe foods, drugs and cosmetics. The service also works closely with the states and other nations in the prevention and control of diseases and in the establishment of community health programs. It is the source of all statistics on health in the United States. The Public Health Service is run by an assistant secretary who supervises all matters concerning general health and correlates the activities in the subdivisions.

Recently this service was reorganized for greater efficiency into the following six divisions: the Centers for Disease Control, the Food and Drug Administration, the Health Resources Administration, the Health Services Administration, the National Institutes of Health, and the Alcohol, Drug Abuse and Mental Health Administration. The Centers for Disease Control, which are located in Atlanta, Georgia, were established in 1973, and their main job is to protect Americans by preventing and controlling diseases and other harmful conditions. They carry out national programs such as the swine flu vaccination program in 1976 and the measles, polio, diptheria and smallpox inoculation for young children in 1977. The centers have also been responsible for warning about the hazards of smoking. They conduct campaigns to eradicate rats and the use of lead-based paint. The latter is the cause of serious illness and sometimes death if eaten, and small children who are apt to chew on anything within their reach must be protected against this lethal danger. Rats carry many diseases which are extremely serious to humans, and, particularly in urban communities, they constitute a very real problem to the nation's well-being. The Centers for Disease Control are also responsible for enforcing the quarantine laws and seeing that clinical laboratories in interstate business maintain high standards. They also assist local and state public health units to identify the cause of diseases such as the Legionnaire's Disease which struck in Philadelphia in 1976 and resulted in many deaths. In addition, the centers have recently undertaken to assist in the battle against occupational hazards and conduct research into ways of eliminating dangers. They work with the World Health Organization of the United Nations and with other foreign governments to control communicable diseases around the world, and the research staff is constantly searching for new vaccines by which disease can be controlled. Even the common cold is under its scrutiny.

The Food and Drug Administration also concentrates on protecting the nation's health. It keeps a constant watch over the dinner tables, medicine cabinets and dressing tables of the United States, enforcing federal statutes establishing standards for food, drugs and cosmetics. The federal government first entered this field in 1906 when widespread appalling conditions in food preparation were disclosed and highly publicized by a group of writers known as the "Muckrakers." In that year Congress passed the Pure Food and Drug Act which forbade the manufacture and sale of adulterated or unsafe foods or drugs and required the pasting of labels on containers stating the contents. The Food and Drug Administration is the arm of the government responsible for carrying out this law and all subsequent related statutes. Today cosmetics, a billion dollar industry, has also been included. In recent years the administration has also assumed responsibility for monitoring radiation levels and determining if electronic devices such as micro-wave ovens and color television sets are safe for consumers. Inspectors all over the United States keep a constant surveillance. Much of the work of the administration is in scientific investigation. Samples of food, drugs, medical devices, face powders, hair dyes, rinses and the like are all tested and must be declared safe before they can be sold. New drugs developed for humans as well as for animals by the chemical and medical supply houses must also pass rigid tests before being adopted. Vaccines for diseases such as polio, which must be made with great care to insure a beneficial reaction, are the special concern of the administration. Each new batch of vaccine must be tested before it can be distributed to doctors for use. As many different drug companies are engaged in the manufacture of drugs and vaccines, the job of testing each new batch is a big one, but it must be done for the safety of those who take them. The job often involves the administration in controversy. Recently, for instance, it declared saccharin, a sugar substitute, to be dangerous because its ingestion in laboratory tests had produced cancer in rats. The announcement caused tremendous consternation among the nation's diabetics who rely on the substance and dieters whose sweet tooth have been assuaged by the diet soft drinks which have been mass-produced for over ten years. The basis for the controversy is in the laws which the administration must carry out which dictate that when a substance given in any amount is suspected of being a cancer-causing agent, it must be stopped. The fact that the rats got a 100 percent dose, whereas a human in a lifetime would never use such a quantity of saccharin caused the uproar. The Food and Drug Administration, however, is only carrying out its mandate, and it is up to Congress not the administration, to change the test requirements if they are, indeed, too stringent. The administration is strictly a watchdog and is in large part responsible for the high standard of food in the United States and the generally good health of the citizenry. No longer can unsanitary, polluted or spoiled food be sold nor can unsafe electronic machines or drugs be foisted on the unsuspecting public. Americans can shop with assurance and have their prescriptions filled with confidence to an extent not common in many other countries.

The Health Resources and the Health Services Administrations have to do with health personnel, the distribution of health resources and the quality of health services across the nation. That we have sufficient and well-trained manpower for the delivery of health services is vital to the public's well-being, and the Bureau of Health Professions in the Health Resources Administration plans and evaluates the development and utilization of those who work in this field. Another section assists local and state governments in providing quality service and makes sure the health facilities are up to federal standards. Through the Bureau of Community Health Services, communities are assisted in figuring out their health requirements and then how best to meet them. Federally funded programs such as Maternal and Child Health, Migrant Health, Family Planning, Community Health Centers, and the National Health Service Corps are administered by this branch. The particular focus is on communities which have few medical or health resources such as the disadvantaged rural areas and the inner cities. The Indian Health Service takes care of all native Americans, providing hospital care and medical services, and lays particular emphasis on preventive measures. As Indians and other native Americans are very susceptible to tuberculosis and other debilitating diseases, the service works to improve water supplies and sanitation in these communities and stresses health education among the residents. This branch is also responsible for carrying out medical and health services for federal employees and for the Federal Bureau of Prisons and the United States Coast Guard. It also maintains a hospital in Louisiana which cares for victims of Hansen's disease (leprosy).

The United States has yet to adopt a comprehensive national health system, but the government is deeply committed to providing as much health care as it can to those who cannot afford private care. Many presidents in recent years have appointed special commissions to investigate national health services and to make recommendations as to how we can improve them. Many of the services such as those described above have come into being as a result of these studies, a recent one being that of the National Health and Manpower Commission authorized by President Johnson in 1966.

Disease for which cures are known can be controlled by quick action, but there are, unfortunately, many illnesses such as cancer for which a cure has yet to be found. Research, therefore, is one of the most important aspects of medicine. In years past American medicine advanced rapidly due to foresighted and kind philanthropists like Johns Hopkins who gave their fortunes to further research in medical schools. Today the United States government has taken on as a national responsibility part of the job of providing funds for medical research to benefit all Americans. Some part of the federal funds go to private medical institutions in the country in the form of grants and fellowships to make it possible for them to conduct research. Other funds have created the National Institutes of Health, the government owned research centers, operated under the Public Health Service. These institutes, of which there are ten at the moment, deal with the health problems most prevalent in the United States today. They are cancer, heart, lung and blood diseases, arthritis, metabolism and digestive disorders, allergy and infectious diseases, child health and human development, dental research, environmental health, general medical sciences, neurological and communicative disorders and stroke, eyes, and aging. Not only do these institutes have vast laboratories in which experiments and research are carried out, but they also have hospital beds and facilities for patients with unique cases. Not just anyone may enter the national hospitals. Any doctor who receives an unusual case may get in touch with the proper institute, and if the case is sufficiently special, the hospital may then take the patient. In this way the doctors and scientists of the National Institutes carry on research while helping many seriously ill people.

A key facility at the National Institutes of Health, located in Bethesda, Maryland, is the National Library of Medicine. It has the greatest collection of medical literature in the world and is constantly being used by researchers from the four corners of the earth. Those who use it are saved hours of laborious poring through card catalogues because the library is equipped with the latest bibliographic devices, MEDLINE and TOXLINE, which are computerized information storage and retrieval systems. In a matter of minutes all information ever published on arthritis, for instance, can be retrieved by an individual doing research on the disease. These modern miracles contribute enormously to medical breakthroughs because researchers not only avoid duplication of effort, but exchange the latest news on findings all over the world which means that they can build on each others' work, speeding the day when cancer, for instance, which is a worldwide problem, will be cured. The library also serves as a training center for medical librarians and supports the translation into English of all medical literature published abroad.

One of the most tragic diseases that can strike people and whose cure is elusive is mental illness. That mental disorders are illnesses has long been recognized, and the government's concern resulted in the establishment of the National Institute on Mental Health some years ago. Only recently, however, have two other areas been classified as diseases and, as such, warranted federal attention. They are alcohol and drug abuse. Actually alcoholism has a long history in America. In the very early years it was associated with the frontier, and as early as 1798 the government recognized the debilitating effect of alcohol on people. The immediate cause of what was called the Whisky Rebellion was that excise taxes were not being paid on corn liquor manufactured by farmers in western Pennsylvania, then very much the frontier. The government in demanding the payment of the tax, however, had an underlying motive—to force the frontier people into productive farming instead of turning corn into liquor. Although the western Pennsylvania farmers did become constructive citizens, as the frontier moved west, so did alcoholism. After the Civil War the problem also became acute among low-income city dwellers who sought to ameliorate their unfortunate living conditions by the bottle. Only in recent years, however, was it realized that alcoholism is not just a bad habit, but a disease which can be cured. In the last decade, largely as a result of the Vietnamese War and the trauma it caused especially among the young people in the United States, the nation suddenly became aware of the severe problem of drug abuse. As mentioned above, the Department of Justice is responsible only for the prevention of the importation, sale and use of drugs and has no responsibility for curing those who have become addicts. In response to these acute problems the then Department of Health, Education and Welfare set up the Alcohol, Drug Abuse and Mental Health Administration in the Public Health Service, thereby incorporating the National Institute of Mental Health which was already in existence. The administration is composed of three institutes, each devoted to one of these problems. They research the causes and work toward eliminating them, and, in addition, support treatment and rehabilitation services for those afflicted. The Institute for Drug Abuse and the Institute on Alcohol Abuse and Alcoholism maintain two hospitals, one in Lexington, Kentucky, and the other in Fort Worth, Texas. These institutes work very closely with state and local services, promote campaigns by which to educate the public as to the dangers of drug and alcohol abuse, and attempt to ameliorate the conditions which produce mental illnesses.

A major and perhaps the best known responsibility of the Department of Health and Human Services is the concern for the social and economic security of the American people. The federal government first assumed this responsibility in the 1930s and since then the initial program has come to include many more areas. During the days of the Great Depression many were jobless through no fault of their own, and many senior citizens, who always have had more difficulty finding employment than younger persons, had their savings wiped out and had nowhere to turn for assistance. The idea was then conceived as part of President Roosevelt's New Deal to provide through the federal government a system of social security for Americans to be used for their old age, for times of illness or for periods of unemployment. Security could be made possible by government insurance programs. The act of Congress bringing this idea into reality was the Social Security Act of 1935. By this act Americans began paying a percentage of their paycheck each month to the government, as do their employers. Self-employed persons may also opt to pay into the social security system. When the employee reaches retirement age, he is entitled to his monthly social security check, providing his income from all sources is not above a certain figure. Social security, therefore, is a retirement sum which gives the worker the promise of security in his older years. The money collected from the employers, the employees and the self-employed is placed in a special trust fund which is invested in interest-bearing government bonds. The payments, then, do not come from the general revenue of the United States. Unemployment and disability insurance operate in the same way, except that the benefits are received whenever necessary. In addition, in the original act of the 1935 Congress, recognizing that many children were suffering because of the poverty of their parents, authorized Aid to Families with Dependent Children. The federal government grants funds for this program to the states which they, in turn, distribute to those who qualify.

The original Social Security Program was administered by an independent agency until 1953 when it was incorporated into the Department of Health, Education and Welfare, and today it is part of Health and Human Services. The Administration is headed by a commissioner who is directly responsible to the secretary, and both he and his staff have been given additional responsibilities by Congress in response to new economic and social pressures which have arisen over the years. In 1965 social security coverage was extended to include medical care for senior citizens. Although inflation affects every segment of the economy, nowhere has it been more devastating than in medical and hospital costs. In addition to inflation, the remarkable advances in medicine since World War II, particularly life-saving devices such as kidney machines, are, sadly enough, extremely expensive. Far too many older persons, who have a greater incidence of degenerative diseases, simply cannot afford the high cost of quality medical services. Congress, therefore, in 1965 enacted Medicare which is an insurance program covering part of the cost of hospitalization for those receiving social security. Those who choose to may pay a small additional premium to receive help with doctors' bills and some other medical expenses. The funds which pay for Medicare come from a proportion of the social security tax. They go into a separate trust fund, and the government assumes part of the cost as well. Medicare has, indeed, been invaluable in assisting the retired by easing the heavy burden of medical bills.

The actual administration of this program and the disbursement of federal funds are the responsibility of the Health Care Financing Administration, a separate entity in the Department of Health and Human Services. This administration also administers the Medicaid Program which Congress enacted at the same time as Medicare. Needless to say, medical costs which were prohibitive for the elderly were also beyond the reach of the nation's most needy citizens, and Medicaid is designed to enable those in the lowest income brackets to receive adequate health care. The federal government finances this program through grants to the states. The Health Care Financing Administration is also responsible for assuring quality in medical services and in nursing home care. Taxpayers' money must go to well-trained professionals and institutions that meet government standards.

Some years later in 1974 the Social Security Administration was given responsibility for the Supplementary Security Income Program which is designed to assist not only the aged, but the blind and the disabled as well. States that supplement the federal funds may contract with the Social Security Administration to handle their payments for them. This coordination results in more efficient handling of the two programs, federal and state, and is beneficial to the recipients. It should be noted that the funds for this program come out of the general revenue and are not part of a special trust.

The Social Security Administration, in addition to its responsibility for these specific programs, also conducts research for the secretary on all aspects of the problems of the aged, the disabled and of poverty in general. The commissioner and his staff propose ways to improve the social and economic security of the nation's less fortunate citizens. The administration is headquartered in Washington, but because its work is directly related to millions living in every part of the nation, there are ten regional offices and 1,300 local ones to deal with individual problems. In case of disagreements over benefits and eligibility there are administrative law judges across the nation who hear cases initially, and an appeals council, and in certain cases, the final decision is reached by the secretary himself.

There is no question that the social security program has

made a tremendous difference to countless Americans. Before 1935 there was no security for those unable to provide for themselves. For the blind and the disabled, government assistance was an unmitigated boon, as it was to those unemployed in times of recession. Children, dependent in every way upon their parents who in many cases were unable to provide for them, benefitted from federal funds. And after 1935 the retirement years no longer loomed bleak and threatening. In the 1970s, however, a totally unanticipated problem suddenly materialized which threatened the very foundations of the social security system, although not of the programs funded from the general revenue. The entire social security system depends on the input of funds by the employed and their employers. Their money is, in effect, a rolling fund, the younger working generation providing the income for those who have retired. Two things could not be anticipated either in 1935 or in later years when amendments were made to provide for increased payments to keep pace with inflation. They were the major drop in the birthrate and the vastly lengthened life-span attributable to advances in medical knowledge. The drop in the birthrate meant that fewer people would be in the labor force in the 1980s and 1990s, and increased longevity meant that many more people would be retired and receiving social security checks for a longer period. The long and the short of it was that the trust fund which provides the cash for the retirement checks would not have the money to meet the demand if the system were to continue to function as originally designed. There were no easy solutions, and, although alarms were sounded in the 1970s, the administration and Congress were loathe to tackle the problem. The wage base for the social security tax as well as the tax itself had been elevated repeatedly, and many believed that they had reached the point of no return. If businesses had to pay more than they considered economically feasible, they would simply let workers go which would further deplete the number of contributors. If the employed were asked to pay too high a tax for the benefit of other persons, it would be politically unpopular. It was suggested that part of the social security benefits be paid from the general revenue, but the problem with that solution is that the Treasury must have enough money to pay the nation's bills, and, if the social security were added, the already large annual deficit in the federal budget would be increased enormously. Another proposed solution was to up the mandatory retirement age for men from sixty-five to seventy. In the 1930s when social security was inaugurated, sixty-five appeared to be the reasonable age for retirement for men (sixty-two for women). Today, again due to better health care, it is questionable whether enforced retirement is necessary or desirable. Many men aged sixty-five do not want to retire as they are in excellent health and enjoy what they are doing. By changing the mandatory age, social security payments would be made to older citizens for a shorter period, which would effect an enormous annual saving for the trust fund. As nothing was done, the funds dwindled, and by 1982 the threat of bankruptcy loomed over the entire social security system. The Reagan administration had no choice but to deal with the crisis. It was indeed a crisis in that social security is an entitlement program. That means that the government is obligated by law to provide the nation's older citizens with the retirement funds to which they had contributed during their working years. In addition, to compound the problem, in the 1970s Congress, in order to protect those on social security from inflation, had legislated cost-of-living adjustments which means that twice-a-year retirement checks are adjusted upwards to reflect rising costs. President Reagan decided to turn the problem over to a commission made up of Republicans and Democrats and apolitical experts in the field. Their assignment was to study the whole system and to recommend to Congress ways by which it could be rescued from the impending bankruptcy. The blue-ribbon panel worked diligently for months, and in a spirit of compromise ended by proposing that the social security tax rate be increased gradually, that the cost-of-living adjustment be postponed temporarily and that the mandatory retirement age for both men and women be upped in the future. Congress, relieved not to have to solve the problem itself, accepted the plan, and, therefore, the retirement program has been secured at least for the immediate future. The future of Medicare, however, is still uncertain at this time in that hospital and health care costs in general are still surging upwards at an unprecedented rate even though the overall rate of inflation has been sharply curtailed. Unless these costs are contained, Medicare will not be able to provide sufficient coverage for retirees. The Reagan administration has suggested several solutions. One is that the price of medical treatments and hospital care for which Medicare gives coverage would be predetermined. Federal payments, therefore, would not be subject to inflation. Another is to encourage the private health insurance business to offer low-cost plans to those sixty-five and over to supplement their Medicare coverage. This idea is in line with President Reagan's philosophy that the private sector should take on more of what in the recent past has become the responsibility of the federal government.

It should also be noted that the entire philosophy of welfare, as well as its present structure, is now under review as well. Originally, the welfare system adopted in the aftermath of the Great Depression was designed to help certain categories of people who were unable to help themselves. Now, forty years later, it is apparent that welfare assistance, which was never designed to be permanent for individuals, but conceived as temporary help, has resulted in the perpetuation of welfare families over several generations. The main reasons are due to the built-in restrictions in the welfare laws. If a person, for instance, on welfare gets a job and earns over a certain amount, he loses his welfare support. Because his standard of living is not improved appreciably by only the little more income he makes working, he loses the incentive to work. Also, the income restriction has worked against the institution of the family which is the unit basic to society. A mother will receive support for her children, but if there is an employed man in the home whose income is counted, she may lose her welfare, and she is often financially better off if the children's father is not in the home. One of candidate Carter's major commitments during the campaign for the presidency in 1976 was to revamp the entire welfare system if he were elected, and he lived up to his promise by proposing a radical new plan to

Congress in the summer of 1977. His program was based essentially on the concept that people want to work and that income assistance should be coupled with employment. The government would undertake to provide jobs if the private sector of the economy could not absorb the able-bodied unemployed; various new ways of income maintenance for the disabled, the elderly and children would be devised; and income tax credit could be earned by those employed in low-paying jobs. Congress, however, failed to enact Carter's plan. The present administration is still grappling with the problem of how to get able-bodied persons off welfare and into productive work. To date, Reagan has not proposed legislation to revamp the system, but his main policies have been to increase the involvement of the private sector in programs such as the Job Training Partnership Program, to tighten considerably the qualifications for welfare recipients, and to urge a major upgrading of the nation's educational standards so that graduates are prepared for the world of work. The whole subject of welfare is exceedingly complex, covering a myriad of deep-rooted sociological and economic problems, and solutions are even more difficult to come by in today's world of high technology in which low-skilled jobs are increasingly scarce.

The Department of Health and Human Services' last area of responsibility involves the welfare of children and is of comparatively recent origin. It is commonly accepted that a father has an obligation to support his children, but all too often a father who has left home fails to meet his responsibilities. Local officials have traditionally had the task of enforcing support laws, because they have been enacted by state legislatures, but with the great mobility of American life, they have had increasing difficulty tracking down delinquents who may be anywhere in the nation. In 1975 Congress set up the Office of Child Support Enforcement. This office is separate from the Social Security Administration, but as the commissioner of the administration is the director of the Child Support Office, there is a very close link between the two organizations. The office works with state authorities to see that absent parents are found and that they pay the amount they are required to for child support. It also assists in determining paternity if necessary. In addition, it is engaged in researching the whole problem of the absent parent and in seeking ways by which family life can be strengthened. This information is shared with the states, and jointly the federal government and state agencies establish policies and programs by which these human tragedies can be averted.

The Department of Health and Human Services, as was stated at the beginning of this chapter, is concerned with the welfare of every single American. Because it spends so much of the taxpayers' dollars, its secretary must be at all times accountable to Congress and to the people at large. The secretary is required by law to make periodic reports to Congress, and he/she devotes a great deal of time in testifying before the many concerned committees on the Hill as well as to making speeches constantly across the country. A nation is only as strong as its constituents. The United States went through a long period in which little federal concern for the lives of individual Americans was necessary because there were endless opportunities available for almost everybody. Today, however, because of many problems—the greatly increased population, the sluggish economy, the concern for human rights, and the general complexity of modern life— the federal government has had to assume an active role in the health and welfare of the American people.

The Department of Housing and Urban Development

Housing and, in fact, all community development in the United States until a few years ago were not concerns of the national government. Quite obviously, with a whole continent before them, generations of Americans simply built homes and cities without government supervision or planning. Interestingly enough, there was only one exception to this rule. Way back in the seventeenth century William Penn, the founder of Philadelphia, was unique in that he was America's first city planner. Before a building was erected in what was to be Philadelphia, Penn had made a master plan in order that the city should be pleasant, safe and uncrowded. The general pattern across the country, however, was that communities just grew helter-skelter, and it was not until very recently that Americans suddenly woke up to the fact that many of their cities, the heart of the commercial and cultural life of the nation, were absolutely unlivable.

The urban blight which besets the United States today did not begin in earnest until the end of the nineteenth century when the Industrial Revolution swept the country, bringing with it ugly factories and overcrowded slum conditions. Air and water pollution began as sewage, smoke and industrial wastes poured forth into the environment without restraint. As cities grew with the rise of modern America, conditions deteriorated commensurately. It was not until the 1930s, however, that national attention was caught by urban problems, and even then it was only because the depression was so severe that the federal government was forced into recognizing that many Americans lived in substandard conditions. President Roosevelt's New Deal, therefore, included some legislation for public housing and for financial help for those who needed it to pay for their homes. After the Second World War, the federal role was greatly expanded in the housing field mainly because there simply were not enough homes for the exploding population of the United States. In the years since the war, because the overall problem of urban and community development has been aggravated by many other factors—such as the awareness of air, water and noise pollution, the civil rights push to eliminate the ghettos, and the gigantic traffic snarls which tie up every major city in the country during the rush hours—the federal government has been forced to face up to its responsibility to the American people to enable them to live in decent surroundings. Therefore, by request of President Johnson, Congress in 1966 established the executive Department of Housing and Urban Development, stating in its declaration and purpose, "the general welfare and security of the Nation and the health and living standards of our people require, as a matter of national purpose, sound development of the Nation's communities and metropolitan areas in which the vast majority of its people live and work."

The department's two main functions are implicit in its

title. It is concerned with providing decent housing for all Americans who cannot afford to buy or rent on their own, and it is concerned with community development. The latter responsibility involves the rehabilitation of communities which have fallen into decay and the planning of new communities so that they are viable and pleasant. The assistant secretary in charge of housing has the task of seeing that low- and moderate-income families and the elderly and the handicapped have decent homes in which to live. He accomplishes this by carrying out legislation which authorizes the government to insure mortgages and loans. Individuals wishing to buy or rent houses, apartments, mobile homes, cooperatives, or condominiums who do not have access to private loans may apply to a HUD approved lender who will then have the mortgage or loan insured by the government. The government also insures mortgages or loans for nursing homes, homes for the elderly, nonprofit hospitals and group medical facilities. This guarantee of financial assistance would be meaningless, however, unless there are, indeed, places to be purchased or rented. To meet the demand for housing, HUD is authorized to give assistance to nonprofit sponsors of low-cost housing by making long-term loans available. It also assists state and local housing agencies to provide low- and moderate-cost housing.

The assistant secretary for housing is also responsible for carrying out the provisions of recent legislation designed to protect the consumer. One such law requires the registration of interstate land sales in order to guard the potential purchaser of real estate in another part of the country against fraudulent land deals. This law was necessary because the public, particularly the elderly seeking retirement homes in the nation's sunny regions, were being bilked by false advertising and other unethical practices. Because mobile homes are now extremely popular, their owners must be assured of safe construction, and the assistant secretary sees that the law establishing the manufactured-housing construction and safety standards is enforced. The Real Estate Settlement Procedures Program came into being not only because of the great disparity in fees charged for property settlements in different parts of the nation, but because of abuses which were found to be all too common against which the ordinary person had no protection. The office of the assistant secretary is also designed to serve the consumer by affording him a place to register his complaints over matters relating to property and to assist those who have bought or rented under a federal program. The staff serving the public in these capacities is under orders to put all communications into simple, direct language that anyone can understand, a much needed order in that most government communications are unintelligible to the average citizen. The particular audience that this office is set up to help consists of women, native Americans, Hispanics, the elderly and the mentally handicapped who are those who have the most difficulty in acquiring homes and are the most vulnerable because they generally do not have business expertise. Lastly, the assistant secretary is responsible for enforcing the Lead-Based Paint Poisoning Prevention Program. As was stated above in the chapter on Health and Human Services, research has identified lead-based paint not only as a serious health hazard if ingested, but a cause of mental retardation as well. It is imperative that small children in particular who tend to chew on anything available be protected, and the use of lead-based paint in homes is therefore prohibited.

The second main area of concern to HUD is community development. Through a variety of different programs the aim is to provide the American people with a healthy environment in which to live and work, and it is a major task in that too many communities across the nation suffer from dilapidation and pollution resulting from decades of neglect. The Office of Community Planning and Development, headed by an assistant secretary, attacks the problem by dispensing several kinds of federal grants to assist communities engaged in rehabilitation. Cities with populations of over 50,000 and central cities and counties with more than 200,000 are called entitlement communities. They receive an annual grant for their federally approved projects which must be designed not only to improve housing, but also to provide economic opportunities for the benefit of low- and moderate-income groups. Smaller cities are not entitled to grants, but they must compete for federal aid which is awarded by HUD on the basis of the greatest need. Each of the projects funded through this program must include environmental considerations so that air, water and noise pollution will be eliminated. In addition, this office also assists those residents who must be relocated when projects are launched. The government pays a reasonable sum to cover the cost to the displaced person of looking for another home or business location as well as the actual move.

The Community Planning and Development Office deals primarily with state and local governments. The federal government, however, is also committed to encouraging the private sector to join in the task of improving the economic and environmental viability of the nation's urban areas. To encourage such participation urban development grants are available to private businessmen who are willing to invest their funds in community projects. Not only will the initial cost be reduced with federal aid, but the investor in a local renewal project will gain when the project is completed and the economic level of the community in which he does business is significantly improved. Individuals may also benefit from another of HUD's programs, urban homesteading. This program enables a person to buy a federally owned building for a minimum sum at a low rate of interest on the promise that he will rehabilitate it. When he has, he receives title to the property. Although, due to the present recession and federal budget cutbacks, the funds available for homesteading have been substantially reduced, the program in past years has been successful, and many communities have not only been considerably improved, but individuals who never thought that they could afford a home now find themselves the proud owner of one.

The Homesteading Program is not the only one to have suffered through budget cuts. One of the most exciting and innovative programs that was authorized in the legislation establishing the Department of Housing and Urban Development was the New Communities Program, the purpose of which was not to rehabilitate old communities, but to build new ones from scratch, an urban designer's dream. The program was administered by the New Community Development Corporation managed by a board of directors, one of whom was the secretary of the department. The corporation made possible financial and technical assistance to approved new communities in inner cities, suburbs and rural areas by guaranteeing bonds issued by public or private developers. Unfortunately, although the concept was bold, in practice it did not work out as planned, and in 1975 Congress virtually ended the program by declaring a moratorium on the corporation's loan guarantees. The few new communities that were actually built before 1975 are still, however, under the jurisdiction of the corporation.

Another important office in HUD is that headed by the assistant secretary for fair housing and equal opportunity. The recent national focus on civil rights has proved that one of the most insidious of the social and economic problems which beset the nation was the pattern of segregation which existed in most urban and suburban communities. Blacks, Orientals, and others for many years were prohibited from buying or renting in certain neighborhoods, if not by law (de jure), then by custom (de facto), and one of the most important of the civil rights laws passed in the 1960s was to assure fair housing. In addition, within the construction business, one of the largest and economically significant industries in the nation, discrimination, particularly against blacks, was widespread, an important contributing factor to the generally lower income status of that minority. The government, therefore, adopted a policy of affirmative action which means that jobs on all construction projects involving federal funds must be open to all workers without regard for race or color. The assistant secretary for fair housing and equal opportunity is the secretary's chief adviser on these matters of civil rights and sees that the federal laws are carried out. The fact that his office is part of the office of the secretary attests to the great importance that is attached to his responsibilities.

Last, the assistant secretary in charge of policy development and research is responsible for investigating the practicality of many new ideas. Would direct cash payments to low-income families for housing be better than the present system of helping them to acquire decent homes? How can houses and mobile homes be made safer? Will urban homesteading work on a large scale? These are a few of the issues this office addresses, and if any experimental idea is deemed feasible the assistant secretary then recommends it to the secretary who may incorporate it in his budget, and if it is adopted housing and urban development may be improved.

HUD, like the other executive departments, is run by the secretary who is the president's chief adviser on all housing and community development matters. He is, of course, assisted by the undersecretary, the assistant secretaries, and the general counsel. As much of the work of HUD is in the field, there are regional offices all over the country, and projects under its jurisdiction are supervised on the spot. One point must be emphasized about the role of this department and that is that it does not take over authority from local governments. It is essentially a center for the coordination of programs for urban renewal and planning and exists primarily to help communities (as well as individuals) to offer more attractive and healthier surroundings. The one area that it does have complete jursidiction over is in insisting on fair housing and equal opportunity to all people regardless of race, color, or creed in any of the many projects around the nation which are federally operated or built with federal funds. The department only began operations in 1966, and it is still too soon to judge whether it will actually succeed in revolutionizing the nation's cities and bringing an end to urban blight. The approach that the department takes, however, of examining and considering all aspects of community life—water, air, sewage, industry, business, residence, open spaces, recreation—is long overdue, and the probability is that federal participation in what amounts to a national housecleaning will result in constructive change for the future. William Penn would probably be vastly amused as well as a little saddened to know that it has taken the United States almost three hundred years to realize that community planning has its value and that "an ounce of prevention is worth a pound of cure."

The Department of Transportation

Nothing is more vital to the well-being and prosperity of the United States today than rapid, efficient and safe transportion. In 1966 Congress, in recognition of this fact, established the Department of Transportation, ordering it to begin serving the American people in 1967. The Department of Transportation, like many of the other executive departments, was not created out of whole cloth, but was initially set up to place under one roof all the already existing agencies and commissions scattered throughout the government concerned with all the various forms of transportation in existence today. The establishment of this new department, therefore, caused major reorganizations among the older departments as they lost responsibilities to Transportation. Since its establishment, however, new functions have been added in response to problems which have developed. The purpose of the department is to provide fast, safe, efficient and convenient transportation at the lowest possible cost for the American people. By having control over all modes of transportation centered in one place and under the jurisdiction of the secretary of transportation, the people of the United States stand to benefit by the coordination of policies and by the concentrated emphasis on technical advances that result from centralization.

The department, like all the others, is headed by the secretary who not only administers the department but performs any job the president asks of him.* The secretary of transportation is assisted by the deputy secretary, five assistant secretaries and the general counsel. These top officials differ from

---

*President Ford left it to his secretary, for instance, to decide whether the Anglo-French supersonic jet, *Concorde*, should be allowed to use Dulles Airport, a federally owned facility outside of Washington, D.C., in nearby Virginia. After a great deal of research into the environmental aspects of the issue, the secretary decided to allow the plane to land and take off from Dulles for a sixteen-month trial period. The British and the French also wanted the *Concorde* to use Kennedy International Airport near New York, but the secretary had no jurisdiction there because Kennedy is owned and operated by the New York Port Authority and it is up to that interstate body to decide.

their counterparts in other departments in that they do not administer the components of the department. They are responsible instead for coordinating such things as general policy, public relations, international affairs and research and technology. Each agency which was transferred to the Department of Transportation retained its own structure and officials. The new tasks that have come under its jurisdiction since 1967 are administered in the same way.

At present there are nine components of Transportation, six transferred from other parts of the government and three new ones. They are the United States Coast Guard, the Federal Aviation Administration, the Federal Highway Administration, the National Highway Traffic Safety Administration, the Federal Railroad Administration, the Urban Mass Transportation Administration, the St. Lawrence Seaway Development Corporation, the Maritime Administration, and the Research and Special Programs Administration.

The United States Coast Guard was transferred from the Department of the Treasury where it had been since 1915. It may seem odd that a maritime unit was in the Treasury, but the nature of many of its duties made it logical for the service to be in the Treasury in peacetime alongside of the Bureau of Customs until the Department of Transportation was created. The Coast Guard is one of the largest of the law enforcement agencies in the country. It is responsible for the enforcement of all the federal laws on the waters under the jurisdiction of the United States government. Recently, when the 200-mile limit was adopted, it was the Coast Guard that apprehended Russian ships and brought them to port for violating the laws restricting the kind of fishing by foreign ships in these waters. The Coast Guard sees that all laws regarding ship inspection and navigation are carried out, and it is responsible for enforcing the revenue, customs and immigration laws. Though wildlife is protected by a division of the Department of the Interior, it is the Coast Guard that protects sea wildlife and carries out the conservation measures deemed necessary by other sections of the government. In Alaska it used to be the members of the Coast Guard who were appointed as United States marshals to carry out the law, but since Alaska became a state, this is no longer the case. Also, the security of ports and the safety of ships at sea are part of the Coast Guard's job. To accomplish the latter, the service maintains lighthouses and lifesaving devices along the coasts of the nation; it builds and maintains the bridges over the nation's navigable waters; it clears waters of derelicts and other objects dangerous to shipping; it efficiently patrols the northern sea lanes, smashing up ice blocks and keeping an eye out for icebergs. In addition, it operates a national safety training program for those who own power boats, and if, by chance, they come to grief on the high seas, it will be the Coast Guard who will come to their rescue. The Coast Guard is also one of the chief sources of information on the broad subject of oceanography, and its vessels conduct research as they patrol the waters bordering the United States. The service also since 1960 has regulated the pilotage on the Great Lakes, maintaining a pool of pilots and setting rates and charges for their services.

Should war break out, the Coast Guard automatically becomes part of the Navy, the primary task of which is to defend the United States on the oceans against all enemies. The members of the Coast Guard are well qualified to become part of the Navy. The Coast Guard Academy in New London, Connecticut, is much like the Naval Academy in Annapolis, Maryland, and its graduates are expert sailors. In peacetime, however, the law-enforcing role of the Coast Guard and its services to those who sail the nation's waters explain its relocation in the Department of Transportation.

The Federal Aviation Administration, formerly an independent agency, has the responsibility for regulating all air commerce in the United States to keep it safe, efficient and prepared, if necessary, for a role in national defense. The administration also encourages the development of civil aeronautics, promotes a national system of airports, and develops and operates the systems of air traffic control and navigational aids within the United States. In conjunction with its responsibilities for the safety of air traffic, the Federal Aviation Administration conducts all examinations and certification of pilots and inspections of aircraft to make sure that they comply with the latest United States safety standards. It also cooperates with other nations in air-traffic control and offers training for foreign nationals in the United States. As air travel becomes more and more popular, the FAA has an increasingly difficult job to perform because as everyone wants to fly, more and more planes are in the air. Airports, particularly in the eastern United States and in the great cities such as Chicago, Houston and Los Angeles, are becoming very congested, and the danger of accidents keeps mounting. It is the Federal Aviation Administration which must try to satisfy the ever growing demand for speedy air service and at the same time insist that at all times the safety of the air passengers is the first consideration. The FAA does not control which private company flies the airplanes or what fares will be. That is the responsibility of the Civil Aeronautics Board, still an independent agency.

The United States is a nation of wheels. A luxury item in earlier times, a car today is a necessity, and many families find that two or even three cars must be maintained in order to meet the demands of family members. In addition, because the lion's share of freight is carried by truck, America's highways are the vital arteries in the national economy. The number of cars and trucks on the superhighways which crisscross the country has increased so much in recent years that the ever increasing tolls of deaths and injuries, not to speak of the cost of repairs, are a national scandal, and because of the importance of motor vehicles to the people of the United States, the federal government has had to be concerned with all the factors involved in automotive safety. Two administrations, therefore, in the Department of Transportation share this responsibility, the Federal Highway Administration and the National Highway Traffic Safety Administration.

The Federal Highway Administration took over the jobs formerly performed by the Bureau of Public Roads in the Department of Commerce and the Corps of Engineers of the United States Army. This administration is now responsbile for the 42,500 miles of interstate and defense highways which have been built since World War II, the federal government paying 90 percent of the cost, the states, 10 percent for an

additional 800,000 miles of federally aided primary, secondary and urban streets, financed on a 75-25 basis, and for the
federal emergency aid in repairing federally aided roads in
disaster areas. The federal share of these programs is paid
for by special highway taxes collected from the users of the
system which are placed in a highway trust fund, thus providing for more highways and improvements as they are deemed
necessary. These highways are engineered to be as safe as
possible for trucks and automobiles and are strategically
placed so that in case of national emergency the armed forces
will be able to move rapidly and efficiently to wherever they
are needed. Not only are they designed to carry the nation's
traffic, but in view of the national concern for the quality of
life, beautification of the interstate system has also been given
a great deal of consideration. Billboards are excluded and
rest areas, gas stations and restaurants are located just off the
highways, usually in carefully landscaped groves. The engineers who design them also take great care not to mar the
beauty of the landscape through which the roads must pass.

Highway construction is only one-half the job of trying to
make automotive travel safe for the American people. The
National Highway Traffic Safety Administration is responsible
for the other half, that of making automobiles, buses and
trucks safe and is charged with implementing all government
policies relating to the automotive industry and to those who
either sit behind the wheel or are passengers. It is the unit of
the government that researches safety measures and is responsible, for instance, for making seat belts mandatory, although
it did have to rescind the order requiring that the seat belt fas-
tening interlock with the starter button because the public
would not accept such an arrangement. It is at present conducting research on the air bag to reduce injuries in crashes.
It also sets standards for safety features by which automobile
manufacturers must abide, and it is continually on the watch
for defects in cars, and, if it discovers any, can require the
manufacturer to remedy them. Although the states are responsible for the inspection of cars and trucks which are licensed within their borders, the federal administration will
conduct a free inspection of an in-depth nature on request.

The inspectors actually take a car apart and examine every piece. Not only does this assure the owner that his vehicle is safe, but it is one of the ways that the administration spots trouble and helps its officials set standards of construction which they then pass on to the manufacturers. Another way in which this unit promotes highway safety is in assisting states and local governments with the cost of safety campaigns, and in this area it works very hard to reduce the number of accidents attributable to the improper use of alcohol and the use of drugs. It also operates a central national register for auto licenses which have been revoked or suspended for more than six months for violations of highway safety codes. No longer can an offender simply leave one state and operate a motor vehicle in another with impunity. It maintains a strict surveillance on all interstate trucking and inspects the machines, removing those that are in hazardous condition from service. In sum, this unit's work is solely in the interest of the millions and millions of car and truck drivers who too often use the nation's highways recklessly.

In addition to its concern for all the aspects of safety on the highways, the National Traffic Safety Administration has had a new job assigned to it as a result of the nation's serious shortage of oil and its dependence on foreign sources. Fuel conservation is of the highest priority, and it is the National Traffic Safety Administration that is responsible for setting the standards for gasoline consumption in cars and trucks which must be adhered to in the near future. Along with the Federal Highway Administration and state governments, it enforces the national speed limit on interstate highways of 55 miles per hour which, as anyone who used to drive at 70 knows, saves a great deal of fuel.

The present state of America's railroads is indeed sad when one thinks of the role they played in the building of the nation after the Civil War. In those years the advance of the Iron Horse across the Great Plains opened up the heart of the country for settlement and made the United States one of the wealthiest nations in the world at the time. One of the most significant events of the nineteenth century was the linking of the rails from the East and West when the golden spike was hammered into place at Promontory Point, Utah, in 1869. The golden age of the railroads continued until the 1920s when automotive traffic began to threaten their position as the nation's leading carriers of passengers and freight, and then in the post–World War II years their decline was hastened by the advent of the air age. Unfortunately, no one was really aware of what the decline of rail traffic was going to mean in the United States in the 1970s. Both automotive and air traffic are totally dependent on the availability of high priced fuel, and, as mentioned above, our oil resources have been seriously depleted and until new supplies, such as offshore fields, can be found and exploited, the nation is dependent on foreign oil and, as such, is extremely vulnerable to other nations' political and economic decisions. Because of these facts of life, the railroads are once again a matter of concern, and the thrust today is to get them revitalized. The federal government in cooperation with private industry is working to this end, and the Federal Railroad Administration in the Department of Transportation is the unit responsible for the federal role. As the National Railroad Passenger Corporation is also involved with rail traffic, it will be discussed in this chapter, although it is a quasi-official agency and not an integral part of the Department of Transportation.

In 1967 the Federal Railroad Administration, which coordinates all government policies concerning the nation's railroads, was created and absorbed the responsibilities for the Bureau of Railroad Safety and Service from the Interstate Commerce Commission, the Office of High Speed Ground Transportation from Commerce, and the operation of the Alaska Railroad from Interior. It establishes safety standards for track, engines, brakes and signals and carries out routine inspections to see that the standards are abided by. It also regulates the transportation of dangerous materials such as explosives, and when accidents of any sort occur, it is this unit which investigates to determine the causes so that they can be prevented from recurring. Much of its work is directed toward the development of advanced equipment so that high speed trains will be possible. In the Northeast in particular, speedy train service would be of great advantage in that the area from Washington, D.C., to Boston, Massachusetts, is extremely congested, the air lanes crowded and the highways jammed with cars, buses and trucks. Distances are not great, and many people would really prefer to ride the trains as depots are in town whereas airports generally are not, and cars are a positive nuisance in a big city as parking becomes increasing difficult to find and is very expensive. So much freight is carried in this northeast corridor that trains could be utilized without seriously cutting into the profits of the trucking industry. The experiments with various types of new equipment and track designed for high speed are conducted in Colorado where the administration maintains a fifty square mile facility which it shares with the Urban Mass Transportation Administration. Another duty of the Railroad Administration, that of operating the Alaska Railroad, is unique in that it is the only instance, apart from the armed forces, in which a government office actually runs a service. The Alaska Railroad differs from the other lines in the United States because it is a government built and operated line. Its primary function is to encourage the settlement and economic development of the state, and for that purpose it maintains 482.7 miles of main track from Seward to Portage Junction with spur lines along the way. This line, though operated by the Federal Railroad Administration, has its tariffs set by the Interstate Commerce Commission which also sets the rates for the privately owned lines in the country. Lastly, the administration also handles all the financial assistance programs authorized by Congress to help the nation's railroads.

No one who lives in an urban or suburban area can be unaware of the traffic jams which characterize rush hours in almost every city in the United States. Not only are cars, trucks and buses almost in a combat situation as they manoeuver for momentary advantage, but noxious exhaust fumes pollute the air and discolor the buildings. Altogether the A.M. and P.M. rush hours are the most unpleasant aspects of modern life, and almost everyone who is subjected to them would like to see things done differently. The reason for the overdependence on automotive vehicles is that although cities have long had subway or elevated trains and bus systems, many are now old, and the cost of operation and maintenance has risen by geometric progression to the point that fares are nowhere near adequate to meet the expenses. The answer to the problems of city and suburban transportation lies in building innovative systems that are swift, clean, efficient, run on time and frequently. The Urban Mass Transportation Administration, established by Congress in 1964, is charged with providing leadership and technical and financial assistance to communities which want to solve their urban transportation problems. It carries out its mission in various ways. It has financed demonstration projects such as the "people mover" rapid rail system in Morgantown, West Virginia, and the new transbus which is an improvement over the standard, exhaust-spewing vehicles in use today. It assists communities with planning mass transportation on an areawide basis with an eye to socioeconomic factors so that all sections can be served at the lowest possible cost. It encourages experimentation with different kinds of traffic flows and parking restrictions to alleviate the jams which clog all but the smallest communities. In addition to providing federal money for either the operating cost of mass transportation or for capital investment by local systems, the administration underwrites part of the expense of advanced training for individuals in the management and design of mass transportation systems. This approach is designed to enable local governments to plan rationally, thus avoiding the uncoordinated hodgepodge of various modes of city transportation which has characterized the past as well as, hopefully, ending the domination of the automobile in urban areas. New subways in San Francisco, California, and Washington, D.C., for instance, have been planned with federal help, and one day we may see high speed monorail type transportation between cities such as Washington and Baltimore and to the airports which serve them.

Until 1981 the Maritime Administration was part of the Commerce Department. It was moved to Transportation in that year under a government reorganization because Congress believed that it was more efficient to include shipping with all the other modes of transportation. The administration is responsible for all aspects of the nation's merchant marine, one of the most important of which is to encourage trade in American ships. Although historically much of America's wealth was derived from its active shipping industry, since World War I the United States has lost a great deal of maritime business to foreign fleets. One reason for this is that American wages for merchant seamen are considerably higher than those of many other countries which adds to the cost of shipping goods in United States vessels. Also, our safely standards are very strict and carefully regulated. Although, of course, it is important in every way for ships to be well constructed, maintained and equipped with the latest technical devices, it again adds to the cost. In addition, the higher wage scale in the United States for shipyard workers is another contributing factor in the overall expense of American shipping. The main thrust, then, of the Maritime Administration is to build and promote American shipping in every way possible to make our merchant marine competitive with those of other nations. To that end the federal government subsidizes many aspects of the merchant marine industry, and the Maritime Administration implements the various parts of this program. It pays, for instance, the difference in cost between operating American ships and foreign ones on essential services, as well as the difference between construction costs in the United States shipyards and those abroad.

Shipping is obviously very important in wartime, and the Maritime Administration has the responsibility of making sure that the nation is prepared in case of a national emergency. At all times the administration maintains a national defense reserve fleet of government owned ships which in times of crisis it operates through agents. It also is empowered to charter United States owned ships to private operators for defense purposes and can requisition privately owned yachts and place them where needed in national emergencies. In order to guarantee that the merchant marine is qualified to serve as an auxiliary to the navy in time of war, the Maritime Administration operates the United States Merchant Marine Academy in Kings Point, New York. Graduates of the academy are not only licensed officers in the merchant marine, but they are also qualified for commissions as ensigns in the naval reserve. Although traditionally the merchant marine has attracted only men to its service, recently women have been admitted to the academy and now serve on merchant ships around the world.

The administration also has the responsibility of deciding what to do with government owned ships for which there is no further use. During both of the world wars the government constructed vast numbers of merchant ships to carry soldiers and supplies abroad. After the wars many of these were sold, but others were "mothballed." That is, they were sealed and left at anchor in various waterways around the country in case they should be needed again. Many are still afloat, but rusted and forlorn. The constant obligation of the Maritime Administration is to generate business for our country's merchant fleet, and if American shippers used our flagships, many of these sad relics could be refurbished and sail again.

It should be noted here that in the United States merchant shipping is the responsibility of both the Maritime Administration and the Federal Maritime Commission, which is an independent agency. The commission does not duplicate the work of the Maritime Administration, however, because its principal job is regulatory. The commission is made up of five members, appointed by the president and confirmed by the Senate, who serve five-year terms. Their task is to set rates for shipping, to set up rules and practices for shippers, to investigate charges of discriminatory rates, and the like. Because the commission is more of a court and the Maritime Administration is more of a promoter, they do not duplicate, but actually complement each other in the task of making the American merchant marine first class.

Another component of the Department of Transportation is the St. Lawrence Seaway Development Corporation. This government owned corporation was established by act of Congress in 1954, and its purpose, now that the seaway is built, is to operate the section between the city of Montreal in Canada and Lake Erie, which is in United States territory. The corporation works closely with the Canadian government with whom the St. Lawrence Seaway project was conceived. The

seaway is one of the most constructive of all government projects going on today in that it enables deep water navigation all
the way up the St. Lawrence River to the Great Lakes, bringing shipping, and therefore profitable trade, into the heart-
land of the continent. Hydroelectric power is also made available to both Canadians and Americans by which their
standard of living is improved. The tolls paid to the corporation by the shippers using the seaway pay for its upkeep and
will eventually make the corporation a profit-making organization.

The ninth component of the Department of Transportation is the Research and Special Projects Administration. It
came into being in 1977 through a reorganization within the
department. Under its jurisdiction are three subdivisions: the
Materials Transportation Bureau, the Transportation Systems Center and the Transportation Programs Bureau. The
latter two are essentially concerned with research into all
aspects involving transportation in the United States with the
aim of making it safer and more efficient in order to better
serve the public. The Transportation Programs Bureau is
also responsible for planning for the use of the nation's
transportation systems in case of national emergencies or for
regions struck by natural disasters. The Materials Transportation Bureau's job is to see that dangerous things such as
explosives, chemicals, and radioactive materials are moved
with great care so as not to endanger others traveling along
the same route. The number of these potentially hazardous
materials has increased over the years to the extent that in
1975 the Materials Transportation Bureau was established to
coordinate the several government agencies that had been
responsible for one or more aspects of the problem. The
bureau is responsible for establishing safety rules for all
forms of transportation, trucks, trains, planes, and for the
pipelines which carry natural gases across state lines. It also
conducts research into ways of improving the containers in
which dangerous materials are carried so as to make them
virtually accident-proof. The bureau sees that all state and
local regulations conform to federal standards and are uniform across the nation so that people traveling the nation's

transportation arteries or living next to them are as safe from accident as the government can possibly make them.

The Department of Transportation has already grown since it became an executive department in 1967 and undoubtedly it will continue to expand its responsibilities as advances are made in the modes by which Americans travel. Helicopters, for instance, may someday become as common as the automobile, and if they do, the regulation of their traffic will become the responsibility of this department. It is also not inconceivable that the secretary will find himself one day regulating interplanetary travel. In the meantime, Americans, who are the most mobile people on earth, are protected to the best of the government's ability by the Department of Transportation's careful monitoring of the present-day means of getting from one place to another.

The Department of Energy

Except for State, War and Navy, and Treasury and Justice, which were established at the beginning of the federal government under the Constitution, the other executive departments have all come into being in response to problems brought about by changing times, and the Department of Energy, created by Congress in 1977, is simply another example of the government meeting new challenges to the security of the American people. What caused President Carter to propose the new department and the Congress to establish it was the sudden realization brought home to the United States during the winter of 1973–74 of the degree to which we are dependent on foreign nations for petroleum which is the lifeblood of American industry. The United States not only must conserve its dwindling supplies of oil if the present standard of living is to be maintained, but must turn back to coal, of which we have plenty, and find new sources of power. It appeared that the most efficient way in which to accomplish these objectives was to consolidate certain energy-related agencies into a cabinet level department with its secretary able to coordinate the programs and evolve a national energy policy.

When the Department of Energy officially came into being in October of 1977, it had under its jurisdiction the Federal Power Commission, the Federal Energy Agency and the Energy Research and Development Administration, hitherto independent, and, in addition, it took responsibility from the Department of the Interior for the five federal hydroelectric power administrations, the Bonneville in Portland, Oregon, the Southeastern in Elberton, Georgia, the Southwestern in Tulsa, Oklahoma, the Alaska in Juneau, and the Western in Denver, Colorado. These administrations operate federal dams which generate electricity and which are also designed for flood control. The electricity from these projects is sold at low cost to the people who live in these regions and has helped them raise their standard of living considerably. They are also protected from the devastation of the floods which before the dams were built used to ravage their communities. The move from the Interior Department has not affected their operation, but it just seemed more logical to place them in the new department as they play a major role in providing energy for a significant portion of the nation.

Neither has the work of the Federal Power Commission changed with its move to Energy, although its name was changed to the Federal Energy Regulatory Commission. Originally set up in 1920 to see that all Americans got sufficient supplies of gas and hydroelectric power for their homes and businesses at reasonable rates wherever they lived, it still carries out the same responsibilities. It sets the rates for oil, gas, and electricity in interstate commerce and establishes standards for the construction of pipelines which carry natural gas and oil to consumers across the nation, and it licenses hydroelectric power installations. In recent years it has also been concerned with environmental standards as well. The commission is still virtually independent. It is administered by a board of five, appointed by the president for a four-year term. The terms are staggered so that at no time is the whole board new to the responsibilities of the commission. The chairman is the chief executive officer responsible for the management and personnel of the commission, and he determines his budget separately from that of the department. He and the board are totally responsible for the day-to-day affairs of the commission, and the secretary of the department has authority over them only in emergency situations.

The Federal Energy Agency and the Energy Research and Development Administration, however, are no longer separate units. The work they did before being absorbed by the Department of Energy has been divided among six new offices, and together these six account for the largest slice of the department's budget. They are the Office of Energy Research, Fossil Fuels, Conservation and Renewable Energy, Environmental Protection, Safety and Emergency Preparedness, Defense Programs and Nuclear Energy.

The Office of Energy Research has responsibility for a myriad of educational programs and works closely with universities which carry out research programs under contract to the government. It is also concerned with determining the generic environmental, health and safety aspects of energy technology, and with the assistant secretary for International Affairs helps arrange for the exchange of scientists between the United States and other nations. The director of this office also sees that duplication in research efforts does not take place, and he assists the secretary in establishing budgetary priorities for research.

Fossil fuels are coal, gas and petroleum, and they are absolutely vital to America's industrial strength upon which is based our high standard of living. Historically, the search for and exploitation of these resources were the domain of private enterprise, and many a fortune was built on the mining of coal, the refining of oil, and the production of natural gas. Today, however, the situation has, unfortunately, changed. Not only is our dependency on fossil fuels enormous, but the supplies are less easily attainable. The shock of the oil embargo imposed by the OPEC nations in the winter of 1973–74 made the American people realize that, because they could no longer count on the importation of cheap oil, they had better conserve their own resources. In addition major efforts had to be made to find new sources of oil, gas, and coal. Because the technology required to find new sources is so terribly expensive, the federal government has taken on the responsibility of underwriting the costs of research. This is the job of the Office of Fossil Fuels, and the technology which results from its work is made available to the private sector for commercialization. In this way each American through his taxes is playing a part in the vital task of reducing the nation's dependency on costly foreign fuels.

Because our own supplies of fossil fuels, no matter how much we improve the means of finding them, are in the end exhaustible, it is imperative that Americans change their profligate ways and make major efforts to conserve energy. This can be done in many ways. Houses, industrial plants, schools, and hospitals, for example, can be weatherized so that thermostats can be turned down. Appliances can be manufactured to work just as well by using far less electricity. Transportation systems can be made more fuel-efficient, and new and renewable sources of energy can be found. Gasohol, for instance, can be produced inexpensively from fermented grain or even garbage, and cars, buses, tractors, etc. can run on it as well as on gasoline. Solar and geothermal heat sources can be harnessed to reduce dependency on gas or oil fired furnaces. To encourage these conservation programs and to stimulate research into renewable energies is the responsibility of the Office of Conservation and Renewable Energy, and it works with state and local governments in planning energy-efficient programs.

It is very important, however, that all energy conservation efforts be compatible with environmental concerns and safety regulations; yet at the same time the nation must be prepared for possible national emergencies such as the one caused by the oil embargo a few years ago which caught the nation totally unprepared. The Office of Environment Protection, Safety and Emergency Preparedness has these responsibilities. To safeguard against fuel shortages, this office manages the nation's three petroleum reserves, the oil stored in abandoned salt mines, shale oil reserves, and the navy's petroleum reserves. The assistant secretary in charge of this office must see that these reserves in no way endanger the safety of communities near them nor harm the environment.

The department also has charge of programs involving nuclear energy which are divided between two offices, the Office of Defense Programs and the Office for Nuclear Energy. The former supervises nuclear weapon research, the development and testing of such weapons as well as their production. It is also responsible for security measures and it has the job of disposing nuclear waste from the weapons program (as well as responsibility for the classification and declassification of information on nuclear weapons). It enforces the regulations concerning the exporting of nuclear materials, and verifies and monitors the provisions of the Nuclear Test Ban Treaty. The Nuclear Energy Office handles research and development of fission energy programs. This involves the office with nuclear reactors, both civilian and military and with the problem of disposing of the nuclear waste from the commercial reactors. When the Nuclear Age began at the end of World War II, most people assumed that it would be the energy source of the future. Although nuclear plants have been built and do supply energy to various parts of the country, many problems have arisen which have caused some very real questions to arise as to the future of nuclear power. One obvious one is the issue of nuclear waste. It remains radioactive for an indeterminate period of time, and this poses a real danger to people and the environment. No one wants a nuclear dump in their backyard. Another is the safety of the nuclear reactor. The accident at Three Mile Island in Pennsylvania several years ago made the nightmare of released radioactivity real. The dangers inherent in nuclear weaponry are obvious, and hence the extreme security measures which surround the development, testing and manufacture of such weapons as well as the constant efforts being made to reach international agreement on the nonproliferation of nuclear armaments and to reach an accord with the Soviet Union on arms control. What appeared to be a boon to mankind has now become a source of great concern. The two offices of the Department of Energy which deal with nuclear programs have, therefore, a grave responsibility.

The Secretary of the Department of Energy has a truly difficult job. As the president's chief adviser on energy, he must devise a national policy not only to protect and preserve our dwindling fossil fuels, but to encourage and promote research into new technologies to produce renewable energy sources. He must see that nuclear programs for weapons and for energy be secure and safe. As energy matters involve all aspects of our national life, the secretary must coordinate the work of his department with almost every other department and agency of the federal government. Perhaps his most difficult task, however, is in convincing the American people that energy conservation is of the utmost importance and that they must, therefore, change their wasteful ways and begin to treat energy as the precious commodity that it is.

The Department of Education

The last of the executive departments, Education, was created by Congress only a few years ago in 1979 in response to President Carter's urging. Its future, however, is somewhat problematic in that during the presidential campaign of 1980 candidate Reagan, a firm believer in a much reduced role for the federal government in national affairs, vowed to dismantle it. When he became president, however, he did appoint a secretary for education, but with the understanding that he would devise a plan whereby the responsibilities of the department could be carried out in other ways than through an executive department. To date, in the fourth year of Reagan's presidency, the department is still functioning, and there does not appear to be a plan to abolish it.

Whether Education remains a cabinet post or not is really not all that important. The fact is that the federal government has long had a vital interest in the subject and undoubtedly will continue to. As long ago as 1862 the government first ventured into the field of education with the passage of the Morrill Act which established Land Grant colleges for the instruction of agricultural and mechanical arts. The federal government gave public lands to the states in the agricultural regions of the country for the colleges and funds for their support. In 1867 the first office for education was set up in Washington in recognition of the fact that no nation can be strong, advanced or follow democratic principles without an educated citizenry. It must be emphasized, however, that historically the responsibility for public education has always been that of the states and local communities within the states and the role of the federal government until recently was confined to the collection of statistics and facts to show the condition and progress of education in the nation. Any information collected by the Office of Education was distributed upon request to improve educational systems and to maintain as far as possible a standard curriculum in the schools throughout the country.

Since World War II, however, the government's role in education has increased enormously for a variety of reasons. Immediately following the war, the G.I. Bill of Rights, passed by Congress to assist veterans in their adjustment to civilian life, provided among other things federal funds for servicemen wishing to continue their education. Not only were their tuitions and books underwritten, but they were granted stipends for their living expenses while completing their studies. This expenditure of public monies necessarily involved the government more closely with the nation's colleges and universities. Later in 1957 the United States was shaken by the launching of Sputnik, the first man-made satellite, by the Soviet Union, and the government became very concerned with the progress of scientific and technological research in this country because it appeared that the Russians had bested us. Scientific and technological research is very expensive, and to encourage it, the government began to make grants to universities around the country to help underwrite the cost. In the 1960s with the tremendous emphasis on equal opportunity in education for all Americans which resulted from the landmark decision of the Supreme Court in 1954 that segregation in public schools was unconstitutional, the federal government had to become involved to an unprecedented degree in order to carry out the law of the land. In addition, in the 1960s President Johnson's hope to create a "great society" further involved the government in many programs all aimed at improving America's education so that every child could have quality elementary and secondary education as well as a college education, if they so desired. Congress responded to this challenge by enacting a number of laws relating to educational opportunities which the old department of Health, Education and Welfare was charged with carrying out. The old Office of Education, which had been placed in that department, was superseded by a new Education Division, which included the Office of an Assistant Secretary, the Office of Education with its new responsibilities and the National Institute of Education. It was this division which in 1979 was removed from HEW and became the new Department of Education.

The primary mission of the department is to see that all Americans—young or adult, particularly those who are disadvantaged or who are members of minority groups—have access to quality education. To that end it has many different areas of responsibility. It devises programs for bilingual education, for instance, which has become necessary in view of the vastly increased numbers of Americans for whom English is a second language. It develops career-education programs, a recent innovation designed to prepare young people for the world of work and to help them make a wise choice of a vocation or a profession. It administers the Teacher Corps which is a program underwritten by the government to train people who are willing to serve in the disadvantaged areas of the nation. The department is also responsible for administering the various direct and indirect financial assistance programs to help needy students to continue their education beyond high school. One is the Pell Grant (the Basic Educational Opportunity Grant), which has enabled many talented young people from impoverished backgrounds to attend college because the government provides up to fifteen hundred dollars toward their expenses. Another is the Work/Study Program which underwrites the cost to an institution of providing jobs for scholarship students so that they may earn while they go to college. The department also makes possible student loans from private banks by insuring the loans. These loans are long term and have low interest rates so that the borrower may complete his education and repay slowly when he has employment. The work of the department is also to a large extent involved with research into all aspects of education. Its goal is to improve our educational system so that America's youth will be prepared to lead constructive and productive lives in the increasingly complex world in which they will live and work as adults.

In addition to supervising the above, the secretary of education has special responsibility for four federally sponsored institutions: Gallaudet College for the Deaf and Howard University, both located in Washington, D.C., the American Printing House for the Blind in Louisville, Kentucky, and the National Technical Institute for the Deaf, a part of the Rochester Institute of Technology in Rochester, New York. Why the first three of these institutions are responsibilities of the federal government is interesting. Each was established to serve a particular segment of the population which had no educational opportunities available at one period in our history. For a long time the United States government had concern for the handicapped, and as early as 1857 Gallaudet's predecessor, the Columbia Institution for the Instruction for the Deaf and the Dumb and the Blind, was established in the District of Columbia. In 1911 by statute it lost its responsibility for the dumb and the blind and became solely concerned with educating the deaf. In 1954 its name was changed to Gallaudet College, and it not only offers a four-year liberal arts program leading to a degree, but also includes the Model Secondary School for the Deaf and the Kendall Elementary School for young deaf children. The college also offers graduate training for persons interested in teaching the deaf. The American Printing House for the Blind was actually founded in 1858 by the legislature of Kentucky and provides, at no charge, braille and talking books and other material for institutions involved in the education of the blind. In 1879 Congress undertook to support it in part, and, although it is administered independently, the secretary of education is the liaison between its president and the government. Howard University was originally founded in 1867 to provide education for blacks in the District of Columbia, which was then under congressional control. At the time blacks were generally unable to acquire a college education, and the federal government recognized its responsibility toward this minority. Today Howard is a major university offering graduate work in a variety of fields in addition to its undergraduate program. It is open to all, regardless of race, national origin, color or creed. In its admission policies it still, however, recognizes a special obligation to blacks. The National Technical Institute for the Deaf is of more recent origin, its doors having opened in 1968, and it is unique in that its establishment is a direct reflection of the modern philosophy of education for the handicapped—mainstreaming. Mainstreaming means that the physically handicapped should no longer be segregated in special institutions, but ought to be in regular schools with their able-bodied peers. The National Technical Institue for the Deaf is an integral part of the Rochester Institute of Technology, a well established college for students without hearing difficulties. Not only does the Institute offer deaf students training in a wide variety of technical fields which provides them with equal career opportunities, but it also, through its outreach program, serves those with hearing impairments both in the United States and abroad.

It will be interesting whether the Department of Education survives as a cabinet-level department, especially in view of the recent national attention focussed on the issue of the standards of our educational system. In 1983, with President Reagan's blessing, a commission was set up to study America's schools and to evaluate their performance. Its final report came as a shock to the nation which for years prided itself on its public school system. The commission found that academic standards were at best mediocre, discipline was lax, and that far too great a percentage of high school graduates lacked competency in the basic skills of reading, writing and computation. It seems unlikely that in view of the necessity of revamping America's educational system, a task that will undoubtedly be very expensive, the federal government can withdraw its support at this time. Making education the responsibility of an executive department gives it stature, and to demote it would seem most unwise.

THE DEVELOPMENT OF THE LEGISLATIVE BRANCH OF THE UNITED STATES GOVERNMENT

In 1787 when the Constitution was written, the framers set forth a plan for the United States Congress or the legislative branch. Each of its two houses was given responsibilities, officers and an organizational plan. As the years have passed, the legislative branch has changed and expanded in much the same manner as has the executive branch. Some of the changes are organizational due to enlarged membership; others have to do with the addition of responsibilities. The size of Congress has expanded since 1789, the year in which the first Congress met. This Congress was made up of senators and representatives from only thirteen states. Today there are fifty states in the Union, sending one hundred senators and four hundred and thirty-five representatives to Washington for every session of Congress. In addition, because the United States has acquired territories and the District of Columbia, each of which has demanded representation, there are also in the House of Representatives the high commissioner of Puerto Rico and delegates from the territories and the District of Columbia. These individuals speak for their constituencies, but do not have a vote in the House, although some may vote in committee. Another change which has taken place since 1789 is the manner in which senators are elected. Originally, the Constitution provided for the election of senators by the state legislatures. In 1913 the Seventeenth Amendment to the

Constitution changed this system, replacing it with the direct election of senators by the citizens of each of the states in the union. Also in 1913 Congress enacted a law setting the number of representatives at four hundred and thirty-five. This statutory limitation was sensible in that if the original system of determining representation solely on population had continued, the House of Representatives would be made up of over a thousand members and would have been totally unwieldy and unable to perform its duties.

As the numbers in Congress have grown, the organization of the legislature has been adapted to handle the greater membership. Both the Senate and the House have added officers to those mentioned in the Constitution to perform duties pertinent to the efficient running of Congress. Although the vice-president is still the president of the Senate as prescribed by the Constitution and the Senate still elects a president pro tempore from its membership in case of the absence of the vice-president or his elevation to the presidency, two other senate positions have been created. The secretary of the Senate is elected by the Senate, and his task is varied. Should the vice-president be absent and the president pro tempore not yet elected, the secretary of the Senate performs the duties of the head of the Senate. The secretary is the custodian of the seal and the gavel of the United States Senate. He draws money from the United States Treasury to pay the senators, the officers and the employees as well as the expenses of running the Senate. He is responsible for administering all oaths to officers of the Senate and to witnesses who appear before that body. He also certifies the ratification of peace treaties and the confirmation of nominees by the Senate to the president of the United States. Every four years he is in charge of the presidential inauguration proceedings at the Capitol, and he is one of those who escorts the president to the rostrum when he addresses a joint session of Congress. Should a senator die in office, it is the secretary who makes the funeral arrangements and escorts congressional committees to the services. Lastly, when foreigners or other dignitaries come to visit the Senate, the secretary brings them to the podium where they are introduced by the president of the Senate to that body.

To keep order in the Senate and in the Capitol Building, the position of sergeant at arms was established. Elected by the Senate, the sergeant at arms manages the Capitol police and the doorkeepers. It is he who collects a quorum of senators (the minimum number required by law to do business) when directed to, and his presence is required at all sessions of the Senate. He also serves subpoenas to persons whose testimony is demanded by the Senate. In addition, he is a member of the Capitol Guide Board, serving as its chairman every other year. In this capacity he makes sure that all visitors to the Capitol are courteously received and given interesting tours by well-trained personnel.

In the House of Representatives the position of clerk of the House has been created to perform certain duties important to the efficiency of that body. The clerk has a continuing job from Congress to Congress. He presides over each new session of Congress until the Speaker of the House is elected. He is the keeper of the House seal, and he prepares the roster of all representatives duly elected to the House. He also witnesses all bills, resolutions and subpoenas for the House.

These officers of Congress, in addition to those mentioned in the Constitution, perform the practical tasks necessary to the smooth functioning of the legislative branch of the government. The amount of business, however, before each session of Congress is so enormous as well as complicated that senators and congressmen could not possibly do all the work themselves. They have, therefore, staffs of their own whose salaries are paid out of government funds. Today congressional staff employees number over nineteen thousand. Representatives have an allowance of $255,144 which means that they have on the average fifteen staff members. The staff allowance for senators varies according to the size of the state they represent, and some have over $900,000 which permits them to hire a great many people. The congressional staffs have extremely interesting jobs. They help prepare legislation, administer the office, handle the voluminous mail from constituents, arrange itineraries for trips and are political liaison officers in their boss's home district or state. These positions attract many young lawyers, political scientists, economists and those just interested in government, and it is not at all unusual for a staffer to enter politics himself after being exposed to the work of Capitol Hill.

The positions described above are all official in that they have been created by each house and are salaried. No discussion of the Congress would be complete, however, without a mention of the role played by the political leaders of the House and the Senate, the Speaker of the House of Representatives and the majority leader of the Senate. The position of the Speaker, to be sure, was established by the Founding Fathers in the Constitution, but because there were no organized political parties at the time, they envisioned it as an administrative function. With the almost immediate advent of political parties, the role of the Speaker became predominantly political as, traditionally, he is always the leader of the majority party in the House of Representatives. In the Senate, because the vice-president of the United States is the president of the body, it was natural that a position was created to provide political leadership in view of the fact that the executive branch can be controlled by one party and the Senate by the other. The majority leader is the political leader of the Senate and is elected by the majority party. The minority party also elects leaders who, although they have obviously far less power than their counterparts of the majority, organize their partisans into an effective opposition which is important in a democracy. The majority leader and the Speaker, as leaders of their party, wield tremendous political power in their respective chambers, and little is accomplished if they are not behind proposed legislation. One might suppose that when the president is of one party and the leadership of Congress of the other that a stalemate would result, but it rarely does because the men who held these extremely important positions are primarily Americans and secondarily politicians and have no desire to destroy the country because of party partisanship.

The committee system has also developed over the years in Congress to help carry out its functions with greater dispatch. Although the Constitution lists carefully the legislative responsibilities for both the House and the Senate, it does not state how these responsibilities should be carried out. With the increased number of members in both houses, it would be almost impossible for each law necessary to the country to be proposed, discussed and formulated by all members at one time. Were that the case, each law would take an unconscionable length of time to be enacted. To avoid such delays, the committee system was devised. In both the House and the Senate there are standing committees on various subjects whose job it is to prepare legislation for consideration by the full membership. In this manner all legislation pertaining to foreign affairs, for instance, is originated, debated and prepared in the proper legislative form by members and staff either of the Foreign Relations Committee of the Senate or the Foreign Affairs Committee of the House. At the moment there are sixteen regular standing committees of the Senate and twenty-two in the House. There are also subcommittees which have been made necessary by the increased amount of legislation which is considered by each session of Congress. It is hard to believe, but roughly twenty-five thousand bills are introduced in each congressional session (two years) of which some seven hundred actually become law. In addition, at any time either house may appoint a special committee if necessary to investigate any situation pertaining to the legislative function of Congress, and there are many joint committees as well, made up of members of the House and the Senate, to consider particular legislative problems of concern to both bodies.

At each new session of Congress the Senate and the House set up their standing committees, and the membership is determined by a vote of each house. This method of selecting committee membership is a recent departure from the system which existed for a great number of years. In the past the leaders of the two largest political parties, the Democrats and the Republicans, held meetings of their party members and apportioned the chairmanships of the committees. The seniority rule prevailed, and the men who had served the most consecutive terms in Congress were those who got the chairmanships of the most prestigious committees. Membership was also determined by seniority, and a new senator or representative regardless of his interests or his expertise had to be satisfied with the least important assignments. Although many senior members of the House and Senate were men of great ability, not all were, and the system had an unfortunate stultifying effect on the Congress and, therefore, on the country. In 1974 a "revolution" was effected by a number of younger members of Congress, many of them newly elected, and they overturned the system, replacing it with the present one by which members may choose their committees and elect the chairmen. This is not only fairer, but makes Congress more receptive to the will of the people who, after all, elect men and women whose ideas they like.

The process by which a legislative proposal becomes law is complicated. Bills, with the exception of those relating to taxes or impeachment which are constitutionally reserved for the House alone, may originate in either the Senate or the House. The systems by which the two bodies deal with proposals differ somewhat. A bill introduced in the Senate goes to the appropriate committee, the chairman of which either places it on his agenda or relegates it to a subcommittee. Wherever, it is next examined in detail and expert witnesses may be called to testify either for or against it. Lobbyists (people who work for private or public interest groups) pressure individual committee members in their offices or in the corridors, trying to get them to make changes advantageous to their groups or to vote for or against the bill. When the bill has been thoroughly analyzed, legislative assistants put it in the proper language, and the committee then goes over it again, section by section, in what is called a mark-up session to make sure that every word and phrase is what they want. Once this is completed, the bill is then placed on the Senate calendar, the date being set by the majority leader in consultation with the minority leader. Debate then takes place in the Senate chamber, and because Senate rules permit each senator to talk for as long as he wants, a bill may be filibustered to death. In recent years the Senate has amended its rules to permit a cloture vote which will limit debate and permit a vote, but because sixty votes are necessary to invoke cloture, it is often very hard to stop a filibuster. Few senators are willing to muzzle one of their number in a debate over a certain bill because at some future time the senator, having voted for cloture, may need the vote of the person he muzzled for the passage of one of his bills. When the Senate is ready to vote, the roll is called, and each senator answers yea or nay.

In the House, bills are introduced and written in the same way by the appropriate committee, but when they come out of committee, they must go to the Rules Committee of the House. This is the most powerful committee in the House because its members determine which legislation will be considered by the whole membership. They can effectively bottle up any proposed legislation that they do not like and keep it from a floor vote. If they do allow a bill out, they determine the amount of time which will be allowed for debate (House rules do not permit unlimited debate) and whether amendments can or cannot be introduced from the floor. The Speaker of the House, who is the majority leader of the House, is as influential as is the majority leader of the Senate in determining the fate of a bill. If he chooses to put his prestige and political clout behind a bill, the chances are great that it will pass. When the House votes, it does so electronically rather than by voice. Each member has a special voting card which he inserts in one of the forty computer terminals on the floor, and his vote is immediately recorded automatically. A running tabulation of the votes is flashed on a screen so that the representatives know which way every member has voted.

When a bill has passed one of the chambers, it goes to the other for consideration. If the House and the Senate differ, a conference is held to effect a compromise, and if one is achieved, the bill is then voted on again by both houses and, if passed, is then sent to the president for his approval. In cases of major legislation the president does not stand aside waiting for congressional action. If he wants a bill to be passed, he sends members of his White House staff as well as cabinet officers to lobby for passage, and very often when the time has come for the vote, the president himself will get on the telephone to key congressmen to urge them to follow his wishes. Presidential pressure is hard to withstand by members of his political party as presidential support at election time is of paramount importance.

If the president should veto a bill, the Congress can by a

two-thirds vote of both houses overturn it, but in recent years few attempts to overturn vetoes have succeeded, as it is difficult to muster a two-thirds vote. Although the Constitution determines that the Congress is the number one branch of the government in that it is the people's voice, the executive branch has, in fact, not only acquired a tremendous amount of power over the years, but in the eyes of the people themselves is the first branch of government. As a consequence, members of Congress have been generally loath to counter the wishes of the president. After the Watergate affair, however, there is a widespread feeling among representatives and senators that they were in part responsible for the aggrandizement of the power of the White House because they had not been exercising their constitutional obligations to maintain the balance of power as carefully as they should have. It should be noted, however, that until 1983 Congress did check executive authority for more than fifty years through the exercise of the legislative veto. Because it became virtually impossible for Congress to spell out in every case specific limitations to the authority granted to the executive in the hundreds of laws enacted every year, it maintained its oversight responsibility by including in statutes where it was applicable its right to veto decisions or orders made by the executive branch with which it disagreed. In 1983 the Supreme Court had occasion to review a case involving the legislative veto, and a majority of the justices decided that it was an unconstitutional violation of the separation of powers devised by the Founding Fathers. Not only has the decision thrown many laws already enacted containing the provision for legislative veto into legal confusion, but to some legal scholars it puts in jeopardy the power of the legislature to guard against an undue expansion of executive authority. At this point, however, it is too soon to tell if the court's decision will have that effect. Surely, in the wake of Watergate, Congress and the people of the United States are well aware of the importance of the checks-and-balances system to preserving our constitutional government.

In addition to its legislative duties, Congress supervises several organizations which at various times Congress itself has placed under its jurisdiction. The first was the Office of the Architect of the Capitol which dates from 1793. In 1800 the

Library of Congress was added, followed by the United States Botanic Garden in 1820. The Government Printing Office was authorized in 1860, and the others, the General Accounting Office, the Cost Accounting Standards Board, the Office of Technology Assessment, the Congressional Budget Office, and the Copyright Royalty Tribunal are all twentieth-century innovations.

Shortly after the federal government began to operate and it was decided to locate the permanent capital of the nation in what is now Washington, D.C., Congress authorized President Washington to appoint an architect to design the Capitol Building. Because funds for the actual construction were not always forthcoming, the Capitol was not finished until 1865, and several architects over the years were in charge of the project. After the Capitol was completed, Congress continued the job of architect of the Capitol, making him responsible for its maintenance and for the upkeep of the grounds. As the numbers of congressmen, plus their staffs, increased, the need for more office buildings arose, and today the architect of the Capitol supervises not only the Capitol and grounds, but also the Senate and House office buildings of which there are five. In addition, he has been given the Library of Congress and the Supreme Court building to care for. He also supervises the operation of the Capitol power plant which provides heat and air conditioning for all these buildings and the botanic garden as well as steam heat for the Government Printing Office, the Folger Library and the city of Washington's main post office which are all located near Capitol Hill. And for some reason he is responsible for the senate dining room.

In addition to all his expanded duties involving the care of buildings, the architect sits on various boards such as the Capitol Guide Board, the District of Columbia's Zoning Commission and the Art Advisory Committee to the Washington Metropolitan Transit Authority, to name a few. His primary task still is to preserve the United States Capitol and, should the Commission of Extension of the Capitol of which he is a member decide to alter the West Front, it will be up to the architect in large part to see that the additions do not spoil the lovely lines designed over a century ago by his predecessors.

The Library of Congress performs to this day an important

task in education for the whole country. In 1800 five thousand dollars were appropriated by Congress to establish a library for the use of the members of Congress. It was thought important to have material at hand for lawmakers to help them in their task. From that limited beginning the Library of Congress has grown into what is really a library for the whole nation, and it is one of the greatest libraries in the world. Not only does it have literary material on every conceivable subject, but it is the largest repository of American first editions as it is the official register of all copyrights in the United States. The library also houses a national collection of music and photographs of interest to the country, and one of the finest collections of manuscripts in the world. Recently it was assigned the American Folklife Center which will add significantly to its material on all aspects of our national culture. In addition, the library has made literary works available for the blind through its "talking books" program. Any visually handicapped person can order any number of books free of charge and it is fair to say that this program has changed the lives of many who are unable to pick up a book at will. Any adult can avail himself of the facilities of the library, and for those who cannot come to Washington, material can be loaned through public and private libraries throughout the nation.

Although the library has come to include many services never thought of in 1800, it still performs the specific function of helping members of Congress through the Legislative Reference Service. This service not only makes available to congressmen all material pertinent to any legislation under consideration, but on congressional demand undertakes in-depth studies into various long-range problems which confront the nation. The library is headed by a presidential appointee who has the title of librarian, but he need not be, in fact, a librarian by profession. It is a position of honor, and generally it is held by an outstanding poet, writer or educator. The Library of Congress is one of the major educational services of the federal government and is of immense value today to all Americans instead of just to the members of Congress whom it was designed to serve at a time when few libraries existed in the nation.

In 1820 the Columbia Institute for the Promotion of Arts and Sciences constituted the first botanic garden. In 1837, however, this institute was abandoned, and botanical interest flagged. In 1842 a United States exploring expedition to the South Seas caused a reopening of the Botanic Garden because it sent many specimens to Washington. Hastily a greenhouse was built to take care of the plants and was placed under the Joint Congressional Committee on the Library for want of a better place. From that humble beginning the present Botanic Garden grew. Originally its purpose was to collect and to grow plants of domestic and foreign sorts for medical use and for horticultural interest. Today the United States Botanic Garden is mainly a place for the exhibition of over ten thousand plants of all varieties, and the garden provides materials for garden clubs and other groups interested in exotic horticulture as well as for students of botany. The staff will also identify any plant from any place in the world for an interested person. The garden no longer performs any real scientific purpose, but is an interesting place for all who enjoy plants and unusual garden effects. The extremely beautiful seasonal exhibitions are one of Washington's most famous tourist attractions.

Perhaps the busiest of all government offices and certainly one of the most important is the Government Printing Office located near the Capitol in Washington. In 1860 Congress recognized the importance to our democracy of making all government documents and records readily available to the public and, therefore, established the Government Printing Office in that year. Unlike the librarian of Congress, the public printer who heads the office must be a professional printer and bookbinder, and he is appointed by the president and confirmed by the Senate. The Government Printing Office publishes every record, document, pamphlet or book produced by the departments and agencies of the government with the exception of the opinions of the Supreme Court of the United States which are printed in the Court building. All material printed by the Government Printing Office is available to the public at modest prices either through the mail or at government bookstores, and over twenty-five thousand items are sold each year. The office also serves the public by making a selected list of important government documents available to public libraries throughout the nation. In addition to its publishing business, the Government Printing Office supplies every federal office across the land with paper, ink, pens, paper clips and other materials upon request.

The work of the General Accounting Office is probably the least glamorous of government functions, but it is of the greatest importance to every citizen of the United States in that it is the auditor of the government's books and, as such, is the guardian of the public's money. Set up in 1921 as an independent, nonpolitical agency, it is run by the comptroller general of the United States and his deputy, both of whom are appointed by the president and confirmed by the Senate. They serve, however, not at the president's pleasure, but for a term of fifteen years. This means that they are not subject to removal from office when an administration changes, and they have, therefore, an independence not shared by other presidential appointees in the executive branch. This independence is vital to their work which is to guarantee that the enormous government expenditures are made for exactly what they are supposed to and that there is no juggling of the books or cheating. Although the General Accounting Office is under the jurisdiction of Congress, it checks congressional appropriations as carefully as it does the expenditures of the executive departments. The office also serves Congress in a multitude of ways, and the comptroller general and his staff undertake special investigations at Congress's request and provide expert testimony at many committee hearings among other things.

The Office of Technology Assessment also was recently deemed necessary by Congress because so much technological change is taking place so rapidly that it is almost impossible to keep up with it all and to evaluate its impact on American life. Congressmen simply do not have the time to keep abreast nor do many have the expertise to assess new developments. They, therefore, set up this office manned by experts to assess technological advances and to try to determine what their effects will be. This is an example of Congress's being foresighted so that it will be prepared to cope with new situations caused by technological changes with appropriate legislation.

The Congressional Budget Office is a recent innovation. As was described above in the section on the Office of Management and Budget in the executive offices of the White House, the Congressional Budget Office was set up to provide Congress with its own assessment of the nation's needs and to give those responsible for setting the budget for the United States an alternative to that prepared by the White House. Because of the billions of dollars that are spent every year by the Government, it is imperative that every dollar be for a truly necessary program, and, as the adage says, many heads are really better than one. The fact that Congress has set up its own budget office is a reflection of the new determination of the legislative branch to fulfill its constitutional role as a separate and equal branch of government and to serve the American people more efficiently by assuming its share of the responsibility for deciding how much money they must pay in taxes and for what services.

The Copyright Royalty Tribunal is also now a part of the legislative branch. It was set up in 1976 by Congress in response to the necessity of seeing that royalties for the copyrighted works enjoyed by the public through various electronic media are duly paid. The authors of records played in jukeboxes, for instance, are entitled to royalties as are the creators of works of art such as sculpture, graphics and pictures which are shown on public broadcasting stations and cablevision. The Copyright Royalty Tribunal not only protects the interests of artists, but it also makes cost-of-living adjustments for non-commercial broadcasting stations in order for them to cope with rising costs due to inflation. The establishment of this new tribunal is another example of the government's constant need to assume new responsibilities to meet the demands of changing times.

Because of the tremendous expansion of the responsibilities of the federal government since 1789, the legislative branch has had to adapt itself to meet the challenges of changing times in much the same manner as has the executive branch. Congress's purpose, however, remains the same as when the first session was gaveled into order, that of enacting the laws by which the nation lives.

THE ORGANIZATION OF THE
FEDERAL JUDICIARY

IT IS VERY surprising in view of the extraordinary importance of the judiciary to the preservation of our constitutional
system to realize how little this branch of the federal government has changed over the two hundred years of its existence.
Whereas the executive and legislative branches would hardly
be recognizable to the Founding Fathers, they would find far
less change if they had to deal with the judiciary. The Supreme Court is now set at nine members, a small increase
from the six that George Washington was authorized to appoint. The district courts now number ninety-one instead of
the original thirteen, and instead of three circuit courts of
appeals, manned by two justices and one district judge, the
twelve courts of appeals in operation today have their own
judges. The duties that these courts perform are very much
the same as when they were first established. The Founding
Fathers would discover, however, that since their day nine
new courts have come into existence to handle special kinds
of cases, a consequence of the enormous growth in the
complexities of life from the eighteenth to the twentieth
century, but they would find that the Supreme Court justices
and the other federal judges still manage to get their work
done with only a few assistants and that the courts run with a
comparatively small staff. The Founding Fathers would undoubtedly be surprised to find that the United States Supreme Court is now housed in an elegant marble building
across the avenue from the Capitol and not far from the

White House, the construction of which many of them lived to see.

In the beginning, and until a generation ago, the Supreme Court had no home and, when it sat, it used a chamber in the Capitol. Only in the 1930s did Congress authorize the construction of a courthouse for the highest bench in the land. Today the nine justices work from the beginning of October to the end of June in the Supreme Court building. There the associate justices have chambers of modest size—a room for themselves, one for their secretaries, another for their two law clerks. The chief justice has more office space and four law clerks because he has several extra duties which justify more help. He is in charge of the administration of the Court and he is the chairman of the Judicial Conference of the United States. The courtroom is in the center of the main floor of the building and is also of modest proportions. The nine justices sit behind the bench with the chief justice in the middle, and members of the Supreme Court bar, who are the only lawyers who can practice before the Court, plead their cases, standing only a few feet in front of them. As is the case with all the courts in the nation, the public is welcome to attend sessions. The staff of the Supreme Court consists of the clerk, the reporter of decisions, the marshal and the librarian. The clerk receives all petitions requesting that cases be heard by the Court, files them, and places them on the docket. The reporter sees that all the records and opinions of the Court are printed, bound and distributed to the proper people. All Court printing is done on the premises to preclude any leaks concerning the Court's decisions prior to their announcement from the bench. The marshal is the executive officer of the Court, and he serves any writs of execution ordered by the Court which, it is interesting to note, are issued not in the name of the Court, but in the name of the United States of America and the president of the United States. The marshal has no powers to enforce writs nor does he have any police authority because once a decision is made, it is the responsibility of the executive branch to see that it is obeyed. He is also responsible to the chief justice for the administration of the Court. The librarian is in charge of the Supreme Court library which houses a large collection of law books for the use of the law clerks and the members of the Supreme Court bar as well as, of course, the justices. These staff members are all appointed by the Court, and each is a position of honor. The justices, the marshal and the librarian are also served by pages. These are young boys and girls who are selected by the Court to act as messengers, running quietly in and out of the courtroom, fetching needed law books or other materials for the justices during a court session and helping in a myriad of ways when the Court is not sitting. These young people, who are educated at government expense, have one of the most coveted jobs in Washington, but one that is generally of short duration. Traditionally, when a page grows taller than the justices' chairs, he or she resigns.

The judges of the courts of appeals and the district courts are similarly assisted by law clerks, clerks of the court, and the United States marshals who, unlike the marshal of the Supreme Court, do have authority to issue subpoenas and to use police powers. The United States attorneys are also closely associated with the district courts and courts of appeals, as they are the government's prosecuting attorneys, but they are responsible to the attorney general. Also serving the district courts are one or more magistrates, probation officers, court reporters, referees in bankruptcy and bailiffs. In some cities these court officers are housed in court houses, but in many cases their work is conducted in federal buildings which house other government operations as well. Many of the federal courthouses which exist for the special use of the United States courts were built during the Great Depression, as was the Supreme Court building in Washington, to give jobs to the unemployed in the construction trade. The number of judges on these courts differ from district to district and circuit to circuit, depending on the business before the courts. In the Southern District of New York, for example, the tremendous number of cases requires many judges, whereas in Maine there are only two. The jurisdiction of the circuit courts covers several states, and to four of them one of the United States territories is assigned as well. The first circuit, for instance, covers Maine, New Hampshire, Rhode Island and Puerto Rico. In the district courts one judge usually hears a case, and in the circuit courts, if there are many judges, three generally sit together on a case, but in cases of great significance the court will sit "en banc" which means that all the judges are present. In addition, the justices of the Supreme Court are each assigned to one of the appeals courts. They do not sit on the court, but if the Supreme Court is not in session and an urgent question arises in a case before a court of appeals which must be answered immediately, an appeal is made to the assigned justice.

The circuit courts of appeals came into being in 1891 to relieve the Supreme Court from having to consider every case on appeal from the district courts. By statute the circuit courts are empowered to review final decision of the district courts. They also review and enforce orders of some of the federal administrative agencies, such as the Securities and Exchange Commission and the Federal Communications Commission. The district courts are the trial courts where a federal case will begin and from which, if there is good reason, appeals may be made either to the circuits or in certain cases to the Supreme Court.

In addition to these courts which hear all cases, civil and criminal, which fall under federal jurisdiction, Congress over the years has created special courts to meet specific needs as they have arisen. The United States Tax Court, for instance, deals with controversies over federal tax laws, particularly the income tax. That tax was expressly forbidden by the original Constitution and could only be legislated after 1916 when the Constitution was amended to permit it. In 1926 Congress set up a board to hear appeals from taxpayers; it was elevated to court status in 1942, and in 1969 its name was changed to the United States Tax Court. It tries cases involving controversies over the amounts owed the government in all federal tax categories, income, gift, estate, etc. Appeals may be made to the United States courts of appeals and to the Supreme Court if it grants a writ of certiorari. Sixteen judges sit on the tax court with the chief judge elected biennially from the group. Retired judges are often called back into service because of the heavy case load, and the chief judge also appoints seven special trial judges to help hear initial pleadings. The court sits in

Washington, but trial sessions are held across the country as a convenience to taxpayers who are at odds with Internal Revenue.

Much older is the United States Court of Claims which was created in 1855. This court handles all claims against the United States arising from the Constitution, acts of Congress or rulings of executive departments. A few examples are: if the government exercises its right of eminent domain, which means the confiscation of property, and if the property owner thinks he has not been paid sufficiently, he can press his claim in this court; claims for back pay by civil servants or the military come to this court also as do claims for refunds from tax payments. In addition, the court hears cases on appeal from Indian tribes who argue the decision of the Indian Claims Commission. The court has jurisdiction across the entire nation, and when a suit is filed against the United States, the initial hearings are held as near to the plaintiff as is convenient. The court, however, sits in Washington and consists of the chief judge and six associates.

The work of the United States Customs Court began in 1890, but it only became a part of the federal judiciary system in 1956. In 1980 its name was changed to the United States Court of International Trade. Unlike the other special courts, this court's main headquarters are in New York City because when it was established, New York was the major port of entry in the country, and the primary function of the court was and still is to hear cases arising under the tariff laws of the nation. The chief judge and the eight associate judges do hold hearings in other major ports of entry today, because, quite obviously, there are many other cities to which imports come. These judges decide cases involving the value of imported goods and the amount of duty owed, among other things, and if the plaintiff is not satisfied with the court's decision, he may appeal the verdict to the United States Court of Customs and Patent Appeals which sits in Washington. This court hears, in addition to tariff cases, appeals from the United States Patent and Trademark Office, the United States International Trade Commission, and the secretaries of commerce and of agriculture under the Educa-

tion, Scientific and Cultural Materials Act and the Plant
Variety Protection Act. Judgments by this court are final
unless the Supreme Court agrees to an appeal.

Three other special courts are the territorial courts, the
United States Court of Military Appeals and the Temporary
Emergency Court of Appeals. The territorial courts in Guam,
the Virgin Islands and the Panama Canal Zone handle federal
as well as local questions which in the states would be in the jurisdiction of the state courts. In Puerto Rico the territorial
court is a district court in that the commonwealth has its own
courts for problems other than those arising under federal
law. In the territories the judges are appointed by the president and confirmed by the Senate, but for an eight-year term.
Those in Puerto Rico are life appointments as are the district
judges in the states. The fact that we have the military appeals
court reaffirms the Founding Fathers' conviction that federal
authority must ultimately belong to civilians and not to the
military. This court of three civilian judges, appointed by the
president and confirmed by the Senate, reviews appeals from
members of all the armed services who have been court-mar-
tialed. These cases include convictions requiring the death
penalty, and those resulting in imprisonment for more than
one year or in a dishonorable discharge. The judges work
closely with the judge advocates general of the armed services
and the general counsel of the Department of Transportation,
who is responsible for legal proceedings against members of
the Coast Guard, and together they are required to report annually to Congress and to suggest improvements in the handling of justice in the military. This court only came into being
in 1950 because prior to that time the United States maintained a comparatively small military in peacetime, and problems of military justice were not as acute as they would become when, due to international tensions, the number of
persons serving in the armed forces had to be greatly increased.

The Temporary Emergency Court of Appeals is very recent
and came into being in 1972 to handle very specific problems
arising under the Economic Stabilization Act passed by
Congress in 1971. Because of the poor state of the economy,

inflation going up monthly, unemployment rising, and the gross national product stagnating, the administration and Congress sought to stimulate it by this act which contained many new regulations which were subject to conflicting interpretations. This special court had to be established in order to adjudicate these disputes because the existing courts' dockets were too crowded to allow for the resolution of problems rapidly enough to fulfill the purpose of the act.

The remaining two special courts are for the District of Columbia, the superior court and the District of Columbia Court of Appeals. These two courts took the burden from the United States district court and the United States court of appeals in local matters that elsewhere would be in the state jurisdiction, cases which overcrowded the calendars of the two federal courts. In 1969, therefore, Congress enacted a court reorganization which provided the residents of the District of Columbia with their own court to hear civil and criminal cases and a court of appeals to make final judgments which can be appealed for proper cause to the United States court of appeals and, if need be, to the Supreme Court, providing that it grants certiorari.

It was mentioned above that the chief justice of the United States is the chairman of the Judicial Conference of the United States. This is the governing body of the United States judicial system. In addition to the chief justice, the conference is made up of the chief judge of each circuit and a district judge from each circuit elected by his peers and the judges of the circuit court in which his district lies, the chief judge of the Court of Claims and the chief judge of the Court of Customs and Patent Appeals. The purpose of the annual conference is to review the state of justice in the nation and to improve its quality. It is assisted in this work by two organizations which report to the conference, the Administrative Office of the United States Courts and the Federal Judicial Center.

The Administrative Office of the United States Courts was set up by Congress in 1939 to administer the entire federal judiciary by carrying out the day-to-day details for the judicial conference. The director and his deputy are appointed by the Supreme Court, not by the president. They are responsible for setting the salaries for court assistants where they are not covered by statute, and they supervise the pensions and annuities paid to widows and dependent children of deceased judges. They are also in charge of the accommodations for the courts and for all their supplies. The director is also responsible for the federal probation officers and magistrates who serve the district courts, and since 1970 he provides for the federal Public Defender Service required by the Criminal Justice Act of that year. This responsibility came in response to the dictate of the Bill of Rights guaranteeing the right of a criminal defendant to counsel. Because this service must be paid for from congressional appropriations, the director prepares its budget as he does those for all the courts, except for the Supreme Court which prepares its own, which are then submitted to Congress. The director and his staff serve the Judicial Conference by preparing annual reports pinpointing the needs of the federal courts and making recommendations for remedies for the conference's consideration. The Federal Judicial Center, a recent innovation, also serves the Judicial Conference. It is more of a "think tank" than an action agency, and its staff studies ways by which justice might be improved in the United States. Its work is supervised by a board chaired by the chief justice and made up of two circuit court and three district judges and the director of the administrative office of the United States courts.

Two subjects have preoccupied the Judicial Conference in recent years, the problem of the tremendously increased case load in all the federal courts, and the question of judges' salaries which have not kept pace with inflation. The problem of too many cases could be solved by the creation of additional judgeships for the district and circuit courts. The burden of work for the Supreme Court justices is perhaps more complicated. In 1948 Congress established the number of associate justices at eight, the chief justice making the full Court nine. The Court had, in fact, for many years had nine members, but the number was not established by law until 1948, and it came about largely to prevent any president from "packing the Court" as President Roosevelt had attempted to do in 1936. Americans not only are very tradition-minded and like the

Court as it has been, but are, in addition, loath to give a president the authority to appoint more justices for fear that politics would endanger the Court's objectivity. In recent years the Judicial Conference, to avoid the political pitfalls of suggesting that the number of justices be increased, has proposed an alternative solution to the overwork of the Court, that of creating a national court of appeals which would relieve the Supreme Court of certain designated types of cases, thereby allowing the justices to address themselves only to cases of great constitutional import. To date, Congress has not responded to the suggestion. It has addressed, however, the problem of judicial salaries, and in 1977 salaries were raised a certain amount. This was a very important step because, as the chief justice of the Supreme Court had pointed out, some of the very best judges in the country were resigning because they could not afford to remain on the federal bench and others who were asked to serve had to refuse for the same reason. It is doubtful, however, that the 1977 salary increases will long be adequate in the face of continuing inflation.

Justice is not an absolute, and the quality of justice for the people of the United States depends to a large extent on the ability, dedication, and integrity of the men and women who serve the federal judiciary.

THE INDEPENDENT AGENCIES

THE EXECUTIVE, the legislative and the judicial branches of the federal government were designed to provide for an effective government for the American people. Since 1789, however, as the size and the responsibilities of the federal government have increased, there have been established other government commissions, agencies and administrations* in Washington in addition to the three constitutional branches. Each has come into being to perform a function by an act of Congress which grants it specific powers. Although they are called independent, these agencies are closely tied to the three branches in that the president appoints the chairmen and the commissioners, the Senate confirms his choices, Congress authorizes their budgets, and, in certain cases, the judiciary may review their decisions. In addition, each agency is required to file a report either once or twice a year with Congress, and the power of Congress to institute special investigations means that the work of these commissions or agencies can be closely followed by the interested committee in Congress. In 1883, with the establishment of the Civil Service Commission Congress began the practice of setting up these extraconstitutional bodies as the most efficient way to provide management and regulation for problems which no existing part of the government was equipped to handle.

These independent agencies are, in general, of three kinds: the strictly regulatory agencies, agencies which administer

---

*Commissions are headed by multi-membered bodies whereas agencies and administrations are run by a single person.

programs authorized by Congress, and the quasi-official, meaning that they are partly private. As there are well over fifty, only a few of each type will be briefly described. Some of the main regulatory ones are: the Interstate Commerce Commission, the Federal Reserve System, the Federal Trade Commission, the Securities and Exchange Commission, the Federal Deposit Insurance Corporation, the Federal Communications Commission, the Equal Opportunity Commission, the Environmental Protection Agency, the Nuclear Regulatory Commission and the Federal Election Commission. Examples of the second kind are: the National Aeronautics and Space Administration, the General Services Administration, the United States Postal Service, ACTION, and the National Foundation for the Arts and Humanities. The Smithsonian Institution and the American National Red Cross will serve to illustrate the quasi-official ones. This partial list has been selected because each deals with a different and new facet of national life which has required federal attention. Had Congress or the executive attempted to perform all these necessary functions, both branches would have been completely bogged down under the weight of detail and, therefore, unable to carry out their essential constitutional duties.

The Interstate Commerce Commission

The Interstate Commerce Commission has an interesting history. It is the second oldest of the federal regulatory agencies as it was set up by Congress in 1887. The ICC was originally only responsible for regulating the nation's railroads. Before the government stepped in, many of the railroads, upon which a large proportion of interstate commerce depended at the time, had engaged in practices such as rebates, different rate schedules for favored customers, etc., and the public was being unfairly treated. The first task, then, of the commission was to set fair rates and to insure good rail service for the benefit of all Americans. In the twentieth century the ICC's regulatory powers were extended to cover all interstate surface transportation: truck, bus, inland and coastal shipping (including that which passed through the Panama Canal), express companies, and such foreign commerce that took place within the United States. The commission was responsible for seeing that the public was well served by adequate transportation at reasonable cost. If carriers disputed the rates set by the ICC, they were entitled to a hearing, but they had to abide by the commission's decision. The ICC also certified all carriers, regulated mergers or purchases of one carrier by another, and decided if rail lines which served few customers were to be continued or not.

For many a decade the American people did not question the regulatory authority of the commission as it appeared to serve their interests. Take moving, for example, as Americans are the most mobile people on earth, and practically everyone has experienced at least one move across state lines. The ICC made the job much easier. No one needed to waste time, for instance, calling different moving companies to compare prices because they were all set by the commission, and the person moving did not have to wonder whether the price charged was correct because it was determined by weight as well as distance. Each moving van crossing state lines had to have its load weighed at an official station and the charge was then computed.

Recently, however, public attitudes toward federal regulation of the transportation industry have changed, and many feel that the public would be better served by more competition between carriers rather than less. In 1980, therefore, Congress responded by enacting three laws, the Motor Carrier Act, the Staggers Rail Act, and the Household Goods Transportation Act, each of which sharply curtailed the regulatory authority of the ICC. Today there is competitive pricing in the trucking and railroad industries, and those planning a move, for instance, would be well advised to shop among moving companies for the best price. The ICC still, however, has authority to prevent discriminatory or unfair pricing, rebates and the like, as they are still illegal. It settles disputes between competing transportation companies, and it still retains authority over mergers, the sale of carriers, and controls the disposition of assets in cases of railroad bankruptcies among other things. Its sharply reduced work-load is reflected in the fact that although eleven commission-ers are authorized, only six man the commission today. Presi-dent Reagan has not filled the five vacancies. Whether deregulation will better serve the public only time will tell, but the fact that it has taken place after almost one hundred years in which regulation was the order of the day is proof that Congress is ever responsive to the public's demands.

The Federal Reserve System

Until 1914 the United States had no central banking system. In 1791, acting on an idea proposed by Alexander Hamilton, the first secretary of the treasury, Congress chartered a United States bank which was a cooperative venture between the federal government which put up one-fifth of the capital and private bankers who put up the other four-fifths. Together they managed the bank until its charter expired in 1811. For five years there was no United States bank, but because the financial affairs of the nation suffered, Congress rechartered it in 1816. The second bank, although it, in fact, did encourage the economic development of the country, was heartily disliked by westerners who felt it was a monopoly dic-tated by eastern bankers, and Andrew Jackson, the first presi-dent from the West, effectively destroyed it by vetoing the bill to recharter it in 1832. The second bank, then, ceased opera-tions in 1836 with the expiration of its charter. In 1862, to en-able the government to meet in part the heavy cost of the Civil War, Congress passed the National Banking Act which set up a system whereby well-capitalized private banks could enter into a mutually profitable relationship with the federal gov-ernment. The government, which required gold to finance the war, sold bonds to the national banks and allowed them to use these bonds, up to 90 percent of their value, as assets upon which to lend money at interest to private citizens. The gov-ernment got the gold, and the banks made money from the interest on their bonds and from the interest paid by bor-rowers. It was a sound system and with modification is still in existence and is regulated today by the comptroller of the currency. The national banking system is not, however, a central banking system, and none existed in the nineteenth century.

By the turn of the twentieth century, it became evident that a central system was necessary to end the erratic fluctuations of the national economy between booms and busts and to assure the circulation of a stable currency to meet the demands of the economy as well. A bipartisan committee was set up by Congress to study the problem, and in 1913 Congress adopted the committee's report and passed the Glass-Owen Act establishing the Federal Reserve System which began operations in 1914.

The Federal Reserve is a bank for banks. If the economy requires more currency to stimulate business, the Fed, as it is called, makes money available to member banks at a low rate of interest. The member banks borrow from the Reserve and then lend at lower interest rates to private borrowers which increases the amount of currency in circulation. To reverse the flow of money if the economy heats up too much, the Fed ups its interest rates and reduces the amount of circulating currency by requiring member banks to pay off their loans. The Fed also regulates the amount of currency in the country by selling and buying government securities. If it sells securities, it decreases the supply of money available for investment, and, conversely, if it buys securities, it is increasing the supply.

The Federal Reserve System also inaugurated a new, decentralized banking system. There are twelve federal reserve banks across the nation which results in a more balanced geographic distribution of funds. If a natural disaster strikes in the West, and ranchers, for instance, must borrow heavily, their local banks are able to borrow funds from their federal reserve branch to meet the sudden demand. The federal reserve branch, if it needs to, can get the additional funds from another federal region. This system has ended the situation which had occurred repeatedly before the establishment of the Federal Reserve System in which banks, particularly in the agricultural regions of the nation, were unable to meet the demands of their customers nor were their customers able in times of disaster or falling prices to repay loans. Bankruptcies were all too frequent, bringing hardship to a great number of Americans.

The Federal Reserve System is managed by a board of seven governors who are appointed by the president and confirmed by the Senate. They serve for fourteen years. The chairman, who is also appointed by the president, has a four-year term but does not resign when a new administration takes office. The chairman is one of the most influential men in Washington because he and the board of the Fed have one of the toughest responsibilities in government. They must first accurately gauge the state of the economy and then adopt a monetary policy which will encourage the stability and growth of our economic life. The Federal Reserve Board is independent of the executive branch, but must work very closely with the president, the secretary of the treasury and the Council of Economic Advisers. If these members of the executive department disagree with the board of the Federal Reserve, it can be a very difficult and tense situation, but the fact that the board is an independent and essentially nonpolitical group is of value in the determination of economic and monetary policies which affect every American.

The Federal Trade Commission

The Federal Trade Commission (FTC) was set up in 1915. Its authority was derived originally from two acts of Congress, the Federal Trade Commission Act and the Clayton Act, both passed in 1914. The purpose of the acts was to maintain the American system of free enterprise in business and to prevent unfair competition or deceptive trade practices. Since 1915 many other acts of Congress have enlarged its jurisdiction. The Export Act, the Wool Products Labeling Act, the Fur Products Labeling Act, the Flammable Fabrics Act, the Lanham Trademark Act, the Truth-in-Lending Act, the Fair Packaging and Labeling Act and the Fair Credit Reporting Act have each added a new function to the Trade Commission's job. The commission carries out these laws in specific ways. The commission sees that free and fair competition in interstate commerce is maintained by preventing price fixing arrangements, agreements or boycotts, by preventing combinations whose purpose it is to restrain free trade, and by stopping all unfair and deceptive practices of any sort. The commission safeguards the public by checking for misrepresentations all advertisements of foods, drugs, cosmetics or therapeutic gadgets. Although all advertisements exaggerate to some extent, they may not mislead the purchaser either in a manner dangerous to him or in a manner calculated to cheat him. Any form of price discrimination, exclusive dealings or tie-in sales are strictly forbidden in the interest of free enterprise. The commission also forbids the mergers of corporations should such combinations be of monopolistic purpose or effect. All fur and wool garments must be properly and honestly labeled to guard the public from fraud. A mink must be a mink and not a dyed muskrat. With the introduction of synthetic fabrics, the commission took on the job of protecting the public against flammable materials. Some of the synthetic yarns, at first, turned out to be highly dangerous in that they would unexpectedly burst into flames, burning the unsuspecting user badly. The commission prevents the sale of any such hazardous fabrics. It also receives and deals with petitions for the cancellation of false trademarks, thereby protecting the consumers from fraudulent products.

In recent years the widespread practice of Americans of buying on credit has caused Congress to pass the Truth-in-Lending Act and the Fair Credit Reporting Act, both of which are implemented by the commission. Before the Truth-in-Lending Act a person buying a car, a household appliance or anything on time was all too frequently misled as to the actual cost of financing, and often to his sorrow he found that he was paying far more than he had originally bargained for. Now every consumer is protected by this law which mandates that the true cost of paying in installments is revealed honestly and in clear language. Bills, for instance, now state that a service charge of 1-1/2 percent per month, or 18 percent annually, will be added thirty days after the bill is presented (every debtor has thirty days in which to pay the full amount). The percentage is that authorized by the government. In addition, so many Americans today use credit cards that Congress in 1970 amended the original act to include federal regulation of the issuance of credit cards, the holder's liability and the fraudulent use of a card by someone other than the rightful owner. Companies simply used to mail a new card when the old one had expired. Now the customer must ask for a new one. Before 1970 if a card was stolen and used, the true owner was liable for the charges run up by the usurper. Now he is liable only for fifty dollars if he has notified the issuer of the card, and penalties have been prescribed for those fraudulently using credit cards for amounts of five thousand dollars or more in interstate or foreign commerce. The Federal Trade Commission is required to enforce these consumer safeguards over retailers or credit unions that are not already covered by federal statutes. Credit is not issued simply on demand for obvious reasons, but the reporting and evaluation of an individual's credit worthiness, if uncontrolled, could lead to an invasion of privacy. Congress, therefore, again in response to a relatively new business practice, passed the Fair Credit Reporting Act to protect the consumer against unfair practices and to permit him to have access to any material which has been collected about him by a credit company or detective agency. This kind of information could be detrimental to a person as he looked for work, for instance, and he must know what it is in order to be able to refute it if it is not accurate.

The commission carries out its functions by issuing "cease and desist" orders to companies or individuals who break any of the trade laws. Although the commission has legislative and judicial functions, it cannot punish offenders. If any infractor refuses to comply with the "cease and desist" order, the offender is then brought to justice in either a United States district court or an appellate court. Not in every case is an order necessary. The commission carries out much of its work by voluntary compliance. When the commission discovers an infringement and points it out to the culprit, more often than not he will willingly stop the offending practice. The "cease and desist" order is for the few who refuse to obey voluntarily.

The work load of the commission necessitates a large and well-organized staff. The commission is headed by five members who are appointed by the president and confirmed by the Senate, each for seven years. No more than three members can be of the same political affiliation at one time. From the five, the president appoints a chairman. Serving under the commissioners is an able staff, the majority of whom are lawyers, each responsible for a specific aspect of the commission's work. Cases come to the Federal Trade Commission through its own investigative department or on appeal by either individuals or companies. Anyone who detects an infringement of a trade law and reports it to the commission is guaranteed secrecy. The name of the person who complains is never disclosed. He may produce his evidence or he may ask the commission to investigate a situation without concrete proof of an infringement. If the violation is real, and there is no voluntary compliance, and a "cease and desist" order is ignored, the United States Department of Justice takes over the case and the offenders are punished by fines, jail terms or both. Free enterprise is guaranteed for all Americans by this commission and rarely does a scheme to defraud the public go undetected.

The Securities and Exchange Commission

One of the immediate causes of the Great Depression of the 1930s was the crash of the New York Stock Exchange which occurred in October of 1929. The crash came about because of many reasons, but two were of major importance. Stocks of questionable value could be offered with impunity because there were no restrictions on the issuance of stock, and stocks could be purchased on margin—that is, the buyer had only to pay a fraction of the price at the time of purchase, with the result that the price went up regardless of the fact that little or no money had exchanged hands. Because the mood of the 1920s was one of exuberance, confidence in business and in the ability of the economy to grow endlessly led a great number of people who in earlier days would not have been interested in investing in the stock market to believe that they would make a killing. The end result was that prices soared to unprecedented heights and bore little relation to the actual value of the companies that had issued them. When it appeared that prices had hit their peak, selling began, and soon became endemic. Within hours, stocks that had had a high paper value were worthless, and those who had invested their savings were wiped out. The crash had a ripple effect on the overall economy, slowing it down until by 1932 it had come to a dead halt.

When President Franklin Roosevelt took office in 1933, one of his strongest convictions was the need to protect the average investor against untoward practices in the securities business, and to that end he urged Congress to pass the Securities and Exchange Act which it did in 1934. The act established the Securities and Exchange Commission (SEC) which is manned by five presidentially appointed commissioners, one of whom is named chairman. The SEC is one of the most important and successful of the New Deal legacies. The law under which it operates requires companies that issue securities for sale through the mail or in interstate commerce to file a statement with the commission regarding all financial information concerning the business and the stock to be issued. Although the commission does not endorse issues which come before it nor in any way guarantee a purchaser success with his investment, the fact that a company must file before selling means that it is highly unlikely that it will offer fraudulent stock. If a company omits filing all the pertinent data required by the law and then offers the issue for sale, it is subject to prosecution. If the individuals involved are found guilty, they are subject to fines, imprisonment or both. The law, in addition, requires that the national stock exchanges be registered with the commission which sets guidelines for their practices as well as for brokers who deal in over-the-counter stocks (stocks that are not sold on the big exchanges) and investment counselors.

The Securities and Exchange Act also authorizes the Federal Reserve Board to establish a required minimum down payment when a stock is purchased and to set a time limit for the full payment. Today, therefore, buying on margin is restricted, and as a result prices cannot be pushed up artificially as they were in the 1920s.

Since the passage of the Securities and Exchange Act and the establishment of the Securities and Exchange Commission, the person interested in investing in the nation's businesses through the purchase of stock is as fully protected as the government can possibly assure. There is, of course, still risk because the market continues to fluctuate in response to the demand for stocks. Confidence in the way the economy is working is a basic factor in the performance of the stock market, and that confidence is based on many different things, both national and international. If confidence begins to slip, prices will generally decline, but dividends do not necessarily decrease as well. Investment in stocks is a way of investing in America and strengthening the free enterprise system, but the wise investor will be sure to avail himself of the information gathered by the Securities and Exchange Commission to avoid making an unwise investment.

The Federal Deposit Insurance Corporation

The Federal Deposit Insurance Corporation (FDIC) came into being as a direct result of the bank failures which occurred because of the Great Depression. Although bank failures had been a fact of life from the beginning of the nation's history, never before had they occurred on the scale of the 1930s, and the fact that so many Americans lost their life's savings prompted federal action. In 1933, therefore, Congress set up this government corporation as an independent agency primarily to insure depositors against losing their money through no fault of their own, and secondarily, to supervise certain aspects of the banking industry to insure against possible bankruptcy. Today the Federal Deposit Insurance Corporation insures each American who has money in a bank under the corporation's jurisdiction up to one hundred thousand dollars.

The corporation does not receive any funding through congressional appropriations, but gets its assets from assessments on deposits held by the banks it insures and from income derived from the investments it makes in government securities. In addition, in case of a tremendous economic collapse, which fortunately has not occurred to date, the corporation is authorized to borrow up to three billion dollars from the United States Treasury.

Thus, Americans since 1933 have been relieved of the worry that bedeviled earlier generations, that of losing their money, because they know that should their insured bank fail, they will be promptly reimbursed by this agency of the federal government. As a result of this guarantee against loss, the ordinary depositor has contributed greatly to the nation's economic growth in that his deposits, particularly in savings accounts, have enabled banks to fund loans for industrial, business and home construction or expansion. The banks covered by this insurance are the national banks, state banks that are members of the Federal Reserve System and other state banks that wish to join and qualify for membership. No one need wonder whether his or her bank is insured because the member banks display prominently the corporation's sign stating that their depositors' accounts are insured by the Federal Deposit Insurance Corporation.

The corporation is run by a board of directors: one, by law, is the comptroller of the currency, and the other two are presidential appointees confirmed by the Senate for six-year terms. The majority of the corporation's staff are bank examiners who work in the field enforcing the regulations which by statute the corporation is authorized to make. In general, these regulations relate to seeing that sound banking practices are followed so that depositors are further protected from possible bank failures. The examiners serve notice if they find a member bank or its individual officers engaged in questionable operations, and, if the bank fails to comply with corrective orders, the corporation may terminate its insurance coverage. In addition, should a national bank overextend its resources and have to go into receivership, its affairs by law are managed by the corporation. If state banks go into receivership, the corporation will act as the receiver only if requested to by the state banking authorities. The work of this federal corporation is of proven value because in its more than forty years of existence it has, in fact, protected depositors, and it has provided such excellent watchdog service that bank failures are now relatively uncommon.

The Federal Communications Commission

If you have ever wondered why it is that each of the channels on your television set or each station on your radio comes through clearly instead of being all muddled up together or that when you pick up the telephone and dial a number anywhere in the nation you are instantly connected, it is because of the Federal Communications Commission (FCC). This independent federal agency came into being in 1934 because of the need to regulate modern communications systems. Only the federal government could take on this task because no other unit could regulate airwaves and wire services which cannot be contained within state boundaries and, indeed, cross the oceans as well, in order to provide orderly and efficient service to the public.

Each new advance in communications has increased the authority of the FCC, and today it is responsible for the regulation of radio and television broadcasting, telephone and telegraph service, cable television, two-way radio, citizen band radio, radio operators and satellite communications. No one can simply start to broadcast, but must appeal to the commission for permission. The commission has a difficult job in that it must balance the requirements for efficient, fast service and the need for economic competition under our free enterprise system. It licenses broadcasters, therefore, for a certain period, and then they must apply for a renewal. With the advent of communication satellites, the commission had to decide how much traffic could be carried by satellite and how much by the older cable systems. These decisions are not easy because technological advances often mean better service, but it would be highly undesirable to cut back services that have been provided by other systems because it would mean financial hardship for all who had invested in the earlier service. The commission, therefore, tries to divide the communications field in an equitable way and at the same time enable the public to enjoy good service at reasonable rates.

In addition to setting rates for telephone service and awarding radio frequencies and television channels, the commission is also responsible for seeing that safety standards are adhered to and that the nation's communications systems are prepared to handle any kind of emergency that might arise. It should be emphasized that regulations set by the FCC do not in any way have to do with program content. The commissioners may deplore the level of offerings (a few years back a commissioner was quoted as saying that much of television was "a cultural wasteland") or they may approve of it, but they may not control it.

The Equal Employment Opportunity Commission

No agency is more illustrative of the revolution which has taken place in American society in recent years than the Equal Employment Opportunity Commission (EEOC). There is no denying that for a long time prejudice against race, color, creed and sex did play a role in employment practices, and blacks, women, Hispanics and other minority groups found themselves excluded from jobs for no other reason than their sex, color, race, age or creed. In the postwar years this inherently unfair and un-American situation became the focal point of widespread dissatisfaction which climaxed in the 1960s, and in 1964 President Johnson called upon Congress to take steps to end this kind of discrimination. The Civil Rights Act passed in that year not only guaranteed equal rights to all Americans, but established the Equal Employment Opportunity Commission to see that the law is enforced.

The commission's primary job is to end discriminatory practices in hiring, promotion and dismissals. Persons who feel they are being discriminated against by employers may appeal to the commission in writing. The commission will then investigate, and if it finds evidence that the charge is true, it will make efforts to remedy the situation through persuasion. The commission itself may also instigate charges of discrimination where its staff have uncovered such practices, and again it tries to solve the problem by informal means. Only if persuasion fails, will the commission turn to the courts and bring suit.

Not only does the commission take action where discrimination has occurred, but it also works to avoid such confrontations by getting employers, private and public, to adopt voluntary programs to make equal employment a reality. The mission of the commission is a particularly sensitive one to carry out. It must be sure that discrimination is, in fact, the true cause of employer action and not the inability of the individual to do the work to the employer's satisfaction.

Because the work of the commission involves the entire nation, the bulk of it is handled in the many field offices in local communities. The headquarters in Washington concerns itself to a large extent with determining policies and providing Congress and the White House with statistical information concerning the employment of minorities. This information is very helpful in determining both the nation's progress toward equal employment opportunities and whether new legislation is required. It should be pointed out that although the Equal Employment Opportunity Commission was set up to deal specifically with the 1964 Civil Rights Act, other federal agencies have also had certain responsibilities for seeing that fair employment practices are carried out. Early in 1978, after he had had a chance to evaluate the nation's progress toward eliminating all job discrimination, Carter came to the conclusion that it would be more effective if EEOC became the job authority in this area. To that end he sent a reorganization plan to Congress and because neither house rejected his proposal within sixty days, it went into effect, and by 1979 all federal anti-discrimination enforcements became the responsibility of an enlarged Equal Employment Opportunities Commission.

The Environmental Protection Agency

Traditionally Americans have been the most profligate of people as far as their natural environment has been concerned. This was so for the obvious reason that from colonial times to the end of the nineteenth century there was a seemingly endless frontier, and Americans, unlike their counterparts in Asia and Europe, did not have to practice conservation or to be concerned with environmental problems. If land wore out or cities became too crowded with the air and water polluted by industrial wastes, people had only to move away. It was not until the beginning of the twentieth century that concern for our natural habitat arose, and it was entirely due to President Theodore Roosevelt who not only saw that conservation of our natural resources was necessary for future generations, but, in addition, was keenly aware of the importance of the quality of life. Only slowly, however, did Americans come to realize the validity of Teddy Roosevelt's concerns, and, unfortunately, only because environmental pollution had become so bad did the federal government respond by creating the Environmental Protection Agency (EPA) in 1970.

The purpose of this agency is to preserve the environment of the United States "for ourselves and our posterity," to quote the Preamble of the Constitution, by carrying out laws enacted by Congress to protect and enhance the environment from all forms of pollution: air, water, noise, solid waste, radiation and pesticides. The agency works to control present pollution by enforcing standards set by Congress. Factory smoke stacks, for instance, must now have scrubbers installed which clean the industrial wastes from the smoke so that the noxious fumes which used to blanket industrialized areas are substantially reduced. Solid wastes can no longer be dumped into the nation's waterways, but must be disposed of in ways which will not endanger the health of people, animals and plant life. Similarly, pesticides such as DDT which were viewed only a decade ago as boons to farmers and outdoorsmen are now forbidden. EPA also sees that nuclear plants meet rigid standards for radiation waste disposal.

Not only does it have responsibility for cleaning up what is already polluted, but the Environmental Protection Agency monitors all new projects planned by federal, state or local governments as well as by the private sector to see that they will not contribute to any sort of new pollution. Statements must be submitted to the agency describing the environmental impact of any new scheme before it is undertaken, and if plans do not meet established standards, EPA must publish its findings so that the public is informed. In instances where

Congress has given it authority, the agency can bring legal proceedings to enforce its judgments. Another important contribution EPA makes is in its research into ways by which pollution can be prevented. It sets up demonstration projects so that new techniques may be implemented by federal, state and local governments and by the private sector.

The agency is headed by an administrator who is appointed by the president and confirmed by the Senate. Unlike many of the heads of the other independent agencies, he serves at the pleasure of the president and resigns if the administration changes. The Environmental Protection Agency's headquarters are in Washington, but most of its work is carried out across the nation through regional offices. Although the agency is very new, its impact on the environment of the United States is already marked. The Potomac River, for instance, which only recently was so polluted that people in the nation's capital were afraid to sail on it for fear of capsizing, is visibly cleaner, and not only do people enjoy boating, but the day is not far off when swimming will be permitted. Salmon, sturgeon and shad are swimming once again in the Hudson and Connecticut rivers because of the success of clean up efforts. Los Angeles, a city known for its smog, now has much cleaner air which is not only obviously beneficial to those who breathe it, but has made air traffic much safer as visibility has been improved. There is still much to be done to make our environment safe and enjoyable, but it can be said that in a very short time the Environmental Protection Agency has made Americans aware of the seriousness of pollution and has advanced the nation toward the goals set forth by President Theodore Roosevelt over seventy years ago.

The Nuclear Regulatory Commission

The Nuclear Regulatory Commission (NRC), established in 1974, is an example of a congressional reorganization to meet changing circumstances. During World War II atomic research was placed by the president in the hands of the Manhattan Engineer District which was responsible for the development of the first atomic bombs which brought the war in the Pacific to an end in 1945. To deal with this new and extremely hazardous source of energy, Congress established the Atomic Energy Commission after the war which, in conjunction with the Defense Nuclear Agency in the Department of Defense, dealt with all phases of atomic power. The Atomic Energy Commission was concerned primarily with research and development of nuclear power for peaceful uses and with its regulation for security and safety. The Defense Nuclear Agency took over the research and development of this new source of energy for military purposes. In the 1970s when the energy crisis first arose, Congress initially established the Energy Research and Development Agency to coordinate research into all sources of energy. The Atomic Energy Commission, as such, was then dismantled, but as its regulatory functions were clearly not related to the new agency's mission, Congress then set up the Nuclear Regulatory Commission with the authority to supervise nuclear plants that are built to generate electric power and to license the export of radioactive materials to foreign countries.

When power companies build plants that use ordinary sources of energy to generate electricity, they do not have to receive government permission, although they must abide by standards for human safety and pollution control. Nuclear reactors, however, can be extremely dangerous to humans and the environment because they involve radioactve material, and, as a consequence, they must be licensed by the government which has had control over nuclear energy since it was first harnessed. Private power companies, therefore, that wish to construct nuclear plants must apply to the commission for permission to build. The commission holds public hearings at which those who oppose a nuclear plant have a chance to speak and the power companies, the opportunity to refute objections. The commission, after hearing all the evidence then decides whether to license the plant or not. If it does grant permission, it is then responsible for enforcing the safety standards that it has established. If an operating plant does not appear to be safe, the commission can order it to close down until the problem is cured.

The commission also conducts research projects designed to

make nuclear reactors and the disposal of nuclear wastes even safer than they are now. Nuclear energy could end the heavy dependence of the United States on petroleum and coal as sources of energy, but until nuclear power plants can be guaranteed to be unfailingly safe, many Americans are reluctant to see their widespread use. The research programs of the Nuclear Regulatory Commission are as vital, therefore, as its regulatory functions which guarantee that plants presently in operation meet the most exacting standards to prevent accidents by which radioactive material will be released.

The Federal Election Commission

A very recent addition to the roster of the independent federal agencies is the Federal Election Commission (FEC) which was established to carry out the provisions of the Federal Election Campaign Act of 1974. The Constitution sets up a democratic republic which, by definition, depends on Americans being willing to run for national office and citizens being willing to support candidates of their choice. What the Founding Fathers, however, could not have possibly foreseen was that the cost of running for national office was to reach proportions unimaginable in the eighteenth century. With the size of the United States and the advent first of radio and then of television, no candidate for national office has a chance unless he can afford to travel extensively and to buy radio and television time as well as all the campaign paraphernalia such as buttons, billboard signs, newspapers ads, and posters. The result has been that the candidate who had the most money to spend, whether from personal sources or from supporters, had an advantage over the one who had less. In addition, in recent years special interest groups such as corporations, labor unions, and the like as well as very wealthy individuals had been providing sizable campaign funds to a candidate sometimes in return for the promise of special favors should he be elected to office. By 1974, particularly in the aftermath of the Watergate revelations, it appeared to Congress that the democratic process was being severely undermined and that campaign reform was necessary.

In that year the first Federal Election Campaign Act was passed with the intent of making federal election campaigns fairer and more democratic by restricting both the amount of money that a candidate can raise and from whom and by requiring that every candidate disclose the amount and source of all campaign contributions. In addition, because of the greatly increased cost of mounting a national campaign, a system of public financing for the presidential nominating conventions and election was devised. Taxpayers who so desire simply check a box on their income tax return indicating their party preference and add a dollar to their tax which is then set aside by the government to be used for the election. Candidates for national office who meet the required standards— enough supporters and a set amount of money raised from them—then receive funds from the government. After the nominating conventions have selected their candidates for president and vice-president, each is given a sum from which to finance the final campaign for the White House which must be accounted for. The Federal Election Commission is the agency with the responsibility of carrying out these provisions of the new law.

The commission, which is bipartisan, is composed of six presidential appointees and the clerk of the House of Representatives and the secretary of the Senate, who are ex officio members. The law dictates that the commission must receive all campaign reports, audit them, and report to both the president and the Congress. It also is authorized to conduct investigations and to subpoena witnesses if necessary. It makes rules and regulations that it considers necessary for carrying out its functions, but they are subject to review by Congress. The commission must also advise Congress on changes which, in its opinion, would improve the system. And it has the power to decide in certain cases where the law leaves room for interpretation whether a candidate has been in compliance or not with the regulations.

Only two presidential elections have taken place since the inauguration of this new system, but it appears to have been successful. The election law has without question reduced the ability of certain groups and individuals to exercise undue influence over presidential candidates by campaign contributions. It seems obvious that in a democracy the president who holds the highest office in the land should be responsive to all who elect him and not only to special interest. In addition, all who want to run for the presidency should have an equal chance and should not be at a disadvantage because they are not rich.

The National Aeronautics and Space Administration

Probably no federal agency is as well known as the National Aeronautics and Space Administration because it has made science fiction come true. Men have walked on the moon; space vehicles are probing Mars, Mercury, Venus and Jupiter; the space shuttle is a reality, and NASA has accomplished these miracles in less than twenty years. Unlike the other independent agencies, NASA owes its creation solely to the advances made by a foreign nation, the Soviet Union, which with its successful launching of Sputnik, the first man-made satellite to orbit the earth, stunned the United States which had considered itself since World War II the first nation in science and technology. Congress responded to this challenge by setting up the National Aeronautic and Space Administration in 1958 with the mandate to coordinate all American scientific and technological research and development into the conquest of space, but, and it is an important but, for peaceful purposes. The United States from the start of its space program determined that no military advantage would be sought and that all knowledge gleaned about the universe would be shared with other nations for the good of all mankind. In the early 1960s President Kennedy stated that the goal of the American space program would be to put men on the moon by 1970, and his faith in American technological capability was vindicated in 1969 when two United States astronauts descended to the surface of the moon, walked about conducting experiments, reascended to join their teammate in their space ship and returned safely to earth with the whole world watching through the miracle of television. In a few years, then, through NASA's brilliant direction the United States had entered the space race and won it.

Shortly after the initial conquest of the moon, however,

manned voyages came to an end mainly because of the tremendous expense involved as well as the fact that space technology had advanced to the point that exploration of the
moon and beyond could be accomplished by guided machines,
and the risk to astronauts obviated. NASA continues its probes
of outer space now by launching rocket-driven space laboratories on long voyages to the distant planets. These machines
send information back to earth which enables astrophysicists
and geologists to learn more about the origin and the makeup
of the universe. In 1983 Viking, one of the United States
space probing vehicles, passed beyond the furthest planet in
our solar system and, to the surprise and delight of space
scientists, has continued its transmissions to earth. It is
headed beyond our solar system and, until its radio goes out,
it will be sending information back to earth about galaxies
hitherto unknown.

Also, NASA research has resulted in the success of the
space shuttle. This first reusable space vehicle operates like a
glider. It is launched into space via retrievable rockets, goes
into orbit above the earth, reenters the earth's atmosphere
through the firing of jet engines aboard, and glides to a
landing either at Edwards Air Force Base in California or at
the Kennedy Space Center at Cape Canaveral, Florida. After
its initial experimental flight, the shuttle now literally shuttles
back and forth routinely and carries payloads which help
defray its cost. Communication satellites belonging to any
nation or company that wishes to pay for the service are
launched from the shuttle. If need be, they can now be
serviced by technicians aboard the shuttle who step out with
their bag of tools exactly as the plumber walks into your
basement to repair the leaky pipe. Researchers can also rent
space aboard the shuttle so that experiments can be carried
out in a weightless atmosphere. These experiments may lead
to the discovery of ways of producing new drugs or chemicals
perhaps for the benefit of mankind.

NASA is also responsible for the spacelab. This is a space
workshop which will stay in synchronous orbit and in which
men and women can live for a period of time carrying out
experiments and research. They will travel to the lab via the

shuttle and return the same way. Soon people will be commuting to space as readily as they commute to another city for a day's business as they do today.

Although much of the glamour and excitement of the 1960s space adventure is over, the National Aeronautics and Space Administration provides one of the most important ongoing research and development programs of the federal government. Already much of what it developed for space travel has been adapted for the benefit of man on earth. Teflon, for instance, which came out of NASA research, is commonly used to line pots and pans to prevent food from sticking—a great convenience—and surgeons use it to reline human hip sockets in operations designed to alleviate the pain and the crippling effects of a form of arthritis. Many kinds of tiny electronic transistors, which have made possible many new devices for everyday earth use, have also come out of space engineering. In addition, every space probe teaches man more about the universe in which he lives and undoubtedly will be of use in coping with environmental and ecological problems of earth. Man's travels into space have already given all human beings a new perspective on this world and how unique it is in the endless realm of space which may, indeed, have the salutary effect of making men realize the importance of preserving their island home from destruction, whether ecological or nuclear.

The General Services Administration

The General Services Administration is the government's housekeeper. It was set up in 1949 in a government reorganization in order to centralize all the many services that the government requires to keep it running smoothly and efficiently. The administration procures all the real estate needed by the federal government in Washington and across the nation and disposes of all the properties no longer needed. It is responsible for all maintenance, improvements and designs for federal office buildings with the exception of those specifically assigned to the Architect of the Capitol. The National Archives of the government are also under its supervision. All the records, papers, documents, etc., of the many offices of the government are gathered, filed and made available to the public through this office. General Services is also the guardian of all of the government's property in addition to real estate, and recently Americans were made particularly aware of this responsibility in the matter of some of former President Nixon's White House possessions which were turned over to this office for safekeeping until their legal status could be determined. The issue involved the whereabouts of certain presents which had been given to the Nixons by foreign governments during his presidency. The law states that such gifts are the property of the United States, and if they are among the former president's personal possessions, the General Services Administration has the authority to remove them and turn them over to the State Department where they will be exhibited for the pleasure of the American people to whom they belong. Another of the functions of the administration is to regulate and to arrange for all government transportation and utilities in Washington and in all other federally controlled areas. The administration really has an enormous, if unglamorous task. It acts as the general coordinator of the myriad of details involved in running the government, and the administrator who runs it must have a large staff to keep track of everything. The administration works very closely with the White House, the executive departments and the General Accounting Office in the course of managing the government's domestic arrangements.

The United States Postal Service

The Postal Service has an entirely different history from all the other independent agencies because until 1971 it was an executive department with the postmaster general a cabinet officer holding the oldest government job in the nation's history. Today it is a government business, run by a board, as are the nation's private corporations, composed of the postmaster general who no longer has cabinet rank, the deputy postmaster general, and nine governors, all of whom are appointed by the president and confirmed by the Senate. The demotion of the Post Office to the status of an independent agency is an

illustration of the effort on the part of the executive and the
Congress to streamline government operations to serve the
public more efficiently and more economically.

Communication between people who live beyond speaking
distance has always been essential, and in the days before the
telegraph, telephone, television and now Telex, mail was the
only means of communication between people who lived at a
great distance. It is not surprising, therefore, that the postal
system in the United States dates back to colonial days. Before
the Revolution the British had a well-organized postal system
in the American colonies. None other than Benjamin Franklin
was largely responsible for its operation. In 1737 he was first
appointed postmaster general of Philadelphia, and in 1757 he
became the co-deputy postmaster general for all the British
colonies. After the outbreak of the Revolution in 1775 the
Continental Congress appointed him the first American postmaster general, and much of the organization of the present
postal system is due to his wise and practical methods in the
days of the rebelling colonies.

The importance of a postal system was so great that even
under the Articles of Confederation in 1777 the otherwise fee-
ble Congress had the sole authority in the new nation to establish post offices, post roads and to issue stamps in order to
pay for them, and, although the Founding Fathers tore up
much of the old government, they continued the authority of
Congress in the Constitution to "establish Post Offices and
Post Roads."

In 1789 the first Congress immediately created the Office of
Postmaster General, but at that time, however, the postmaster
general had no department nor was he of cabinet rank. One
of the postmaster general's prerogatives was to appoint all the
postmasters who ran the post offices across the nation, and in
1829 when Andrew Jackson, the "people's president," took
over the White House, the political significance of this authority was not lost on him. He, therefore, began the tradition of
appointing a close political ally to the position and having him
attend cabinet meetings. The job of postmaster general, then,
took on a political connotation, and until 1971 the postmaster
general was responsible for dispensing a large part of the po-

litical patronage for the president as well as for the operations of the Post Office Department. Interestingly enough, this extra task of the postmaster general played an important part in determining the final outcome of the contested presidential election of 1876 because in 1872 Congress had belatedly endorsed the postmaster general's cabinet status by creating the Department of the Post Office. In 1876 the electoral college had not been able to choose the president because the vote of several states had been contested, and the nation approached the inaugural date with the issue still unresolved. At the eleventh hour Samuel Tilden, the Democrat, agreed to Republican Rutherford B. Hayes' having the presidency provided he promised to do two things: one, to remove the last of the federal troops from the South, thus ending the post–Civil War occupation, and two, to appoint a Democrat to the position of postmaster general, thereby restoring the party to political respectability. Hayes subsequently did both.

Throughout much of the nation's history the Post Office was the key government department as far as communications were concerned, and as the nation expanded across the continent, postal service kept abreast by developing innovative ways of delivering the mail. The pony express became legendary in the nineteenth century, assuring speedy service between East and West. When the railroads linked the coasts, the mail began traveling in special cars, guarded by armed postal employees from potential robbers who roamed the still largely unpopulated western plains and mountains. In the twentieth century air mail service was inaugurated with the advent of the air age, and in the 1960s as technology advanced, the Post Office adopted new techniques to enable it to deal with the enormous increase in the amount of mail it had to handle. The famous Zip Code was devised to speed up mail delivery. Every city, town, county and hamlet in the United States is assigned a number, and all articles of mail in order to reach their destinations promptly must bear the correct number. Big cities are assigned one primary code number, 100 in the case of New York, and then, in addition, two other digits to designate to the central post office to which section of the city or of the nearby suburbs the letter or package must be delivered. At the same time automation was introduced to sort out the tremendous volume of mail in a speedy and efficient way. In many major cities no human hand touches the mail until the postman carries it to the door of the addressee.

Although the Post Office Department tried heroically to conquer the problems presented by the ever increasing amounts of mail—by requiring the Zip Code, by introducing automation and by continually increasing the price of postage—unfortunately the expense involved in delivering the mail quickly and efficiently soared higher and higher, and the federal government sustained ever growing deficits every year. The time came when the only possible thing to do was to turn the Post Office Department into a government owned corporation and to try to run it as a business. Congress, therefore, in 1971 brought the history of the venerable department to a close and established the United States Postal Service as an independent agency.

The corporation is run by the board which sits in Washington and is responsible for making policy and for seeing that the eighty-eight billion pieces of mail that it handles annually are delivered promptly and efficiently. Although the familiar blue-grey uniformed postmen still walk their routes, they are no longer civil servants, but are unionized, as are their counterparts in the nation's industries, and negotiate contracts with the management of the corporation. In addition to seeing that mail is delivered, the board of the Postal Service has certain law enforcement powers. The mails cannot be used for the transmittal of obscene literature; they may not be used for lotteries which are a form of gambling; they may not be used for fraudulent purposes; and they cannot be used for shipping liquor or flammable goods. Postal inspectors have the responsibility of checking the mail and making sure that it is not being used illegally. If an unlawful use is detected, the postal officials turn the case over to the Department of Justice for prosecution.

The cost of mail service is still a major problem as every year the Postal Service runs an enormous annual deficit which Congress must subsidize. The solution is not an easy one. Americans want their mail, but they do not want to pay the

entire cost which would send postage rates soaring to prepos-
terous heights. Each new president when he takes office has to
face the problem, and President Carter was no exception. He
first suggested that first-class mail, which is primarily personal
correspondence, be kept at the rate of thirteen cents and that
second- and third-class postage be increased. This solution
might have reduced the amount of what is called "junk" mail,
which fills the mailman's bag to capacity and enabled him to
carry a lighter load, thereby allowing him to make his round
more speedily, but unfortunately this idea was resisted by
many heavy users of the Postal Service such as the mail order
industry and magazine publishers. They do not want the
price of postage to rise any more than does the person who
writes a letter. Unfortunately, the only immediate solution,
therefore, was to up the price of first-class mail to fifteen
cents, and subsequently to twenty. Undoubtedly, costs will
continue to rise, and both the executive and legislative branches are searching for a more permanent solution to the
problem of delivering the mail. To date no plan has been
agreed upon.

ACTION

One of the most striking characteristics of the American
people is their willingness to volunteer their time to help others. From colonial times to the present people have cooperated to solve each other's problems whether it be to raise
a barn or to assist a neighbor in trouble. With the exception of
the quasi-official agency, the American Red Cross, government had not in the past used volunteers in carrying out government programs, but today ACTION has the responsibility
of utilizing the generosity of Americans to give their time in
order to benefit society both at home and abroad.

John F. Kennedy was the first president to recognize the
singular potential of this spirit of volunteerism toward explaining the nature of the American people to those abroad,
and one of the first suggestions he made to Congress resulted
in the establishment of the Peace Corps, perhaps the most revolutionary program undertaken by the nation since 1789. The

law which set up the Peace Corps in 1961 stated that the purpose was "to promote world peace and friendship through a Peace Corps, which shall make available to interested countries and areas men and women of the United States qualified for service abroad and willing to serve, under conditions of hardship if necessary to help the peoples of such countries and areas meeting their needs for trained manpower, and to help promote a better understanding of other peoples on the part of the American people." Volunteers for the Peace Corps (there were over six thousand serving abroad in sixty-five countries in 1977) are carefully chosen and trained for a period of months either by private agencies or on college campuses and then serve abroad for two years. All kinds of skills are utilized by the Corps, construction workers, farmers, teachers, doctors, veterinarians, engineers and nurses, to name a few, and although there is little financial reward for volunteers (they receive a very small stipend) the satisfaction derived from the experience has been universal. It is fair to say that the program has kindled the imagination of the American people and awakened in a large number the desire to serve the cause of international understanding and good will. One of the better known alumnae of the Peace Corps was "Miss Lillian," President Carter's mother, a fact that would have undoubtedly pleased President Kennedy.

The success of the Peace Corps was so immediate that President Johnson continued the idea of his predecessor, turning it to work on the domestic front, and Congress, responding to his urging, established VISTA, Volunteers in Service to America, in 1964. VISTA volunteers work in the many areas of the United States which are economically, culturally and educationally deprived in the same way that the Peace Corps works abroad. Anyone can join this program and will receive training, and then give one to two years of service. In the years that the program has been in operation, literally thousands of Americans have participated, and the communities, which range from inner-city ghettos to Appalachia to Indian reservations to migrant labor camps, that have received VISTA volunteers have not only benefitted enormously in the practical sense, but their residents have also come to realize that the United States is a nation that cares about its less fortunate citizens.

The success of the Peace Corps and VISTA resulted in a demand for further projects, and President Nixon by executive order set up ACTION in 1971 as an independent agency with responsibility for organizing and administering all government sponsored volunteer programs, including the Peace Corps and VISTA. ACTION today administers a number of truly innovative and imaginative programs which not only provide important services to many people in need, but, in addition, give the volunteers themselves a sense of their own usefulness which is particularly of value to older citizens who so often no longer feel needed. The Foster Grandparents Program is aimed at children who either have no families or whose families have no time for them. The grandparents who volunteer simply act as grandparents, giving that extra bit of attention and love. The Retired Senior Volunteer Program offers those who have retired the opportunity of using their professional or work experience to help others to do better in their jobs, and the Senior Companion Program brings older persons into a one-to-one relationship with people who need help. The Vietnam Veterans Leadership Program recruits veterans of that war who have successfully adjusted to civilian life to volunteer their time to help those who still bear the searing scars of their experience. ACTION also, through the Urban Crime Prevention Program, works with nonprofit community organizations in medium to large cities to make low- and moderate-income neighborhoods safe for their inhabitants. Because it is the national center for volunteerism, ACTION acts as a coordinator as well as an innovator of projects that can best be carried out by volunteers. It provides information on all types of programs designed to train volunteers so that they can perform their duties with expertise. ACTION can perhaps best be described as the agency that harnesses human power to solve many of the problems that face the nation.

Because ACTION programs are entirely manned by volunteers, its paid staff is one of the smallest of all the independent agencies. It is run by an administrator and a handful of assistants who work in Washington and in the regional offices around the nation. The Washington headquarters' main concern other than making policy for the agency is to get ACTION's modest budget through Congress so that it can continue its admirable service. Although it has been in operation only a few years, ACTION is one of the most important of the independent agencies in that it has rekindled the traditional American spirit of generosity and has channeled it into constructive programs dedicated to serving human needs. In addition, it has proved beyond a doubt that money is not the only thing that will solve human problems in a highly complex and sophisticated society.

The National Foundation of the Arts and Humanities

The National Foundation of the Arts and Humanities is an example of a totally different sort of federal agency. It was established recently solely to promote the arts and the humanities for the cultural advancement and enjoyment of the American people. The United States until 1965, the year Congress set up the National Foundation, was one of the few great nations in the world whose government had not been keenly involved in the promotion of the national culture. It was largely due to Mrs. Jacqueline Kennedy Onassis who, when she was the First Lady, pressed for such an agency that Congress became aware of the importance of support for the arts and humanities and established the foundation. The agency's work is divided between the National Endowment for the Arts and the National Endowment for the Humanities. Each has its own staff, and coordination between the two is the responsibility of the Federal Council on the Arts and the Humanities which is composed of fourteen members including the chairmen of the two endowments. What each endowment does is to promote cultural and intellectual development by awarding grants to individuals, state agencies, art groups, theaters, universities, colleges, museums and the like as well as to television, radio and film producers. With this government support many new, innovative artistic and intellectual achievements are made possible which enrich our cultural life. It must be emphasized, however, that the foundation does not in any way determine the style or content of what the artists and scholars it supports produce. The foundation simply encourages the development of the talents of gifted Americans.

The Smithsonian Institution

The Smithsonian, a quasi-official government agency, is a unique institution in every way. It is a vast complex of museums, the national zoo, and research centers located in Washington, D.C., across the nation and in many foreign countries. It is also a publisher of note, producing a popular magazine, scholarly journals, books, and pamphlets and provides a forum for symposiums on all sorts of scientific, technological, cultural and intellectual inquiries designed to further knowledge of all aspects of the human experience. The Smithsonian is also an exception among federal agencies in that it owes its origins to the extraordinary generosity of an Englishman who never set foot on the soil of the United States. In 1829 Mr. James Smithson of London left a sizable amount of money to the United States in his will for "an establishment for the increase and diffusion of Knowledge among men." Congress, however, did not respond immediately to the bequest, and it was not until 1846 that the institution was actually established by law.

The original institution was housed in one building on the Mall in front of the Capitol, called the Castle because of its crenellated towers, in which were exhibited collections of paintings, artifacts, and the like which were usually simply donated. For a long time the Smithsonian had the reputation of being the nation's attic because it contained a hodgepodge of many assorted objects, but over the years as its collections grew, order came out of chaos, and today there are ten museums directly under the Smithsonian as well as the National Gallery of Art, the gift of Andrew Mellon to the American people, and the John F. Kennedy Center for the Performing Arts which is associated with the institution. Each has a separate board of directors. The Natural History Museum, the Museum of American History, the National Collection of

American Art, including the Renwick Gallery, the National Portrait Gallery, the Hirshhorn Museum of Painting and Sculpture, the Freer Gallery of Oriental Art, the Air and Space Museum and the Anacostia Museum are all in Washington, and the Cooper-Hewitt Museum of Design and Decorative Arts has recently opened in New York. Each collection contains either the finest examples of art, both American and foreign, or paintings and other objects pertinent to the history of the United States. The National Portrait Gallery, for instance, has a sizable collection of portraits of the presidents of the United States and of many other citizens whose contributions to one of the many facets of American life have been outstanding. The Air and Space Museum contains not only the space capsules in which our astronauts flew to the moon, but the *Spirit of St. Louis,* Charles Lindbergh's famous plane, and many other planes and objects depicting the history of flight. And the Museum of American History has the original models of American inventions such as Eli Whitney's cotton gin which revolutionized American society and industry. Every museum is well worth visiting, and the problem which confronts every tourist is having enough time to see everything.

The National Zoological Park consists of two large acreages. The zoo proper is in Washington in Rock Creek Park and houses all kinds of interesting specimens of living birds and animals from all over the world, including the famous pandas, the gift of the Peoples' Republic of China. The Wild Animal Breeding Farm is located in Front Royal, Virginia, and there research is carried out on animal behavior as well as special breeding projects designed to insure that species endangered in their natural habitats will continue to exist for the benefit and enjoyment of future generations. Although most people think of a zoo as simply an interesting place to visit, to scientists and veterinarians a zoo is an important research facility, and zoo directors in every nation are in constant communication, sharing information and trading animals so that the world does not lose rare species.

In conjunction with its research work the Smithsonian also maintains the Chesapeake Bay Center for Environmental

Studies, the Smithsonian Tropical Research Institute in Panama, and the Smithsonian Astrophysical Observatory in Cambridge, Massachusetts, in association with Harvard University. It also works with the government of Nepal in a project to protect the few remaining white tigers. The knowledge acquired through all of the research projects of the Institution is available to all interested persons, and to make it easier for individuals to keep abreast of developments, the Smithsonian Science Information Exchange was recently established as a nonprofit corporation in the District of Columbia. It has also been responsible for the International Exchange Service, established as long ago as 1849, through which all official United States publications are made available abroad.

The Smithsonian also administers many varied educational programs for the benefit of the general public. Smithsonian personnel, for instance, give courses in the museums which anyone can take for a modest fee and scholarships are available for those who cannot pay. A wide variety of movies, lectures, tours, etc., are constantly being offered in Washington, and certain traveling exhibits are mounted for the enjoyment and edification of those not in the Washington area. Overseas trips to fascinating places—Cape Horn, the Greek Islands, Iran, Siberia, etc., to cite a few—organized by the Smithsonian are another popular offering. In fact, to list all the activities of the Smithsonian would be impossible for a book of this scope. Suffice it to say that this quasi-official institution has something of interest for everyone, and that it is fully appreciated is attested to by the millions of visitors it entertains each year.

This enormous complex has clearly carried out Mr. Smithson's instruction to found an establishment for "the increase and diffusion of Knowledge," and it obviously has grown well beyond the capacity of the original bequest. Today, the Smithsonian is funded by an annual appropriation from Congress and by the American people who support it by gifts and bequests, by membership in the Smithsonian Associates program, by subscribing to the magazine, and by purchasing many of the distinctive objects available in the museum stores and book shops. The job of administering the Smithsonian is the responsibility of the secretary of the institution who is selected by the Board of Regents, made up of the chief justice of the United States, the vice-president, three senators, three members of the House of Representatives and nine outstanding citizens of the United States who are appointed by a joint resolution of Congress. The secretary, who traditionally has been a noted scientist, probably has the most interesting, exciting, and challenging job in Washington.

The American National Red Cross

The American Red Cross was originally founded by Clara Barton, a nurse of Civil War fame, in 1881. Until 1905 it was a private organization, administered by volunteers, manned by volunteers and funded by voluntary contributions. Its initial purpose was to help all the needy in the United States who were either at home or in hospitals. In 1905 Congress made it a quasi-official agency of the United States government and authorized it to work with the International Red Cross in carrying out the provisions of the Geneva Convention* which the United States had signed.

The change of status to quasi-official from private really only meant minor changes. The title was changed to American National Red Cross, and the president of the United States was authorized to appoint eight of the fifty-person board that runs the organization, one of the presidential appointees being the honorary chairman. The organization is still manned by volunteers except for a small paid staff, and it is still almost exclusively funded by voluntary contributions. Its responsibilities, however, have expanded over the years. It is the agency which assists people when national and international disasters occur. It provides volunteer aid in time of war to the wounded or sick. It acts as a means of communication between members of the armed forces and their families when necessary. In wartime it also works to see that the provisions of the Geneva Convention are followed, and in the recent war

---

*The Geneva Convention is an international agreement dating from 1864 which sets standards for the treatment of prisoners of war and which guarantees neutrality for noncombatants such as nurses and hospital employees.

in Vietnam the Red Cross worked hard to get information from the North Vietnamese government concerning Americans missing in action. In peacetime, in addition to always being prepared to help victims of natural disasters both at home and abroad, it runs a great many services for the benefit of the American people. Its Blood Program is one of its most essential services. The Red Cross not only supplies the bloodmobiles where volunteer donors give their blood, but processes it and distributes it to hospitals. It also carries out research programs aimed at discovering better and safer ways of treating blood so that it may be stored for long periods of time. It administers the Grey Lady Program, volunteers who provide a variety of services for those in hospitals such as helping to entertain children, reading to patients, writing letters and bringing mobile stores to bedsides. The Red Cross trains nurses' aides who assist hospital personnel by relieving them of many of the nonmedical, but important duties. The Red Cross is also invaluable in chauffeuring outpatients who need treatment to and from hospitals. Among the many educational programs run by the organization, the lifesaving course is one of the best known, but there are others devoted to health care in general. These courses as well as the other services of the Red Cross are free, and, because they contribute so much to the welfare of the American people, everyone, hopefully, will respond generously to the Red Cross appeals for support. The Red Cross along with ACTION exemplifies one of the best characteristics of Americans, their willingness to help others without monetary reward.

As was stated above, this is only a partial list of all the agencies, commissions, administrations and boards that have been authorized by Congress at various times to do a particular job. The ones described, however, give a fair picture of the enormous variety of government responsibilities that must be attended to, but would overburden the executive and legislative branches were they to try to handle them. It also should be clear that the government is constantly being reorganized with the intent of providing better service to the public. Whenever it seems appropriate, for instance, to set up a new executive department, existing agencies concerned with matters which will be under the jurisdiction of the new cabinet officer are simply transferred to his department. Health and Human Services, for example, absorbed the older Social Security and Food and Drug Administrations. The Federal Aviation Administration became part of the Department of Transportation, and the Federal Power Commission has lost its independent status with the establishment of the Department of Energy. Conversely, when a department no longer seems necessary, it is dismantled and its responsibilities carried out in a more efficient way. Such was the case with the Post Office.

It may appear that there is a lot of duplication, but a close examination will show that there is not so much actual duplication as there is a division between different aspects of a similar responsibility. The Federal Trade Commission, for example, is responsible for preventing violations of federal law from occurring, whereas the Anti-Trust Division of the Department of Justice is charged with prosecuting offenders after the violation has taken place. In any event, Congress, by establishing these agencies, has enabled the federal government to stay abreast of current problems without changing the basic structure of the government as designed by the Founding Fathers.

THE FEDERAL GOVERNMENT
AND THE CITIZEN

THIS BOOK is only a brief and by no means complete discussion of some of the many parts of the United States government and how they work. It is extraordinary to think that the Constitution whose Preamble is only one sentence and whose body is but a few pages could be the foundation of the enormous and complicated structure that is the nation's federal government today. The size of the government may be overwhelming and seem far removed from the short outline of the Constitution, but its increase in size has not meant that the government has veered from the purpose stated in the Preamble. To realize the phrase "in order to form a more perfect union" has been the purpose of each new addition to the federal government. As life has grown more complex with new economic, social, scientific, technological and international developments with which the local and state governments were not designed to deal, there has been repeatedly the need to increase the responsibilities and duties of the federal government. A backward glance over the years that the government of the United States under the Constitution has been in existence proves that the government has met the challenge of new situations, often by adding a department or an agency in order to accept the new responsibility so that the needs of the American people are met. At the same time, however, constant care is taken to prevent unrestricted growth, and reorganizations are continually taking place to make the federal government a better servant of the people. Each new president is fully aware of his responsibilities to streamline the government, and President Reagan is no exception. In the 1980 campaign he promised, if elected, to make the federal government more efficient and less of a burden to the American people.

There is no denying, however, that to carry out its fundamental responsibilities to the American people, the United States government has had to enter into the lives of every American today to an extent inconceivable to the Founding Fathers. Much that we take completely for granted is only available and possible for us because of the activities of the many branches of the federal government. This book is filled with proof of this statement.

Take orange juice, for example, one of the most common of breakfast items. How can this everyday beverage reflect the interest and workings of the United States government? Before that orange arrives at the breakfast table, many departments of the federal government have had something to do with it. First, the housewife at the market before she buys the fruit can choose between several grades of oranges each for a different price. Why? The Congress of the United States has passed legislation requiring the grading of fruit according to size and color; the price is fixed accordingly—the larger the orange, the higher the price. Naturally the orange grower wants to produce the best produce in order to get more profit. How can he grow the best fruit? He can go to the United States Department of Agriculture. Agricultural research centers are largely responsible for the development of fertilizers, sprays and methods of grafting trees which all result in the growing of better fruit. Other divisions of the department provide on-the-spot help to the farmer in planning his grove or in providing machinery, perhaps for spraying. The National Weather Service also contributes to the growing of the orange. Advance warnings of frost will help the farmer. He puts smudge pots in the groves in order to keep his trees from being frostbitten. Once an orange is grown and harvested, the United States Department of Agriculture inspectors grade the fruit, attesting to its size and color. Marketing services, also provided by the Agriculture Department, can help the grower to sell his fruit to the best advantage. Once the grower has sold his fruit to the wholesaler, it must travel to markets all over the country. At this point the Interstate Commerce Commission enters the picture. Because the fruit must cross state borders, the trucking and railroad industries are regulated by the federal government. Rates, health and sanitation codes, and refrigeration temperatures are all standardized for the protection of the transport companies and for the consumers who buy the fruit at the local markets. When the fruit is unpacked at its destination and the retail price affixed, inspectors check to see that price and quality correspond correctly. By the time the orange is in the consumer's kitchen, it has been almost constantly under the surveillance of the United States government. Because of this government concern, the orange is all it should be, and the person who drinks its juice does so casually and in complete confidence that the fruit is pure and wholesome, probably never thinking of the many federal government employees whose labors have brought that orange to his table.

This is but one detailed example of the way in which the United States government affects the life and business of Americans. There are also many other ways by which we are made aware of the federal government in our daily lives. Take a look in your telephone directory, for instance, and count the listings under the United States government. In your own community you will find a myriad of federal offices all there to help you—the F.B.I., the Internal Revenue Service, the Equal Employment Opportunity Commission, the Department of Agriculture, the Department of the Interior, to name a few, and, if you live either in a port of entry or near the coasts, you will also find the United States Customs Service, the State Department's Passport Office, and the Coast Guard. And, naturally, the National Weather Service and the United States Postal Service operate nationwide.

In addition, every day we all can know exactly what is happening in Washington and what role the United States is playing in the world because of the intense coverage by the news media. The president himself frequently gives interviews to the press and holds at various times televised press conferences. His press secretary (or his assistants) briefs the news media once a day routinely, and more often if an important story is breaking. Each of the executive departments through its secretary or his public affairs officer reports constantly on the activities of his office. Decisions of the Supreme Court, complicated as they may seem, are always carefully reported in detail because each has a direct and important impact on the lives and the affairs of the American people. Not only do reporters cover Capitol Hill, but in recent years important committee hearings have been televised, an extremely significant development in our democracy. The televising of the Judiciary Committee of the House of Representatives impeachment investigation in 1974, for instance, which was viewed by millions, played a vital part in the events leading to President Nixon's resignation from office. Americans knew exactly what the evidence was and, as they watched the members of the committee carrying out their constitutional responsibility, they could not help having their faith in our democratic process renewed.

It goes without saying that for those who have the opportunity to visit Washington the federal government is there for them to experience at first hand. Although it is impossible for the president to be available to every American citizen, anyone with important business may make an appointment to see him. The White House is open for tours during certain hours because it belongs to the American people. The galleries in the Senate and the House of Representatives are there expressly for the purpose of enabling the public to witness the proceedings on the floor, and congressmen and senators welcome guests from their districts and states. The Supreme Court sessions are always open to the public because justice in the United States is not a secret proceeding, and for those who are interested in the history of the Court, there is a fascinating exhibition of memorabilia of past justices as well as the originals of many of the great opinions which have changed the course of history. And one of the most interesting of all exhibits is in the National Archives, the original Declaration of Independence and the Constitution. The federal government does, in fact, belong to the American people.

When the extent, as well as the necessity, of the United States government's activities are known and understood, it then becomes apparent that to support this government is the responsibility of every citizen. The great size of the government explains the need for many taxes. Every government employee must be paid; every government building must be maintained; new buildings must be built; and every government program must be carried out both domestically and abroad. Money is fundamental to the success of the government, and the cost must be met. Tax money, to a very great extent, pays the bills. Without the money collected in revenue, it would be impossible to have a government. Instead of a nation whose citizens are among the most prosperous in the world today, there would be a weak and disorganized country without the power to stand for freedom against tyranny. Though taxes are unpleasant to pay, it is the duty of every citizen to share the cost of the benefits which he receives from the federal government.

The citizen is not only called upon to pay his fair share of the taxes, but he is also responsible for another and equally important contribution to his government—interest in it. Democratic government can only succeed if the citizenry is willing to take the responsibility of being interested in and informed about the problems of government and in voting. The United States federal government is made up essentially of elected representatives of the people. Those who are appointed to important executive positions are chosen by the president who is elected, and they must be confirmed by the elected representatives of the people in Congress, the senators. If the people of the United States are not interested in voting and taking democratic responsibility, they will pay the consequences. They will have to accept people in government whom they have not chosen. An alert and interested electorate is the greatest safeguard of liberty. The Constitution so ordered the federal government that the people have the greatest power. If they refuse to accept this great responsibility, they will no longer have democracy, but if they choose to exercise their privileges as one of the freest peoples on earth, they will, in turn, maintain good and honest government, truly dedicated to serving the best interest of the public. That the American people understand their responsibility to safeguard their freedom by supporting the Constitution was more than adequately proved by the Watergate affair, and they can be justly proud that they vindicated the faith of the Founding Fathers in the efficacy of a government "of laws and not of men."

THE CONSTITUTION
OF THE UNITED STATES
OF AMERICA

We the People of the United States, in Order to form a more perfect Union, establish Justice, insure domestic Tranquility, provide for the common defense, promote the general Welfare, and secure the Blessings of Liberty to ourselves and our Posterity, do ordain and establish this Constitution for the United States of America.

ARTICLE. I.

Section. 1. All legislative Powers herein granted shall be vested in a Congress of the United States, which shall consist of a Senate and House of Representatives.

Section. 2. The House of Representatives shall be composed of Members chosen every second Year by the People of the several States, and the Electors in each State shall have the Qualifications requisite for Electors of the most numerous Branch of the State Legislature.

No person shall be a Representative who shall not have attained to the Age of twenty five Years, and been seven Years a Citizen of the United States, and who shall not, when elected, be an Inhabitant of that State in which he shall be chosen.

[Representatives and direct Taxes shall be apportioned among the several States which may be included within this Union, according to their respective Numbers, which shall be determined by adding to the whole Number of free Persons, including those bound to Service for a Term of Years, and excluding Indians not taxed, three fifths of all other Persons]. The actual Enumeration shall be made within three Years after the first Meeting of the Congress of the United States, and within every subsequent Term of ten Years, in such Manner as they shall by Law direct. The Number of Representatives shall not exceed one for every thirty Thousand, but each State shall have at Least one Representative; and until such enumeration shall be

290

made, the State of New Hampshire shall be entitled to chuse three, Massachusetts eight, Rhode-Island and Providence Plantations one, Connecticut five, New-York six, New Jersey four, Pennsylvania eight, Delaware one, Maryland six, Virginia ten, North Carolina five, South Carolina five, and Georgia three.

When vacancies happen in the Representation from any State, the Executive Authority thereof shall issue Writs of Election to fill such Vacancies.

The House of Representatives shall chuse their Speaker and other Officers; and shall have the sole Power of Impeachment.

SECTION. 3. The Senate of the United States shall be composed of two Senators from each State, [chosen by the Legislature thereof,] for six Years; and each Senator shall have one Vote.

Immediately after they shall be assembled in Consequence of the first Election, they shall be divided as equally as may be into three Classes. The Seats of the Senators of the first Class shall be vacated at the Expiration of the second Year, of the second Class at the Expiration of the fourth Year, and of the third Class at the Expiration of the sixth Year, so that one third may be chosen every second Year; [and if Vacancies happen by Resignation, or otherwise, during the Recess of the Legislature of any State, the Executive thereof may make temporary Appointments until the next Meeting of the Legislature, which shall then fill such Vacancies].

No Person shall be a Senator who shall not have attained to the Age of thirty Years, and been nine Years a Citizen of the United States, and who shall not, when elected, be an Inhabitant of that State for which he shall be chosen.

The Vice President of the United States shall be President of the Senate, but shall have no Vote, unless they be equally divided.

The Senate shall chuse their other Officers, and also a President pro tempore, in the Absence of the Vice President, or when he shall exercise the Office of President of the United States.

The Senate shall have the sole Power to try all Impeachments. When sitting for that Purpose, they shall be on Oath or Affirmation. When the President of the United States is tried, the Chief Justice shall preside: And no Person shall be convicted without the Concurrence of two thirds of the Members present.

Judgment in Cases of Impeachment shall not extend further than to removal from Office, and disqualification to hold and enjoy any Office of honor, Trust or Profit under the United States: but the Party convicted shall nevertheless be liable and subject to Indictment, Trial, Judgment and Punishment, according to Law.

SECTION. 4. The Times, Places and Manner of holding Elections for Senators and Representatives, shall be prescribed in each State by the Legislature thereof; but the Congress may at any time by Law make or alter such Regulations, except as to the Places of chusing Senators.

The Congress shall assemble at least once in every Year, and such Meeting shall [be on the first Monday in December,] unless they shall by Law appoint a different Day.

SECTION. 5. Each House shall be the Judge of the Elections, Returns and Qualifications of its own Members, and a Majority of each shall constitute a Quorum to do Business; but a smaller Number may adjourn from day to day, and may be authorized to compel the Attendance of absent Members, in such Manner, and under such Penalties as each House may provide.

Each House may determine the Rules of its Proceedings, punish its Members for disorderly Behaviour, and, with the Concurrence of two thirds, expel a Member.

Each House shall keep a Journal of its Proceedings, and from time to time publish the same, excepting such Parts as may in their Judgment require Secrecy; and the Yeas and Nays of the Members of either House on any question shall, at the Desire of one fifth of those Present, be entered on the Journal.

Neither House, during the Session of Congress, shall, without the Consent of the other, adjourn for more than three days, nor to any other Place than that in which the two Houses shall be sitting.

SECTION. 6. The Senators and Representatives shall receive a Compensation for their Services, to be ascertained by Law, and paid out of the Treasury of the United States. They shall in all Cases, except Treason, Felony and Breach of the Peace, be privileged from Arrest during their Attendance at the Session of their respective Houses, and in going to and returning from the same; and for any Speech or Debate in either House, they shall not be questioned in any other Place.

No Senator or Representative shall, during the Time for which he was elected, be appointed to any civil Office under the Authority of the United States, which shall have been created, or the Emoluments whereof shall have been encreased during such time; and no Person holding any Office under the United States, shall be a Member of either House during his Continuance in Office.

SECTION. 7. All Bills for raising Revenue shall originate in the House of Representatives; but the Senate may propose or concur with Amendments as on other Bills.

Every Bill which shall have passed the House of Representatives and the Senate, shall, before it become a Law, be presented to the President of the United States; If he approve he shall sign it, but if not he shall return it, with his Objections to that House in which it shall have originated, who shall enter the Objections at large on their Journal, and proceed to reconsider it. If after such Reconsideration two thirds of that House shall agree to pass the Bill, it shall be sent, together with the Objections, to the other House, by which it shall likewise be reconsidered, and if approved by two thirds of that House, it shall become a Law. But in all such Cases the Votes of both Houses shall be determined by yeas and Nays, and the Names of the Persons voting for and against the Bill shall be entered on the Journal of each House respectively. If any Bill shall not be returned by the President within ten Days (Sundays excepted) after it shall have been presented to him, the Same shall be a Law, in like Manner as if he had signed it, unless the Congress by their Adjournment prevent its Return, in which Case it shall not be a Law.

Every Order, Resolution, or Vote to which the Concurrence of the Senate and House of Representatives may be necessary (except on a question of Adjournment) shall be presented to the President of the United States; and before the Same shall take Effect, shall be approved by him, or being disapproved by him, shall be repassed by two thirds of the Senate and House of Representatives, according to the Rules and Limitations prescribed in the Case of a Bill.

SECTION. 8. The Congress shall have Power To lay and collect Taxes, Duties, Imposts and Excises, to pay the Debts and provide for the common Defence and general Welfare of the United States; but all Duties, Imposts and Excises shall be uniform throughout the United States;

To borrow Money on the credit of the United States;

To regulate Commerce with foreign Nations, and among the several States, and with the Indian Tribes;

To establish an uniform Rule of Naturalization, and uniform Laws on the subject of Bankruptcies throughout the United States;

To coin Money, regulate the Value thereof, and of foreign Coin, and fix the Standard of Weights and Measures;

To provide for the Punishment of counterfeiting the Securities and current Coin of the United States;

To establish Post Offices and post Roads;

To promote the Progress of Science and useful Arts, by securing for limited Times to Authors and Inventors the exclusive Right to their respective Writings and Discoveries;

To constitute Tribunals inferior to the supreme Court;

To define and punish Piracies and Felonies committed on the high Seas, and Offences against the Law of Nations;

To declare War, grant Letters of Marque and Reprisal, and make Rules concerning Captures on Land and Water;

To raise and support Armies, but no Appropriation of Money to that Use shall be for a longer Term than two Years;

To provide and maintain a Navy;

To make Rules for the Government and Regulation of the land and naval Forces;

To provide for calling forth the Militia to execute the Laws of the Union, suppress Insurrections and repel Invasions;

To provide for organizing, arming, and disciplining, the Militia, and for governing such Part of them as may be employed in the Service of the United States, reserving to the States respectively, the Appointment of the Officers, and the Authority of training the Militia according to the discipline prescribed by Congress;

To exercise exclusive Legislation in all Cases whatsoever, over such District (not exceeding ten Miles square) as may, by Cession of particular States, and the Acceptance of Congress, become the Seat of the Government of the United States, and to exercise like Authority over all Places purchased by the Consent of the Legislature of the State in which the Same shall be, for the Erection of Forts, Magazines, Arsenals, dock-Yards, and other needful Buildings;—And

To make all Laws which shall be necessary and proper for carrying into Execution the foregoing Powers, and all other Powers vested by this Constitution in the Government of the United States, or in any Department or Officer thereof.

SECTION. 9. The Migration or Importation of such Persons as any of the States now existing shall think proper to admit, shall not be prohibited by the Congress prior to the Year one thousand eight hundred and eight, but a Tax or duty may be imposed on such Importation, not exceeding ten dollars for each Person.

The Privilege of the Writ of Habeas Corpus shall not be suspended, unless when in Cases of Rebellion or Invasion the public Safety may require it.

No Bill of Attainder or ex post facto Law shall be passed.

No Capitation, or other direct, Tax shall be laid, unless in Proportion to the Census or Enumeration herein before directed to be taken.

No Tax or Duty shall be laid on Articles exported from any State.

No Preference shall be given by any Regulation of Commerce or Revenue to the Ports of one State over those of another: nor shall Vessels bound to, or from, one State, be obliged to enter, clear, or pay Duties in another.

No Money shall be drawn from the Treasury, but in Consequence of Appropriations made by Law; and a regular Statement and Account of the Receipts and Expenditures of all public Money shall be published from time to time.

No Title of Nobility shall be granted by the United States: And no Person holding any Office of Profit or Trust under them, shall, without the Consent of the Congress, accept of any present, Emolument, Office, or Title, of any kind whatever, from any King, Prince, or foreign State.

SECTION. 10. No State shall enter into any Treaty, Alliance, or Confederation; grant Letters of Marque and Reprisal; coin Money; emit Bills of Credit; make any Thing but gold and silver Coin a Tender in Payment of Debts; pass any Bill of Attainder, ex post facto Law, or Law impairing the Obligation of Contracts, or grant any Title of Nobility.

No State shall, without the Consent of the Congress, lay any Imposts or Duties on Imports or Exports, except what may be absolutely necessary for executing it's inspection Laws: and the net Produce of all Duties and Imposts, laid by any State on Imports or Exports, shall be for the Use of the Treasury of the United States; and all such Laws shall be subject to the Revision and Controul of the Congress.

No State shall, without the Consent of Congress, lay any Duty of Tonnage, keep Troops, or Ships of War in time of Peace, enter into any Agreement or Compact with another State, or with a foreign Power, or engage in War, unless actually invaded, or in such imminent Danger as will not admit of delay.

ARTICLE. II.

SECTION. 1. The executive Power shall be vested in a President of the United States of America. He shall hold his Office during the Term of four Years, and together with the Vice President, chosen for the same Term, be elected, as follows

Each State shall appoint, in such Manner as the Legislature thereof may direct, a Number of Electors, equal to the whole Number of Senators and Representatives to which the State may be entitled in the Congress: but no Senator or Representative, or Person holding an Office of Trust or Profit under the United States, shall be appointed an Elector.

[The Electors shall meet in their respective States, and vote by Ballot for two Persons, of whom one at least shall not be an Inhabitant of the same State with themselves. And they shall make a List of all the Persons voted for, and of the Number of Votes for each; which List they shall sign and certify, and transmit sealed to the Seat of the Government of the United States, directed to the President of the Senate. The President of the Senate shall, in the Presence of the Senate and House of Representatives, open all the Certificates, and the Votes shall then be counted. The Person having the greatest Number of Votes shall be the President, if such Number be a Majority of the whole Number of Electors appointed; and if there be more than one who have such Majority, and have an equal Number of Votes, then the House of Representatives shall immediately chuse by Ballot one of them for President; and if no Person have a Majority, then from the five highest on the List the said House shall in like Manner chuse the President. But in chusing the President, the Votes shall be taken by States, the Representation from each State having one Vote; A quorum for this Purpose shall consist of a Member or Members from two thirds of the States, and a Majority of all the States shall be necessary to a Choice. In every Case, after the Choice of the President, the Person having the greatest Number of Votes of the Electors shall be the Vice President. But if there should remain two or more who have equal Votes, the Senate shall chuse from them by Ballot the Vice President.]

The Congress may determine the Time of chusing the Electors, and the Day on which they shall give their Votes; which Day shall be the same throughout the United States.

No Person except a natural born Citizen, or a Citizen of the United States, at the time of the Adoption of this Constitution, shall be eligible to the Office of President; neither shall any Person be eligible to that Office who shall not have attained to the Age of thirty five Years, and been fourteen Years a Resident within the United States.

In Case of the Removal of the President from Office, or of his Death, Resignation, or Inability to discharge the Powers and Duties of the said

Office, the Same shall devolve on the Vice President, and the Congress may by Law provide for the Case of Removal, Death, Resignation or Inability, both of the President and Vice President, declaring what Officer shall then act as President, and such Officer shall act accordingly, until the Disability be removed, or a President shall be elected.

The President shall, at stated Times, receive for his Services, a Compensation, which shall neither be encreased nor diminished during the Period for which he shall have been elected, and he shall not receive within that Period any other Emolument from the United States, or any of them.

Before he enter on the Execution of his Office, he shall take the following Oath or Affirmation:—"I do solemnly swear (or affirm) that I will faithfully execute the Office of President of the United States, and will to the best of my Ability, preserve, protect and defend the Constitution of the United States."

SECTION. 2. The President shall be Commander in Chief of the Army and Navy of the United States, and of the Militia of the several States, when called into the actual Service of the United States; he may require the Opinion, in writing, of the principal Officer in each of the executive Departments, upon any Subject relating to the Duties of their respective Offices, and he shall have Power to grant Reprieves and Pardons for Offences against the United States, except in Cases of Impeachment.

He shall have Power, by and with the Advice and Consent of the Senate, to make Treaties, provided two thirds of the Senators present concur; and he shall nominate, and by and with the Advice and Consent of the Senate, shall appoint Ambassadors, other public Ministers and Consuls, Judges of the supreme Court, and all other Officers of the United States, whose Appointments are not herein otherwise provided for, and which shall be established by Law: but the Congress may by Law vest the Appointment of such inferior Officers, as they think proper, in the President alone, in the Courts of Law, or in the Heads of Departments.

The President shall have Power to fill up all Vacancies that may happen during the Recess of the Senate, by granting Commissions which shall expire at the End of their next Session.

SECTION. 3. He shall from time to time give to the Congress Information of the State of the Union, and recommend to their Consideration such Measures as he shall judge necessary and expedient; he may, on extraordinary Occasions, convene both Houses, or either of them, and in Case of Disagreement between them, with Respect of the Time of Adjournment, he may adjourn them to such Time as he shall think proper; he shall receive Ambassadors and other public Ministers; he shall take Care that the Laws be faithfully executed, and shall Commission all the Officers of the United States.

SECTION. 4. The President, Vice President and all civil Officers of the United States, shall be removed from Office on Impeachment for, and Conviction of, Treason, Bribery, or other high Crimes and Misdemeanors.

ARTICLE. III.

SECTION. 1. The judicial Power of the United States, shall be vested in one supreme Court, and in such inferior Courts as the Congress may from time to time ordain and establish. The Judges, both of the supreme and inferior Courts, shall hold their Offices during good Behaviour, and shall, at stated Times, receive for their Services, a Compensation, which shall not be diminished during their Continuance in Office.

SECTION. 2. The judicial Power shall extend to all Cases, in Law and Equity, arising under this Constitution, the Laws of the United States, and Treaties made, or which shall be made, under their Authority;—to all Cases affecting Ambassadors, other public Ministers and Consuls;—to all Cases of admiralty and maritime Jurisdiction;—to Controversies to which the United States shall be a Party;—to Controversies between two or more States;—between a State and Citizens of another State;—between Citizens of different States,—between Citizens of the same State claiming Lands under Grants of different States, and between a State, or the Citizens thereof, and foreign States, Citizens or Subjects.

In all Cases affecting Ambassadors, other public Ministers and Consuls, and those in which a State shall be Party, the supreme Court shall have original Jurisdiction. In all the other Cases before mentioned, the supreme Court shall have appellate Jurisdiction, both as to Law and Fact, with such Exceptions, and under such Regulations as the Congress shall make.

The Trial of all Crimes, except in Cases of Impeachment, shall be by Jury; and such Trial shall be held in the State where the said Crimes shall have been committed; but when not committed within any State, the Trial shall be at such Place or Places as the Congress may by Law have directed.

SECTION. 3. Treason against the United States, shall consist only in levying War against them, or in adhering to their Enemies, giving them Aid and Comfort. No Person shall be convicted of Treason unless on the Testimony of two Witnesses to the same overt Act, or on Confession in open Court.

The Congress shall have Power to declare the Punishment of Treason, but no Attainder of Treason shall work Corruption of Blood, or Forfeiture except during the Life of the Person attainted.

ARTICLE. IV.

SECTION. 1. Full Faith and Credit shall be given in each State to the public Acts, Records, and judicial Proceedings of every other State. And the Congress may by general Laws prescribe the Manner in which such Acts, Records and Proceedings shall be proved, and the Effect thereof.

SECTION. 2. The Citizens of each State shall be entitled to all Privileges and Immunities of Citizens in the several States.

A Person charged in any State with Treason, Felony, or other Crime, who shall flee from Justice, and be found in another State, shall on Demand of the executive Authority of the State from which he fled, be delivered up, to be removed to the State having Jurisdiction of the Crime.

[No Person held to Service or Labour in one State, under the Laws thereof, escaping into another, shall, in Consequence of any Law or Regulation therein, be discharged from such Service or Labour, but shall be delivered up on Claim of the Party to whom such Service or Labour may be due.]

SECTION. 3. New States may be admitted by the Congress into this Union; but no new State shall be formed or erected within the Jurisdiction of any other State; nor any State be formed by the Junction of two or more States, or Parts of States, without the Consent of the Legislatures of the States concerned as well as of the Congress.

The Congress shall have Power to dispose of and make all needful Rules and Regulations respecting the Territory or other Property belonging to the United States; and nothing in this Constitution shall be so construed as to Prejudice any Claims of the United States, or of any particular State.

SECTION. 4. The United States shall guarantee to every State in this Union a Republican Form of Government, and shall protect each of them against Invasion; and on Application of the Legislature, or of the Executive (when the Legislature cannot be convened) against domestic Violence.

ARTICLE. V.

The Congress, whenever two thirds of both Houses shall deem it necessary, shall propose Amendments to this Constitution, or, on the Application of the Legislatures of two thirds of the several States, shall call a Convention for proposing Amendments, which, in either Case, shall be valid to all Intents and Purposes, as Part of this Constitution, when ratified by the Legislatures of three fourths of the several States, or by Conventions in three fourths thereof, as the one or the other Mode of Ratification may be proposed by the Congress; Provided [that no Amendment which may be made prior to the Year One thousand eight hundred and eight shall in any Manner affect the first and fourth Clauses in the Ninth Section of the first Article; and] that no State, without its Consent, shall be deprived of its equal Suffrage in the Senate.

ARTICLE. VI.

All Debts contracted and Engagements entered into, before the Adoption of this Constitution, shall be as valid against the United States under this Constitution, as under the Confederation.

This Constitution, and the Laws of the United States which shall be made in Pursuance thereof; and all Treaties made, or which shall be made, under the Authority of the United States, shall be the supreme Law of the Land; and the Judges in every State shall be bound thereby, any Thing in the Constitution or Laws of any State to the Contrary notwithstanding.

The Senators and Representatives before mentioned, and the Members of the several State Legislatures, and all executive and judicial Officers, both of the United States and of the several States, shall be bound by Oath or Affirmation, to support this Constitution; but no religious Test shall ever be required as a Qualification to any Office or public Trust under the United States.

ARTICLE. VII.

The Ratification of the Conventions of nine States, shall be sufficient for the Establishment of this Constitution between the States so ratifying the Same.

DONE in Convention by the Unanimous Consent of the States present the Seventeenth Day of September in the Year of our Lord one thousand seven hundred and Eighty seven and of the Independence of the United States of America the Twelfth IN WITNESS whereof We have hereunto subscribed our Names,

Go WASHINGTON—
Presid^t. and deputy from Virginia.

New Hampshire.

JOHN LANGDON,   NICHOLAS GILMAN.

Massachusetts.

NATHANIEL GORHAM,   RUFUS KING.

Connecticut.

WM. SAML. JOHNSON,   ROGER SHERMAN.

New York.

ALEXANDER HAMILTON.

New Jersey.

WIL: LIVINGSTON,   WM. PATERSON,
DAVID BREARLEY,   JONA: DAYTON.

Pennsylvania.

B FRANKLIN,   THOMAS MIFFLIN,
ROB^T MORRIS,   GEO. CLYMER,
THOS. FITZSIMONS,   JARED INGERSOLL,
JAMES WILSON,   GOUV MORRIS.

Delaware.

GEO: READ,   GUNNING BEDFORD, jun,
JOHN DICKINSON,   RICHARD BASSETT.
JACO: BROOM,

Maryland.

JAMES MCHENRY,   DAN OF S^T THOS. JENIFER,
DAN^L CARROLL.

Virginia.

JOHN BLAIR— JAMES MADISON JR.

North Carolina.

WM. BLOUNT, RICH'D DOBBS SPAIGHT,
HU WILLIAMSON.

South Carolina.

J. RUTLEDGE CHARLES COTESWORTH PINCKNEY,
CHARLES PINCKNEY, PIERCE BUTLER.

Georgia.

WILLIAM FEW, ABR BALDWIN.
Attest: WILLIAM JACKSON, *Secretary.*

The text of the Constitution, as given above, is from the engrossed copy signed by thirty-nine framers, which is now enshrined in the National Archives and Records Service, General Services Administration, Washington, D.C. The official records relating to the Amendments, which follow, are also permanently located in the National Archives.

The parts included in brackets have since been changed because of amendments or obsolescence.

AMENDMENTS

The first ten Amendments were ratified December 15, 1791, and form what is known as the Bill of Rights

ARTICLES IN ADDITION TO, AND AMENDMENT OF, THE CONSTITUTION OF THE UNITED STATES OF AMERICA, PROPOSED BY CONGRESS, AND RATIFIED BY THE LEGISLATURES OF THE SEVERAL STATES PURSUANT TO THE FIFTH ARTICLE OF THE ORIGINAL CONSTITUTION

ARTICLE [I]*

Congress shall make no law respecting an establishment of religion, or prohibiting the free exercise thereof; or abridging the freedom of speech, or of the press; or the right of the people peaceably to assemble, and to petition the Government for a redress of grievances.

ARTICLE [II]

A well regulated Militia, being necessary to the security of a free State, the right of the people to keep and bear Arms, shall not be infringed.

*Only the 13th, 14th, 15th, and 16th articles of amendment had numbers assigned to them at the time of ratification.

ARTICLE [III]

No Soldier shall, in time of peace be quartered in any house, without the consent of the Owner, nor in time of war, but in a manner to be prescribed by law.

ARTICLE [IV]

The right of the people to be secure in their persons, houses, papers, and effects, against unreasonable searches and seizures, shall not be violated, and no Warrants shall issue, but upon probable cause, supported by Oath or affirmation, and particularly describing the place to be searched, and the persons or things to be seized.

ARTICLE [V]

No person shall be held to answer for a capital, or otherwise infamous crime, unless on a presentment or indictment of a Grand Jury, except in cases arising in the land or naval forces, or in the Militia, when in actual service in time of War or public danger; nor shall any person be subject for the same offence to be twice put in jeopardy of life or limb; nor shall be compelled in any criminal case to be a witness against himself, nor be deprived of life, liberty, or property, without due process of law; nor shall private property be taken for public use without just compensation.

ARTICLE [VI]

In all criminal prosecutions, the accused shall enjoy the right to a speedy and public trial, by an impartial jury of the State and district wherein the crime shall have been committed, which district shall have been previously ascertained by law, and to be informed of the nature and cause of the accusation; to be confronted with the witnesses against him; to have compulsory process for obtaining Witnesses in his favor, and to have the assistance of counsel for his defence.

ARTICLE [VII]

In Suits at common law, where the value in controversy shall exceed twenty dollars, the right of trial by jury shall be preserved, and no fact tried by a jury, shall be otherwise reexamined in any Court of the United States, than according to the rules of the common law.

ARTICLE [VIII]

Excessive bail shall not be required, nor excessive fines imposed, nor cruel and unusual punishments inflicted.

ARTICLE [IX]

The enumeration in the Constitution, of certain rights, shall not be construed to deny or disparage others retained by the people.

ARTICLE [X]

The powers not delegated to the United States by the Constitution, nor prohibited by it to the States, are reserved to the States respectively, or to the people.

ARTICLE [XI]

The Judicial power of the United States shall not be construed to extend to any suit in law or equity, commenced or prosecuted against one of the United States by Citizens of another State, or by Citizens or Subjects of any Foreign State.

ARTICLE [XII]

The electors shall meet in their respective states and vote by ballot for President and Vice-President, one of whom, at least, shall not be an inhabitant of the same state with themselves; they shall name in their ballots the person voted for as President, and in distinct ballots the person voted for as Vice-President, and they shall make distinct lists of all persons voted for as President, and of all persons voted for as Vice-President, and of the number of votes for each, which lists they shall sign and certify, and transmit sealed to the seat of the government of the United States, directed to the President of the Senate;—The President of the Senate shall, in the presence of the Senate and House of Representatives, open all the certificates and the votes shall then be counted;—The person having the greatest number of votes for President, shall be the President, if such number be a majority of the whole number of Electors appointed; and if no person have such majority, then from the persons having the highest numbers not exceeding three on the list of those voted for as President, the House of Representatives shall choose immediately, by ballot, the President. But in choosing the President, the votes shall be taken by states, the representation from each state having one vote; a quorum for this purpose shall consist of a member or members from two-thirds of the states, and a majority of all the states shall be necessary to a choice. [And if the House of Representatives shall not choose a President whenever the right of choice shall devolve upon them, before the fourth day of March next following, then the Vice-President shall act as President, as in the case of the death or other constitutional disability of the President.] The person having the greatest number of votes as Vice-President, shall be the Vice-President, if such number be a majority of the whole number of Electors appointed, and if no person have a majority, then from the two highest numbers on the list, the Senate shall choose the Vice-President; a quorum for the purpose shall consist of two-thirds of the whole number of Senators, and a majority of the whole number shall be necessary to a choice. But no person constitutionally ineligible to the office of President shall be eligible to that of Vice-President of the United States.

ARTICLE XIII

SECTION 1. Neither slavery nor involuntary servitude, except as a punishment for crime whereof the party shall have been duly convicted, shall exist within the United States, or any place subject to their jurisdiction.

SECTION 2. Congress shall have power to enforce this article by appropriate legislation.

ARTICLE XIV

SECTION 1. All persons born or naturalized in the United States, and subject to the jurisdiction thereof, are citizens of the United States and of the State wherein they reside. No State shall make or enforce any law which shall abridge the privileges or immunities of citizens of the United States; nor shall any State deprive any person of life, liberty, or property, without due process of law; nor deny to any person within its jurisdiction the equal protection of the laws.

SECTION 2. Representatives shall be apportioned among the several States according to their respective numbers, counting the whole number of persons in each State, excluding Indians not taxed. But when the right to vote at any election for the choice of electors for President and Vice President of the United States, Representatives in Congress, the Executive and Judicial officers of a State, or the members of the Legislature thereof, is denied to any of the male inhabitants of such State, being twenty-one years of age, and citizens of the United States, or in any way abridged, except for participation in rebellion, or other crime, the basis of representation therein shall be reduced in the proportion which the number of such male citizens shall bear to the whole number of male citizens twenty-one years of age in such State.

SECTION 3. No person shall be a Senator or Representative in Congress, or elector of President and Vice President, or hold any office, civil or military, under the United States, or under any State, who, having previously taken an oath, as a member of Congress, or as an officer of the United States, or as a member of any State legislature, or as an executive or judicial officer of any State, to support the Constitution of the United States, shall have engaged in insurrection or rebellion against the same, or given aid or comfort to the enemies thereof. But Congress may by a vote of two-thirds of each House, remove such disability.

SECTION 4. The validity of the public debt of the United States, authorized by law, including debts incurred for payment of pensions and bounties for services in suppressing insurrection or rebellion, shall not be questioned. But neither the United States nor any State shall assume or pay any debt or obligation incurred in aid of insurrection or rebellion against the United States, or any claim for the loss or emancipation of any slave; but all such debts, obligations and claims shall be held illegal and void.

SECTION 5. The Congress shall have power to enforce, by appropriate legislation, the provisions of this article.

ARTICLE XV

SECTION 1. The right of citizens of the United States to vote shall not be denied or abridged by the United States or by any State on account of race, color, or previous condition of servitude.

SECTION 2. The Congress shall have power to enforce this article by appropriate legislation.

ARTICLE XVI

The Congress shall have power to lay and collect taxes on incomes, from whatever source derived, without apportionment among the several States, and without regard to any census or enumeration.

ARTICLE [XVII]

The Senate of the United States shall be composed of two Senators from each State, elected by the people thereof, for six years; and each Senator shall have one vote. The electors in each State shall have the qualifications requisite for electors of the most numerous branch of the State legislatures.

When vacancies happen in the representation of any State in the Senate, the executive authority of such State shall issue writs of election to fill such vacancies: *Provided,* That the legislature of any State may empower the executive thereof to make temporary appointments until the people fill the vacancies by election as the legislature may direct.

This amendment shall not be so construed as to affect the election or term of any Senator chosen before it becomes valid as part of the Constitution.

[ARTICLE [XVIII]

[SECTION 1. After one year from the ratification of this article the manufacture, sale, or transportation of intoxicating liquors within, the importation thereof into, or the exportation thereof from the United States and all territory subject to the jurisdiction thereof for beverage purposes is hereby prohibited.

[SECTION 2. The Congress and the several States shall have concurrent power to enforce this article by appropriate legislation.

[SECTION 3. This article shall be inoperative unless it shall have been ratified as an amendment to the Constitution by the legislatures of the several States, as provided in the Constitution, within seven years from the date of the submission hereof to the States by the Congress.]

ARTICLE [XIX]

The right of citizens of the United States to vote shall not be denied or abridged by the United States or by any State on account of sex.

Congress shall have power to enforce this article by appropriate legislation.

ARTICLE [XX]

SECTION 1. The terms of the President and Vice President shall end at noon on the 20th day of January, and the terms of Senators and Representatives at noon on the 3d day of January, of the years in which such terms would have ended if this article had not been ratified; and the terms of their successors shall then begin.

SECTION 2. The Congress shall assemble at least once in every year, and such meeting shall begin at noon on the 3d day of January, unless they shall by law appoint a different day.

SECTION 3. If, at the time fixed for the beginning of the term of the President, the President elect shall have died, the Vice President elect shall become President. If a President shall not have been chosen before the time fixed for the beginning of his term, or if the President elect shall have failed to qualify, then the Vice President elect shall act as President until a President shall have qualified; and the Congress may by law provide for the case wherein neither a President elect nor a Vice President elect shall have qualified, declaring who shall then act as President, or the manner in which one who is to act shall be selected, and such person shall act accordingly until a President or Vice President shall have qualified.

SECTION 4. The Congress may by law provide for the case of the death of any of the persons from whom the House of Representatives may choose a President whenever the right of choice shall have devolved upon them, and for the case of the death of any of the persons from whom the Senate may choose a Vice President whenever the right of choice shall have devolved upon them.

SECTION 5. Sections 1 and 2 shall take effect on the 15th day of October following the ratification of this article.

SECTION 6. This article shall be inoperative unless it shall have been ratified as an amendment to the Constitution by the legislatures of three-fourths of the several States within seven years from the date of its submission.

ARTICLE [XXI]

SECTION 1. The eighteenth article of amendment to the Constitution of the United States is hereby repealed.

SECTION 2. The transportation or importation into any State, Territory, or possession of the United States for delivery or use therein of intoxicating liquors, in violation of the laws thereof, is hereby prohibited.

SECTION 3. This article shall be inoperative unless it shall have been ratified as an amendment to the Constitution by conventions in the several States, as provided in the Constitution, within seven years from the date of the submission hereof to the States by the Congress.

ARTICLE [XXII]

SECTION 1. No person shall be elected to the office of the President more than twice, and no person who has held the office of President, or acted as

President, for more than two years of a term to which some other person was elected President shall be elected to the office of the President more than once. But this Article shall not apply to any person holding the office of President when this Article was proposed by the Congress, and shall not prevent any person who may be holding the office of President, or acting as President, during the term within which this Article becomes operative from holding the office of President or acting as President during the remainder of such term.

SECTION 2. This article shall be inoperative unless it shall have been ratified as an amendment to the Constitution by the legislatures of three-fourths of the several States within seven years from the date of its submission to the States by the Congress.

ARTICLE [XXIII]

SECTION 1. The District constituting the seat of Government of the United States shall appoint in such manner as the Congress may direct:

A number of electors of President and Vice President equal to the whole number of Senators and Representatives in Congress to which the District would be entitled if it were a State, but in no event more than the least populous State; they shall be in addition to those appointed by the States, but they shall be considered, for the purposes of the election of President and Vice President, to be electors appointed by a State; and they shall meet in the District and perform such duties as provided by the twelfth article of amendment.

SECTION 2. The Congress shall have power to enforce this article by appropriate legislation.

ARTICLE [XXIV]

SECTION 1. The right of citizens of the United States to vote in any primary or other election for President or Vice President, for electors for President or Vice President, or for Senator or Representative in Congress, shall not be denied or abridged by the United States or any State by reason of failure to pay any poll tax or other tax.

SEC. 2. The Congress shall have power to enforce this article by appropriate legislation.

ARTICLE [XXV]

SECTION 1. In case of the removal of the President from office or of his death or resignation, the Vice President shall become President.

SEC. 2. Whenever there is a vacancy in the office of the Vice President, the President shall nominate a Vice President who shall take office upon confirmation by a majority vote of both Houses of Congress.

SEC. 3. Whenever the President transmits to the President pro tempore of the Senate and the Speaker of the House of Representatives his written declaration that he is unable to discharge the powers and duties of his office, and until he transmits to them a written declaration to the contrary, such powers and duties shall be discharged by the Vice President as Acting President.

SEC. 4. Whenever the Vice President and a majority of either the principal officers of the executive departments or of such other body as Congress may by law provide, transmit to the President pro tempore of the Senate and the Speaker of the House of Representatives their written declaration that the President is unable to discharge the powers and duties of his office, the Vice President shall immediately assume the powers and duties of the office as Acting President.

Thereafter, when the President transmits to the President pro tempore of the Senate and the Speaker of the House of Representatives his written declaration that no inability exists, he shall resume the powers and duties of his office unless the Vice President and a majority of either the principal officers of the executive department or of such other body as Congress may by law provide, transmit within four days to the President pro tempore of the Senate and the Speaker of the House of Representatives their written declaration that the President is unable to discharge the powers and duties of his office. Thereupon Congress shall decide the issue, assembling within forty-eight hours for that purpose if not in session. If the Congress, within twenty-one days after receipt of the latter written declaration, or, if Congress is not in session, within twenty-one days after Congress is required to assemble, determines by two-thirds vote of both Houses that the President is unable to discharge the powers and duties of his office, the Vice President shall continue to discharge the same as Acting President; otherwise, the President shall resume the powers and duties of his office.

ARTICLE [XXVI]

SECTION 1. The right of citizens of the United States, who are 18 years of age or older, to vote shall not be denied or abridged by the United States or any State on account of age.

SEC. 2. The Congress shall have the power to enforce this article by appropriate legislation.

PROPOSED EQUAL RIGHTS AMENDMENT
(Proposed by Congress March 22, 1972) — Defeated

SECTION 1. Equality of rights under the law shall not be denied or abridged by the United States or by any State on account of sex.

SEC. 2. The Congress shall have the power to enforce, by appropriate legislation, the provisions of this article.

SEC. 3. This amendment shall take effect two years after the date of ratification.

INDEX